YOUNG STUDENTS

Learning Library

VOLUME 19

Sled–Swaziland

WEEKLY READER BOOKS
MIDDLETOWN·CONNECTICUT

PHOTO CREDITS

Young Students Learning Library is a trademark of Field Publications.

ISBN 0-8374-6049-2

CONTENTS

SLED A sled is a form of transportation still used in areas of the world that have snowy winters. Sledding is a popular winter sport.

A common type of sled consists of a platform attached to parallel runners. The platform of the sled is usually made of wood. The runners are made of smooth steel. Many sleds have a bar across the front that is used for steering. Pulling the right side of the bar slightly toward you makes the sled turn right. Pulling on the left side makes the sled turn left. A rope is often attached to the front of the sled. This makes it easy to pull the sled back up a hill.

You can ride down a hill on a sled in either a sitting or lying position. If the sled is long enough, more than one person can sit on it. The front rider should hold the rope so that it doesn't slide under the runners and slow the sled down. Make sure everyone is on the sled each with the legs around the waist of the person in front. Then have someone else give you a push from the top of the hill.

When you lie down on the sled, you get a faster ride. Run with the sled held in front of your chest. Then throw the sled down and flop down on top of it quickly. This kind of ride is called a belly-whopper.

Several kinds of sleds have no runners. One of these is shaped like a big, round, shallow bowl usually made of polished aluminum or fiberglass. This kind of sled is sometimes called a *flying saucer*. A flying saucer is made for just one person. You sit in it and steer by leaning to one side or the other. The *toboggan* is another kind of runnerless sled. It has a flat bottom constructed of long wooden boards held together by crossbars. The front end curves up in an arch. To steer, all the passengers must lean in the direc-

◀ A river market in Thailand. These boats are loaded mainly with bananas. (See SOUTHEAST ASIA.)

tion of the turn.

The racing toboggan, or *luge*, has metal runners. The rider sits on it, leaning backward. On the skeleton toboggan, used by racers on the famous Cresta Run track in Switzerland, the rider lies down, head first.

The *bobsled* has two sets of runners—one on the front and one on the back. The person who sits in the front steers the bobsled by means of a bar or a wheel. The person who sits in the back controls the brakes. Bobsleds always travel on hollowed-out runs down a hillside. Steep banks are built along the sides of the run to keep the sleds from shooting off the twisting course. Bobsleds can go more than 90 miles (145 km) an hour.

Sometimes after a snow in the city, a side street on a hill is closed to traffic. Then it is safe to go sledding in the street. Otherwise, never go sledding in the road. Most sleds have no brakes. The only way to stop them is by dragging your feet.

ALSO READ: OLYMPIC GAMES, SPORTS.

SLEEP Scientists do not know exactly what causes sleep, but they have learned much about what sleep is. Sleep is a state of unconscious rest. It is necessary for good health, because during sleep the body recovers from the previous day's activities. The rest you get in sleep enables you to be alert

▲ These children are well wrapped up in warm winter clothes, ready to enjoy riding on their sleds.

▲ The best place to enjoy a toboggan ride is on a special track made on a snowy slope.

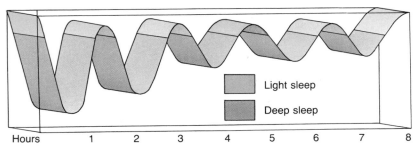

▲ *As you sleep, you change from periods of deep sleep to periods of light sleep. After 6–8 hours of sleep, the periods of light sleep become longer until you finally wake up.*

Light sleep

Deep sleep

Hours 1 2 3 4 5 6 7 8

People who go for more than 36 hours without sleep become irritable and confused. If they manage to stay awake for more than 60 hours, they may begin to "see" and "hear" things that are not there.

Different animals spend different lengths of time sleeping. Lions, for example, sleep for 16 hours daily; giraffes sleep only 20 minutes a day. Scientists do not know why there should be such large differences.

and active the following day.

When you wake up in the morning, you usually cannot remember what happened when you were asleep. Perhaps you remember a dream, but the rest of your sleep was a kind of darkness in which nothing seems to have happened. But several things happen to your body while you are sleeping. As you sink deeper into sleep, your muscles relax more and more. Your heartbeat becomes slower. Your temperature and blood pressure go down. The brain also slows down, sending fewer messages that cause you to think or act consciously. About five times during the night you change from periods of deep sleep to periods of light sleep.

Although most of your body processes slow down, your mind becomes active from time to time, and you dream. The stage of sleep in which dreaming occurs is called REM, for *r*apid *e*ye *m*ovement. Scientists know about this stage because they have found that when a sleeper is dreaming, the eyeballs move beneath the eyelids. Doctors have found that dreams often reveal a great deal about a person's problems and anxieties.

As you begin to wake up, your temperature and blood pressure rise to normal. Your heartbeat and breathing increase to normal and you wake up.

Scientists have found that sleep is partly controlled by a part of the brain called the *hypothalamus*. Whatever the cause, sleep provides essential rest for both the body and the mind.

ALSO READ: BRAIN, DREAM, METABOLISM, PSYCHOLOGY.

SLIME MOLD   see FUNGUS.

SLOTH   The sloth of Central and South America is a slow-moving furry animal that lives hanging upside-down from a tree branch. It eats and sleeps while hanging upside-down, and it sleeps most of the day. Its food is mostly leaves, shoots, and fruits.

Green *algae*, tiny growing plants, stick in the sloth's fur and make the animal look green in wet weather. These algae, and the sloth's long, shaggy hair make the sloth hard to see in the trees. Sloths move awkwardly on the ground, but surprisingly they can swim. The word "sloth" also means laziness and inactivity, which may explain how the animal got its name.

The only time a sloth moves fast is when it meets another sloth on the same branch. Then the two sloths fight each other to see which one stays on the branch. A female sloth gives birth to one young sloth at the beginning of the dry season.

The two kinds of sloths that exist today are often called two-toed and three-toed sloths, although the "toes" or "fingers" are really long, curved claws. The larger sloth is the two-fingered *unau* of Central America. It has no tail and is about two feet (60 cm) long. The unau eats leaves and fruit of several trees. It has sharp

▼ *The three-toed sloth, or ai, uses its claws to cling to the tree branches.*

teeth and can strike quickly with its claws. The smaller *ai* of South America is from 20 to 24 inches (50–60 cm) in length and has three claws on each hand. It eats the leaves and flowers of the wild cecropia tree.

Once many kinds of giant ground sloths, some as big as elephants, lived in South America.

ALSO READ: ANIMAL, MAMMAL.

SMELL

The organ of smell in human beings is called the *olfactory* organ. This organ is made up of special cells located in the back of the nose. Odors (smells) are caused by molecules of substances. When you breathe some of the molecules into your nose, they dissolve in the moisture that covers the lining of your nose. This solution then stimulates the receptor cells of the olfactory organs. The cells send a message to the brain, and the brain recognizes an odor.

Smell is important in our enjoyment of food. The flavor of food is a mixture of taste and smell. Taste only tells you if the food is salty, sour, bitter, or sweet. The rest of the flavor comes from smell. Smell is less important to human beings than it is to animals. Smell is the most important sense for some kinds of animals, such as dogs, wolves, and bears. These animals learn as much about their surroundings through their sense of smell as human beings learn through the sense of sight.

But smell is still important to human survival as well as human pleasure. Smelling can disclose dangers that are not obvious to other senses, such as leaking natural gas.

ALSO READ: NERVOUS SYSTEM, NOSE, SENSE ORGAN, TASTE.

SMITH, JOHN see AMERICAN COLONIES, POCAHONTAS, VIRGINIA.

SMITH, JOSEPH (1805–1844)

Joseph Smith was the founder of the Mormon Church, or the Church of Jesus Christ of Latter-day Saints. He is regarded as a prophet by the members of that church. Smith was born in Sharon, Vermont. He later moved to Palmyra, New York. There, he claimed to have had a series of visions. He said that the angel Moroni had appeared to him and told him that he would find a book of holy writings buried nearby.

In 1827, Smith announced that he had found golden tablets on which were written the history of the church of Christ in America. He published the writings, called the *Book of Mormon*, in 1830. That same year, he founded the Mormon church. Smith moved with his followers to Kirtland, Ohio, in 1831. They later went to Missouri and finally to Nauvoo, Illinois.

In 1843, Smith started the practice of *polygamy* (having more than one wife at the same time) in the Mormon church. Some Mormons refused to accept the practice and started a newspaper to fight the idea. The newspaper office was destroyed, and Smith was blamed. Local citizens began to protest against the Mormons, and Smith was jailed in Illinois on a charge of treason. He died when an angry mob broke into the prison and shot him.

ALSO READ: CHRISTIANITY, LATTER-DAY SAINTS, PROTESTANT CHURCHES.

SMITHSONIAN INSTITUTION

If you visit Washington, D.C., you can see giant pandas at the zoo and also the airplane named the *Spirit of St. Louis* that Charles Lindbergh flew when he crossed the Atlantic Ocean alone. You would be seeing just a small part of the Smithsonian Institution. The pandas are at the National Zoological Park, and the airplane is in

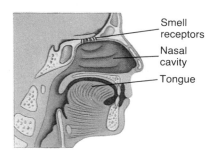

▲ *The receptor cells in your nose and mouth are stimulated by incoming molecules in the air you breathe. They can detect more than 10,000 different odors. Your tongue adds to your sense perception by recognizing four main kinds of taste. Bitterness is tasted at the back of the tongue, sourness at the sides, and sweetness at the front. Saltiness is tasted all over, but especially at the tip.*

▲ *Joseph Smith, founder of the Church of Jesus Christ of Latter-day Saints.*

▲ *The Egyptians burned incense. Here, an Egyptian king offers smoking incense before the statue of a god (about 1300 B.C.).*

▲ *The North American Indians smoked tobacco. The tomahawk pipe* (left) *could also be used as a weapon. In Japan* (right) *laborers smoked long-stemmed pipes.*

▲ *A Japanese* geisha *girl smoking a pipe. Tobacco was brought to Japan by the Portuguese in 1596.*

▲ *Pipe smoking was fashionable among women in the 1700's. The Turkish or Indian* hookah *pipe* (right) *filters the smoke through a vessel filled with water.*

the National Air and Space Museum, two of the many divisions of the Smithsonian.

The Smithsonian Institution was established by Congress in 1846. The idea and the money for its beginning came from James Smithson (1765–1829). Smithson was a rich English scientist. When he died, he left all his money to the United States government. He wanted the government to build a place where scientists could do research and study, and where all people could come and learn something about science.

The scientists who work for the Smithsonian Institution have gone on expeditions all over the world. They have made discoveries in archeology, astronomy, aeronautics, geology, biology, physics, chemistry, and other fields. Astronomers have use of the Smithsonian Astrophysical Observatory. The Smithsonian Institution has a large library of scientific books and magazines, and publishes many of its own.

The Smithsonian Institution is governed by a board of regents, which consists of the U.S. Vice-President, the chief justice, three U.S. senators, three U.S. representatives, and six nonofficials. The secretary of the institution is the executive director.

Samuel Pierpont Langley, an astronomer and aeronautical pioneer, was secretary from 1887 until 1906. During this time, the National Zoological Park and the Astrophysical Observatory were established.

In the buildings of the Smithsonian, you can see a space capsule, exhibits on Indian life, a real locomotive steam engine, and many other interesting things. At the National Gallery of Art, you can see paintings and sculptures by many of the world's great artists. Portraits of many famous Americans can be found at the National Portrait Gallery. Oriental works of art are at the Freer Gallery. The Smithsonian also has museums of natural history and of technology.

Concerts, films, and lectures are often presented in the various Smithsonian buildings. In the summer, folk arts festivals and other events take place on the mall outside the Smithsonian.

ALSO READ: MUSEUM, OBSERVATORY, ZOO.

SMOG see AIR POLLUTION.

SMOKING Smoking is the drawing in and puffing out of smoke from burning tobacco in cigarettes, cigars, and pipes. It can damage people's lungs and hearts, leading to serious illness, and can make people cough and feel short of breath.

The U.S. Public Health Service published a report on January 11, 1964, stating that cigarette smoking is an important cause of lung cancer and other deadly diseases. Cigarette packages must bear a printed warning that smoking is dangerous. The government's warning was issued only after ten of the country's outstanding doctors studied scientific evidence for more than a year. When their studies were finished, all ten doctors agreed that the warning should be issued.

Tobacco smoke contains tiny amounts of *tars* and *nicotine*. Tars take form as the tobacco burns. Tars coat the lungs, and then the cilia, the "cleaning brushes" of the lung's bronchial tubes, cannot brush out germs and dust as they should. Nicotine is a drug contained in tobacco leaves. It makes the heart beat faster and also speeds up breathing.

The use of tobacco for smoking probably began with the American Indians. Christopher Columbus saw the Indians smoking. In the 1500's, explorers took the dried leaves of the tobacco plant to Europe. Smoking soon became fashionable in the courts of Europe. Cigarettes were made popular by the Turks in the 1800's.

Cigarette smokers often inhale the tobacco smoke into their lungs. They are more likely to be affected by the harmful substances in smoke than cigar and pipe smokers who usually do not inhale. But pipe and cigar smokers absorb nicotine that might injure the heart. They also risk the danger of developing cancer of the mouth or lips. Some of the diseases linked with smoking besides lung cancer are emphysema, chronic bronchitis, and heart disease. Smoking is also a health risk to nonsmokers who breathe smokers' smoke, called *side smoke*.

Scientists have found that people who smoke when they are very young die much earlier than people who don't smoke at all. It is also true that smoking stains teeth and fingers, causes bad breath, and makes clothes smell bad.

ALSO READ: DRUG ABUSE, HEALTH, TOBACCO.

SNAILS AND SLUGS Snails and slugs belong to a large group, or phylum, of animals called *mollusks*. Mollusks are soft-bodied animals that usually have shells. Slugs do not look like snails because they have no outer shells. However, they are related to them. Snails and slugs make up a class of mollusks called *gastropods*, a word that means "stomach-footed." They get this name because they move around by creeping, or gliding, on a part of their body that seems to be their stomach. It is really a foot. Some land snails and slugs give off a slippery trail of slime that helps them skid along more easily.

Snails and slugs live in all parts of the world. They are found in jungles, forests, deserts, swamps, lakes, rivers, and all parts of the ocean. Certain snails spend their lives in the tops of tropical trees. There are thousands of kinds of snails and slugs, which are found in many sizes and colors.

Snails and slugs eat many kinds of food. Many eat plant matter. Others eat decaying meat or catch live prey. To help them get their food, snails and slugs have teeth that are like no others in the animal kingdom. Their teeth are arranged in a line, along the *radula*, a part of the body that is something like a tongue. Some snails have many hundreds of teeth. Others have only a few. The teeth act like saws as the radula moves across the food. They cut away particles of the food, which the radula then pulls back into the animal's stomach. The teeth of meat-eating snails are sharper than the teeth of plant eaters. The cone shell snails, which live in the Indian and Pacific Oceans, can inject poison with their teeth.

The shells of snails usually curl into a spiral shape. Some, however, look more like little cones. Limpets, for instance, look like tiny volcanoes. Ordinary land snails in the United States are usually small. They live in damp places, around decaying wood or other vegetation. A snail's eyes are on extending stalks on top of its head.

▲ *Superheroes don't smoke! The use of comic-strip characters to make the "don't smoke" message helps young people to realize the health dangers associated with smoking.*

▼ *Slugs are mostly active at night. The slug's shell is not large enough to give the animal any protection from enemies.*

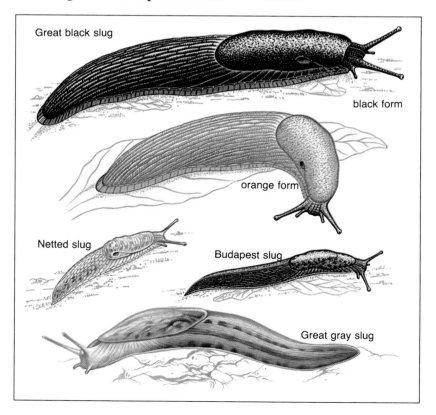

Great black slug

black form

orange form

Netted slug

Budapest slug

Great gray slug

Garden snail (land)

Great ram's horn (water)

Roman snail (land)

Great pond snail (water)

▲ *Snails are protected by shells. The shell is built up, coil by coil, from substances produced in the snail's body. All snails have one or two pairs of stalklike feelers on their heads.*

The common garden snail is the fastest moving kind of land snail. Its top speed is about 0.03 miles per hour (about 55 yards or 50 meters per hour).

Certain European land snails are prized as food. The French call them *escargots*, and they are raised for market. Some tropical land snails grow to be very large. A giant land snail of Africa, *achatina*, grows to be more than eight inches (20 cm) long. Land slugs are related to land snails. They are often garden pests because they eat parts of leafy plants. Some land slugs eat earthworms and insects. Snails that live in fresh water (lakes and ponds) have either lungs or gills. Snails that live in the ocean have only gills.

The shells of sea snails are usually thicker than those of land snails. They take a great variety of shapes, including spirals, cones, and cups. Conchs, whelks, tritons, limpets, and abalones are all snails that live in the ocean. Some are large, like the 24-inch (60-cm) horse conch of the Atlantic Ocean. Many have beautiful shells, decorated with complicated patterns and bright colors.

Sea slugs are marine snails. They do not need the protection of shells because many are poisonous and other sea animals will not eat them. Many sea slugs are also brilliantly colored. Sea slugs eat small bits of coral from the bottom of the ocean floor.

ALSO READ: ANIMAL, ANIMAL FAMILY, ANIMAL KINGDOM, ANIMAL MOVEMENT, AQUARIUM, MOLLUSK, SHELL.

SNAKE Many people are afraid of snakes. They think that snakes are slimy and dangerous. In fact, most snakes are dry to the touch and harmless. Even the poisonous kinds kill only for food. A snake is a reptile—a cold-blooded, air-breathing animal with a backbone and a scaly skin. A snake's body is long and narrow and almost always legless. Pythons and boas have tiny leg remnants like spurs, but these are no longer used for locomotion. Unlike other reptiles,

snakes do not have ear openings or eardrums and cannot hear sounds in the air. They have ears inside their skulls and can hear only when the skull bones pick up vibrations from the ground. A snake's eyes are always open. Snakes do not have moveable eyelids, so they can't blink.

Like all reptiles, snakes are covered with scales. Every so often, the snake sheds its skin. It loosens the skin around its lips by rubbing against a rough surface, then peels the skin back from its head to its tail. Underneath is a new skin.

The fact that a snake is cold-blooded does not mean that its blood is always cold, but that its body temperature changes with the temperature of its surroundings. A snake can keep quite warm if it lives in a warm climate and keeps active. Snakes live in all the warmer areas of the world, but some snakes live as far north as the Arctic Circle. Some snakes live in the water. Some live on the ground or in burrows. Some live in trees. Snakes live in wet places and in dry deserts.

Most snakes give birth by laying eggs. A mother snake usually just lays her eggs and crawls away. The warmth of the sun incubates the eggs. The baby snakes are able to take care

▼ *The egg-eating snake can unhinge its jaws to swallow an egg. Bones in the throat then break the egg, and the snake spits out the shell fragments.*

of themselves as soon as they hatch. Snakes that lay eggs are *oviparous*. This word comes from two Latin words that mean to bring forth eggs.

A few snakes, including the common garter snake, are born alive. The mother's eggs stay in her body until the baby snakes inside are developed. The unborn snakes do not get nourishment directly from the mother's body, as mammals do. These snakes are *ovoviviparous*, from the Latin words that mean to bring forth live young from eggs.

Snakes are many different sizes. The pythons and boas of the tropical jungle may grow as long as 30 feet (9 m). Some blind burrowing snakes are only a few inches long.

Snakes usually move with a *serpentine* motion—pushing against rocks, twigs, and bumps in the ground and weaving forward in a series of curves. Water snakes swim with the same weaving motion. Some snakes can move with a *concertina* motion—they grip the ground with their neck and slide the rest of the body forward like a folding concertina. Large, heavy snakes often crawl straight ahead like a caterpillar, gripping the ground with their flat belly scales and humping along. Snakes called sidewinders live in deserts where the sand is too loose to push against. The sidewinder twists its body into loops and "rolls" sideways. When it has unrolled, it touches its head down, curls into new loops, and unrolls again.

Some snakes can climb trees. They have ridges on the outside of their broad belly scales. The ridges catch on the tree bark and act as a brace. A tree snake can span distances and move from tree to tree by tightening muscles until its body is as rigid as a stick.

All snakes eat meat. Many snakes simply grab their victims and swallow them. Some snakes kill their prey first by constriction or squeezing. Poisonous snakes kill with poison. They all swallow animals whole, and some-

Indian cobra

European grass snake swallowing a frog

Baby coral snakes

▲ *There are some 1800 species of snakes. Here are three quite different species.*

times alive. A snake has a double row of sharp teeth in its upper jaw and a single row in its lower jaw. These teeth slant backward toward its throat. The teeth are not for chewing but for holding the prey tightly and pulling it down the snake's throat. A snake's jaw is hinged so it can open wide, wide enough to swallow an animal larger than the snake itself. The snake's skin can stretch like a balloon to hold large prey. A snake may take a long time to swallow an animal, and some snakes eat only once every few weeks.

The snake's tongue is long and forked at the end. It is not for tasting. It is for touching things and helping the snake to smell. It is also perfectly harmless.

Constrictors and Poisoners Pythons and boas, the two largest snakes, are constrictors. The king snake and the bull snake are also constrictors. The constrictors seize the animal, usually by the head, then coil around it, and squeeze. If they feel a pulse, they squeeze again. The pressure stops the animal's breathing and cuts off its circulation. The snake then swallows its prey.

Poisonous snakes have hollow teeth called *fangs*. The snake jabs its fangs into the victim and tightens the muscles around its poison glands. The poison, or *venom*, is squirted through

▲ *In India, people "charm" snakes. The animal cannot hear the music but follows the movement of the pipe. The charmers know when to stop before the cobra strikes at the pipe.*

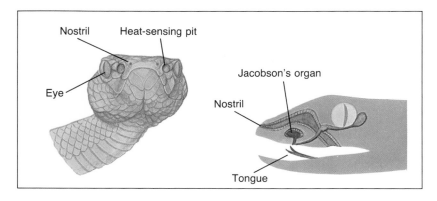

Nostril Heat-sensing pit

Eye

Jacobson's organ

Nostril

Tongue

▲ *A snake "tastes" the air with its flickering tongue. It has special sense organs, called Jacobson's organs, in the roof of its mouth (above right). These "read" the chemical samples picked up by the snake's tongue and tell the snake what is going on around it. Some snakes, such as pit vipers and rattlesnakes, can also detect heat, by means of special heat-sensing pits on their heads (above left). These help them to detect prey even in darkness.*

There are many stories of large animals and even human beings being swallowed whole by large snakes. It is believed that the largest recorded "swallowing" was by an African python. An antelope weighing 130 pounds (59 kg) was removed from its stomach. A 26-foot (8-m) anaconda was found to have in its stomach a caiman (alligator) nearly 7 feet (2 m) long. But anacondas do not have to eat very often. After consuming a big meal, they can go for up to a year without eating.

the fangs into the victim. Venom can attack the blood or the nerves. Snakes are grouped by the kind of venom they use.

Vipers produce venom that destroys red blood cells and breaks down the walls of blood vessels. Rattlesnakes, copperheads, water moccasins (or cottonmouths), and bushmasters are vipers. Adders are also vipers. Cobras and coral snakes produce venom that attacks the nervous system, paralyzing the nerves controlling the heart and the breathing muscles.

Most snakes are harmless to people. They eat mostly rats, mice, frogs, and insects. Some snakes eat other snakes, and many snakes are helpful in controlling insect and rodent pests.

People often have strong feelings about snakes. Snakes have long been associated with evil. In the Biblical story of Adam and Eve, the snake tempts Eve with the forbidden fruit in the Garden of Eden. On the other hand, many ancient cultures considered snakes to be wise. They were thought to have powers to cure disease and prolong life. The symbol of medicine has two "healing serpents" wound around a staff. Hopi Indians in Arizona still do a ceremonial rain dance with live snakes held between their teeth. The Hopis believe that the snake's zigzag shape resembles lightning, so the snake can carry a message to the rain god.

Most snakes are beneficial. No snake is intentionally harmful. About the last thing any snake wants to do is be near, let alone kill, a human being.

Remember, snakes don't chew their food, they swallow it whole. And few snakes are large enough to swallow even a small human being. A snake will attack a person only if it thinks the person is about to attack it. You should be careful of snakes but not afraid of them. Since poisonous snakes *are* dangerous, do not touch or play with any snake you see.

ALSO READ: LIZARD, REPTILE.

SNEEZE When you sneeze, you suddenly and violently blow your breath out through your mouth and nose. You do this by strongly contracting the chest and stomach muscles that you use when breathing in and out. Sneezes are caused by irritation of the tissue that lines the nose. The irritation may be due to a cold or to breathing in dust or pollen. Many people who suffer from allergies, such as hay fever, are prone to sneezing fits in the summer when the pollen count is very high. Sneezing is a *reflex action*. This means that you cannot make yourself sneeze just by trying, and once a sneeze has begun, you cannot stop it. Sometimes, you may feel a sort of tickling in the upper part of your nose just before you sneeze. When you feel this, you may have time to stop the sneeze by pressing a finger directly under your nose.

When you have a cold, sneezing can spread your cold germs into the air, and nearby persons may catch your cold. A sneeze can propel germs as far as 15 feet (almost 5 m). To prevent this, you should always sneeze into a tissue or handkerchief.

ALSO READ: ALLERGY, BREATHING, COMMON COLD, DUST, NOSE.

SNOOKER see BILLIARD GAMES.

SNOW see RAIN AND SNOW.

SNOWMOBILE

A snowmobile is a motorized sled used to travel over snow and ice. The winter sport of "snowmobiling" is popular in the northern United States and Canada.

The snowmobile was developed from the first engine-propelled toboggan in 1927. A modern snowmobile is a machine with skis under the front end and revolving tracks underneath. The track moves the machine across the snow in the same way that tracks move a bulldozer. A snowmobile is run by an internal combustion engine. The driver steers with handlebars. Many snowmobiles can go 50 miles (80 km) per hour and faster.

Most people ride snowmobiles for recreation. They like the thrill of driving a fast machine and going places that a car cannot go in winter. Snowmobiles are used for transportation in some rural areas. Fish and game wardens and forest rangers use snowmobiles to patrol large areas where roads are scarce. Fur trappers use them to check their traps. Ski patrols use them to rescue injured skiers. Telephone line workers, lumberjacks, and ranchers also use snowmobiles.

Riding in a snowmobile can be dangerous. Passengers can drown when snowmobiles break through the ice on rivers and lakes. Snowmobiles sometimes collide with cars on roads. They sometimes hit rocks or other obstacles covered by snow in fields or in the woods. This can cause the machine to flip over. Even if the driver is not hurt, he or she may still be in trouble. A snowmobile is too heavy for one person alone to turn right side up easily. The driver may be stuck somewhere miles from home in very cold weather.

Conservationists think snowmobiles should be regulated more closely. People are becoming concerned about the threat to wildlife by these loud machines. Their noise terrifies deer and small animals who are used to silence in winter. Sometimes the animals panic. They run until they die from exhaustion.

ALSO READ: CONSERVATION, SKIING.

SOAPS AND DETERGENTS

Soaps and detergents are substances used for washing and cleaning. People have known how to make soap for thousands of years, at least since the time of the Roman Empire. Until soap making became a big industry, most people made soap at home for their own use. Animal fats were boiled with wood ashes which contain lye, a substance that is an *alkali*. The alkali reacted with the fats, making soap. This kind of soap was very harsh, unlike the soap people buy today. In modern soap making, the animal fats (or vegetable oils) are combined with water at a high temperature and pressure. Milder alkalis are used making soap that is easier on the skin. Perfume and coloring are also added to soap. Deodorants are added to some kinds of soap.

Detergents are cleaning substances that are *not* made from fats and oils. Detergents are made from synthetic (man-made) ingredients. Detergents clean better than soap in hard water. Hard water contains salts that react with soap to prevent effective cleansing. Detergents by themselves do not make suds, but suds are not necessary for cleaning. Substances that make suds are added to detergents because most people do not think their clothes are being cleaned unless they see suds.

Water cannot penetrate the oil and grease molecules of dirt by itself. The cleansing action of soaps and detergents is due to their ability to get between these molecules. This enables the water to loosen dirt particles and wash them away. Soaps and detergents also bind oil and grease particles to the water droplets, which prevents the objects being washed from becoming soiled again before

▲ *In the winter, snowmobiles are ideal as a means of transport as well as fun.*

▼ *Soap bubbles do not burst as easily as ordinary bubbles. An ordinary air bubble bursts when it rises to the surface, because of the squeezing force of the water. Soapy water forms a film around the air inside and does not squeeze the air so hard. Therefore, the bubble will float above water.*

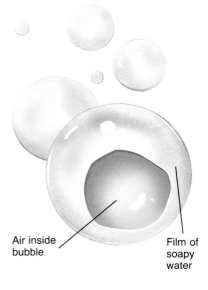

Air inside bubble

Film of soapy water

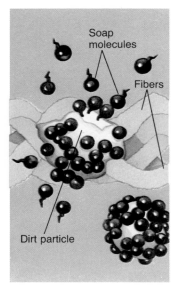

▲ *Soaps and detergents work by dissolving the grease that makes dust and dirt stick to the fibers of clothes. Ordinary water does not clean well because grease and water do not mix. The soap molecules attach themselves to water molecules at one end and to grease molecules at the other end. In this way, the soap links the grease and water, so the grease is dissolved and washes away with the water.*

the dirty water is rinsed out of them.

As soapy water goes to sewage-treatment plants or into rivers, bacteria change the soap to harmless substances. Therefore, soap is said to be *biodegradable*. Detergents contain substances called phosphates, which are not biodegradable. As a result, they remain unchanged in water and pollute it. Phosphates can indirectly kill plants and fish living in the water. Because of this danger, detergents without phosphates have been developed.

ALSO READ: ECOLOGY, SURFACE TENSION, WATER POLLUTION.

SOCCER Baseball, basketball, and football are the most popular sports in the United States. But in many other countries in the world, soccer is the big game. Soccer is quite different from American football, but it is often called football in other countries.

In soccer, one team tries to kick a ball into the goal of its opposing team, thus scoring one point, called a goal. The goal is guarded by a *goalkeeper*, the only team member permitted to handle the ball with the hands. All the other players must either kick the ball, or, when possible, try to hit it with their heads, called *heading*.

Soccer is played on a grass field up to 120 yards (109 m) long and 80 yards (73 m) wide. Goals are located in the middle of each end of the field. They consist of posts eight feet (2.5 m) high and 24 feet (7.3 m) apart, joined at the top by a crossbar. A net is attached to the back of the crossbar and posts and pegged to the ground behind them.

There are 11 players on a soccer team. Each team has a goalkeeper, the remainder are defensive backs, midfielders or halfbacks, and forwards. Also on the field are the officials—the *referee* and two *linesmen*. The officials watch for *fouls*—such as holding, tripping, pushing, and blocking opponents. In the case of a foul, a *free kick* may be awarded to the offended team. A free kick is taken from the place where the foul was committed. If this was inside a box 18 yards (16.5 m) from the goal called the *penalty area*, the free kick is taken in front of the goal from a spot 12 yards (11 m) away.

The soccer ball is filled with air and measures about 28 inches (71 cm) around. Soccer players wear jerseys, shorts, knee-high stockings, and soccer shoes with cleats. A game usually lasts for two halves of 45 minutes each.

A soccer player's size is not as important as his or her speed, agility, and coordination. The players must work together as a team. But at the same time, there are plenty of opportunities in both passing and scoring for individuals to show their skill.

A game like soccer was played by the Chinese about 2,500 years ago. The Romans played a similar game and brought it to England about A.D. 200. But not until 1863 were rules established for the playing of soccer, which was an amateur sport at that time. The first professional soccer teams were organized in England in 1885. The game then spread quickly throughout the world. The World Cup games, held every four years, were started in 1930, with competi-

Field diagram labels: 120 yds, 20 yds, 44 yds, 75 yds, 10 yds, Goal area, Penalty spot, 8 yds, Penalty arc, Penalty area

tion between national teams from many countries. In the United States, soccer was mainly an amateur sport until professional teams began to play in the North American Soccer League in 1968. This was suspended in 1985.

ALSO READ: FOOTBALL, SPORTS.

SOCIALISM Socialism is an economic system based on state ownership of the vital means of production and important natural resources and utilities—including land, mines, railroads, water, gas, and power companies. Socialists believe that this system will solve many of the problems of modern society, including unemployment and poverty.

Modern socialism differs from Communism. Communists believe that the government should control the means of production and rule in a dictatorial manner for "the good of the people." Under a dictatorship, people have little personal or political freedom. Usually, only one party—the ruling party—is allowed to exist. Modern socialists believe in a democratic form of government, in which people can elect public officials. Communist governments maintain that their aim is to establish a completely socialist society. However, the governments of most of the Communist nations in Europe, such as the Soviet Union, developed from the socialist parties of those nations.

Socialist ideas are not new. Plato, the ancient Greek philosopher, discussed some socialist ideals in his work, *The Republic*. The French philosophers, Comte de Saint-Simon and François Fourier, and the English reformer, Robert Owen, expressed socialist beliefs during the 1700's and early 1800's. Karl Marx, the German philosopher and economist, developed his theory of "scientific socialism" in 1848, but his name later became more closely associated with Communism.

The socialist movement became prominent after the Industrial Revolution took hold in Europe in the 1800's. Factory workers were dissatisfied with the capitalist system, under which they labored long hours for their employers with little pay and no benefits. For example, if workers became ill or were injured on the job, they were fired. Their families were left without income. This led to workers setting up labor unions that fought for better pay and conditions.

Today, socialist ideas are applied in many countries. The extent to which governments own the means of production varies greatly. In some countries, such as Sweden, the government controls several key industries, such as the communication and transportation industries. But many other industries are privately owned and are operated for individual profit. In socialist countries, free medical care is available for all. Day nurseries are provided at little or no cost for the children of working mothers. In the United States, few industries are government owned.

The Tennessee Valley Authority, however, is one example of a successful socialist enterprise in the United States. The TVA is a government corporation that operates dams, electric power plants, and flood-control systems within the Tennessee River Valley.

▲ *Soccer is played on every continent. Every four years, when the World Cup competition is played, millions of fans watch it on TV.*

▼ *Socialism is an ancient idea, but it gained support in the 1800's. During the Industrial Revolution, workers in the new factory cities lived in poor overcrowded dwellings, earned low wages, and worked long hours in dangerous conditions. Socialism was supported by those seeking a better life for all.*

▲ *Robert Owen, a Welsh socialist, founded a number of small communities that were run on socialist principles. One was in New Harmony, Indiana.*

Socialism has never been as strong in the United States as it has been in Europe. In the 1920 presidential election, the Socialist candidate, Eugene V. Debs, received 920,000 votes. Since then, Socialist strength in the United States has declined.

ALSO READ: CAPITALISM; COMMUNISM; ECONOMICS; GOVERNMENT; LABOR UNIONS; MARX, KARL; SOCIAL SECURITY; SOVIET UNION; SWEDEN.

SOCIAL SECURITY Social Security is a U.S. government program providing money and medical care for people who are disabled, unemployed, or too old to work. It may also provide these benefits for the *dependents* (husbands, wives, and children) of unemployed, disabled, or deceased workers.

Most countries have some type of social security program. The United States adopted its program, Old Age, Survivors, Disability, and Health Insurance (OASDHI) in 1935. It is financed by contributions from workers and their employers. When a person starts working, he or she must apply for an account at the Social Security Administration. The Social Security Administration then establishes an account for that person and issues the person a card with his or her account number printed on it. Payments are deducted from the worker's paycheck. The worker's employer makes equal payments. Self-employed people also pay a certain amount of their earnings for social security.

If workers become disabled or retire, they are entitled to cash benefits from the Social Security Administration. The government pays them or their families a certain amount of money each month. The amount paid depends on how long the workers have worked, their earnings, and their age. If workers die, their dependents receive cash payments.

Since its adoption, the Social Security program has changed very much. Cash benefits have increased, and the amounts paid into the social security fund by workers and employers have also increased. A health insurance program, called Medicare, has been established. This program provides health insurance for people aged 65 and over. This insurance pays most of the cost of doctors, hospitals, and medicines that may be needed by these older people.

ALSO READ: GOVERNMENT, INSURANCE, PUBLIC HEALTH, SAVINGS.

SOCIAL STUDIES The term "social studies" refers to the studies in human relationships taught in school. Social studies are also called *social sciences*. A great many fields of study come under this heading. Social studies deal with every aspect of life and community living. They include the study of anthropology, government, economics, history, geography, and sociology. Social studies teach students how the people of the world work, learn, govern, play, and worship.

Social studies show how people's lives are changed by wars, political movements, new developments in technology, and new inventions. One very important goal of a social studies program is to teach students what they need to know to be good citizens. Students of social studies learn about both their rights and their responsibilities as members of a community and citizens of a state and country.

The teaching of social studies begins in the elementary grades, where the various kinds of social studies are usually presented in one general course. Students are taught about their community—how it is run and the responsibilities of each member of the community. They also learn about other countries in social studies classes.

History and *geography* form the basis of social studies in the elementary school. History teaches about past events and how they have affected mankind and our life today. Studying the history of other lands and of our own country helps us to understand ourselves.

In geography, students discover facts about the world in general and their country and others in particular. For example, they learn what crops are grown where and what different countries are like. Students also study government in social studies, beginning with the nearby local community and continuing up to the national government. The *legislative* (law-making), *executive* (presidential policy), and *judicial* (judges and courts of law) branches of the government are studied. Students investigate our system of laws and the way our leaders are elected. Current events often make up part of the subject matter.

In the secondary grades, social studies courses become more specialized. Students usually study one particular subject at a time. For example, they may have an individual course in United States history, world history, economics, or political science. *Civics* courses introduce pupils to the study of citizenship and government. *Economics* is the study of the making and distribution of goods and their later use. *Political science* is the study of politics and government. *Anthropology*, the study of mankind, includes elements of biology, economics, political science, and sociology. *Penology*, the study of prisons, is usually included in general *sociology* courses. The religions of the world are sometimes included in social studies programs. Many high schools offer students a course in which current affairs and problems of national concern are discussed and debated.

ALSO READ: ECONOMICS, GEOGRAPHY, HISTORY, SOCIOLOGY.

SOCIAL WORK In all communities, there are some people who are unable to take care of themselves. People who are sick and cannot work need financial help and medical care. Physically and mentally handicapped people need help in learning basic

skills and in finding jobs. Youngsters without homes, old people without families, people who come from other countries and cannot speak any English—all these people need some type of help. Social work is a means of helping these people in an organized way. Specially trained people called *social workers* perform this work.

People have always tried to help others in times of need. Until the 1900's, the help was given only by religious organizations as charity, or temporarily by a government (usually local). In recent years, social work has become better organized. Social workers do more than just give money and food when it is needed. They are trained to help people with emotional and psychological problems. They also work to change the social and economic conditions causing people's problems. Social workers today are trained in special two-year university courses after they graduate from college.

There are three main kinds of social workers. The first is called a *caseworker*. He or she works directly with the person or family in trouble.

▼ *Many social workers supervise young children in nurseries or day care centers, particularly in remote areas. These children are playing in one such remote area in north-west Saskatchewan, Canada. Such isolated communities need the help of group workers.*

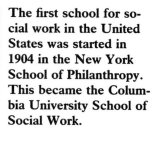

The first school for social work in the United States was started in 1904 in the New York School of Philanthropy. This became the Columbia University School of Social Work.

In 1947, the American Friends Service committee and the British Friends Service council received the Nobel peace prize. They won the award for relief work on the continent of Europe after World War II.

Some caseworkers work at government welfare or public-assistance agencies. Their job is to distribute financial aid and help people with their individual problems. Caseworkers whose work is connected with hospitals are called *medical caseworkers*, and those who work with people who have emotional problems are called *psychiatric caseworkers*. They help patients make the adjustment from living in a hospital or institution to living at home. They also help the families of those people who have to live in an institution or in a hospital.

The second type of social worker is the *group worker*. He or she is in charge of groups of people rather than individuals. The group worker works on community projects for people of all ages. He or she often functions in a church, community center, or settlement house—those places that offer workrooms and meeting rooms to people in a community. Group workers lead recreational activities. They may also supervise small children in a nursery or day care center, or organize community projects.

The third type of social worker is the *social planner*. The social planner plans the activities of social work agencies, helps raise funds for those activities, and conducts research on social and economic problems. He or she may also plan new laws that help the needy.

ALSO READ: ADDAMS, JANE; CAREER; SOCIOLOGY.

SOCIETY OF FRIENDS

The Society of Friends is a branch of the Christian religion. Its members are called Friends, or Quakers. An English religious leader, George Fox, founded the Society of Friends around 1650, a time when there was much dispute about the practices of the Christian faith in England. Fox believed in an "inner light." He felt that people can know God within their own souls and be guided by God. A judge gave the name "Quaker" to Fox, when he accused him of quaking, or trembling, before God.

Quakers do not have ministers to lead their congregations, nor do they have regular church services. They gather at "meetings" and pray in silence. Any member of the congregation may stand up and speak during a meeting. Quakers are usually pacifists; that is, they are against any form of war or violence. They were among the first people to speak out against slavery. One of the most important organizations run by the Quakers is the American Friends Service Committee. This committee organizes educational projects for peace and runs relief services for the needy. The Quakers also have excellent schools and colleges.

The Society of Friends came to America in the 1650's. They were often persecuted for their beliefs. William Penn, a Quaker, founded the Pennsylvania colony in 1682, and thousands of Quakers settled there. Today, there are about 210,000 Quakers throughout the world, including about 120,000 in the United States.

ALSO READ: PENNSYLVANIA, RELIGION.

▼ *Lam Peter Church, built in 1749, is a Friends' Meeting House in Lancaster County, Pennsylvania.*

SOCIOLOGY Sociology is the science that studies human society. (A society is a group of persons who share the same interests and way of life.) The words "sociology," "society," and "social" all come from the Latin word *socius,* meaning "companion," or "the companionship of human beings together." Scientists called *sociologists* study how human society began, how it developed, and how people live in groups. Sociologists gain their information by collecting facts, studying historical records, and observing people. Sociology is one of the social sciences. It overlaps with other social sciences—such as anthropology, economics, political science, and psychology—but it focuses on social behavior and group relationships.

Sociologists study the various levels of a society. Everyone is part of several groups in a society. The child is part of the family group. The family is part of a neighborhood group. Religious and school organizations make up other local groups. The town or city is another, larger group. Beyond that there are state and regional groups, national groups, and—the largest group of all—the world society. All of these groups have an effect on the people who live within them. Each group has special rules of behavior, laws, and customs. For example, different governments create different ways of life for the people who live under them. People living in very hot or dry climates do not live the same kind of life as those living where it is almost always cold or wet. People living in cities live different kinds of lives than those living in small towns or on farms in the country.

Sociologists attempt to discover how people in each level of a society behave. They study how people work and play, how they learn, worship, and think. They find out what people buy and what pleases them or displeases them. Sociologists study how

These two children enjoying friendship are both American, sharing the same language and way of life. However, their skin color shows they are originally from different cultures. Sociologists study such differences in our society.

people communicate with one another and how they are affected by their environment. They examine a society's *mores,* the customs or moral standards it considers important. The institutions of a society are studied. An *institution* is a pattern of group behavior that has become important to a society. Marriage and the family group are institutions. They have their own set of customs, or ways, that have become accepted as natural and right by society. Sociologists study many social problems, such as crime and prejudice, and try to find reasons for them and possible solutions. The aim of sociology is to discover as much as possible about people and their relationships.

Sociology as a specific science is not very old, but its roots go back to the ancient Greek writers. A French philosopher named Auguste Comte made it a separate science in the 1830's, when he recommended the scientific study of society. Before that time, the study of human society was treated as part of philosophy. (Philosophy is the study of knowledge, truth, and wisdom.) Comte thought that sociology should be studied on its own, not as a part of another science. An English philosopher, Herbert Spencer, continued Comte's research. In 1882, Spencer published a book called *Principles of Sociology,* which had a great influence on later sociologists. In his book, Spencer (influ-

The French philosopher Auguste Comte gave sociology its name: the study of relationships. He joined the Latin word *socius* (meaning "relationship") to the Greek word *logos* (meaning "study").

▲ *The family is a basic unit in society. In some African societies, the mother is the most important family member. Sociologists study family life in different societies in order to better understand human behavior.*

enced by Darwin's theory of evolution) maintained that social behavior and customs evolve from simple to complicated forms, just as animals do. As the new study of sociology grew, it developed into many different branches. Some sociologists study human ancestors and racial groups. Others study geography or population and their effects on human beings. Some emphasize the use of statistics. The study of human psychological behavior (the way the mind works) is another important part of sociology. More specialized studies in sociology are being investigated today. The study of prisons, *penology*, and the study of crime, *criminology*, are special fields of sociology.

ALSO READ: ANTHROPOLOGY, CIVILIZATION, CULTURE, CUSTOMS, ECONOMICS, GEOGRAPHY, HISTORY, PHILOSOPHY, POPULATION, PSYCHOLOGY, RELIGION, SOCIAL STUDIES, STATISTICS.

SOCRATES (about 469–399 B.C.) Socrates was a great Greek philosopher (thinker) and teacher. He never wrote a book or established a regular school, but his beliefs and teachings have had an important effect on the development of philosophy.

Socrates believed that virtue was knowledge, and that a person who

knew what was right would not act unjustly. Socrates did not think money and possessions were important. He wore only one garment, both in winter and summer. One time, at a fair, he remarked, "How many things there are that I do not need!"

Socrates was born in Athens, the son of a sculptor. He also became a sculptor and then a soldier. He fought bravely in several battles during the Peloponnesian War between Athens and Sparta. Socrates spent most of his life wandering through the marketplaces and streets of Athens, talking and teaching. He developed a method of teaching, now known as the *Socratic method*. He questioned his pupils thoroughly, helping them to discover the answers to their questions. One of Socrates' best pupils was Plato, another great Greek philosopher. Most of what is known about Socrates comes from the writings of Plato. Another pupil was Alcibiades, who became a famous general and politician.

Some Athenian citizens became angry with Socrates and charged him with neglecting the gods and misleading young people. They put Socrates on trial and condemned him to death. He was ordered to drink a cup of hemlock, a deadly poison. Socrates could have escaped, but he chose to spend his last hours with his friends. He then courageously drank the hemlock.

ALSO READ: ATHENS; GREECE, ANCIENT; PHILOSOPHY; PLATO.

SOFTBALL see BASEBALL.

SOIL Soil is the loose material on the Earth's surface in which plants grow. Soil is made up primarily of *humus* (partial decay of dead plants and animals) and small particles of rock. Humus provides many of the chemical elements needed for plant

▼ *Socrates* (left) *with friends, enjoying conversation. The philosopher spent his last hours in this manner, before drinking poison.*

growth. The rock particles are classified according to size. Sand is made up of grains of rock materials such as silica. Silt consists of smaller rock particles. Clay is a sticky material made up of the smallest particles of rock. Soil also contains water, some gases, and living organisms.

Fertile soils (good for growing crops) are fairly equal mixtures of sand, clay, and humus. If soil is very sandy, it is too loose to hold water well. If it has too much clay, water and air cannot pass through the soil very easily. (Think how sticky clay is when it is wet.) An excess of some kinds of humus makes soil too acid and too loose to support plant roots.

Several factors are involved in soil formation. They combine to create many kinds of soils. Time is, of course, an essential factor. It takes thousands of years for rocks to weather and break up and for soil to form. The make-up of a soil depends to a great extent on the kind of rock that is breaking up and providing part of the soil. The soil that rests on limestone is different from the soil

that comes from granite. Climate is equally important in the make-up of soil. The cold and humid climate of the eastern part of the United States produces soils different from those found in the hot, dry climate of the western United States. Climate also determines the kinds of plants that can grow in an area, and this influences the kind and amount of humus produced. Soil formation is influenced by the amount of rainfall an area loses or retains, so the slope of an area is important. The living organisms in soil also influence the kind of soil formed.

Soil is a very valuable natural resource. Without soil, or with only very poor soil, plants and the animals that eat plants could not survive. Since it takes thousands of years for only two or three feet of soil to form, it is very important to take care of soil. Erosion of fertile soil by water and wind action must be prevented. When soil is used repeatedly for growing crops (particularly the same crop year after year), minerals in the soil are used up. With proper care, soil can be kept good for growing crops. Fertilizers, organic matter (compost), and crop rotation help to make soil fertile again.

ALSO READ: AGRICULTURE, CONSERVATION, EROSION, FERTILIZER, NITROGEN, SAND.

▲ *Rain washes all but a thin layer of plant food deep down into this forest soil.*

▲ *Grassland soil soaks up less rain than forest soil. Plant food stays near the surface, feeding the grasses.*

▲ *Desert soil quickly loses moisture through evaporation. All that remains is a salty crust where few plants grow.*

▼ *In the past, many trees were felled to enable fertile soil to be plowed for crops. But the soil soon lost its fertility. Exposed to the weather, it was eroded (worn away) by wind and water. In the end, only barren desert was left, as shown here in North Africa.*

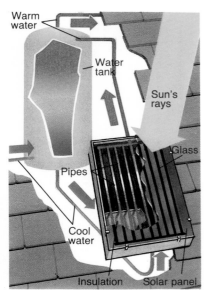

▲ *Solar panels on the roofs of houses trap the sun's rays. The sun's heat warms water flowing through the panels, to produce hot water for washing and heating.*

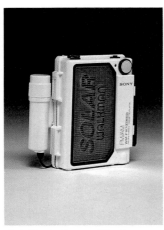

▲ *This is the world's first solar-powered portable stereo. It has a built-in rechargeable battery, powered by a solar cell.*

SOLAR ENERGY We depend on solar energy—the rays of light and heat that come from the sun—for life. We can make additional use of solar energy to provide us with energy to heat our houses and offices and to power machines. It's a good source of energy because it is clean and costs no more than the price of the machinery that collects it.

Solar panels on the roofs of buildings capture the sun's heat rays. They heat water passing through tubes inside the panels. This hot water is then used for washing or heating. Solar panels may not provide all the energy a home needs, but they help to reduce heating costs.

In sunny regions, such as California, solar power stations use the sun's heat rays to generate electricity for homes. They have mirrors that direct the sun's rays on a central boiler. The boiler turns water into steam, which is then used to power an electric generator.

Solar cells turn the sun's light rays directly into electricity. Each cell does not give a strong current, but large panels of cells can produce useful power. Solar cells are used on many satellites and spacecraft as there is perpetual sunlight in space. Solar power has also been harnessed for experimental road and air transport. You can see solar energy in action on the many pocket calculators that now use this power source.

SOLAR SYSTEM The solar system is made up of the sun and all the bodies that are in orbit around the sun. This includes the planets, satellites of the planets, asteroids, comets, meteoroids, interplanetary dust and gases, and other matter.

The sun is a *star*, a mass of hot gas. It is a very ordinary star, not especially large or bright. It looks much brighter than other stars only because it is so much closer to Earth. The next

▲ *A photograph of the planet Jupiter, taken by the Voyager 2 spacecraft.*

nearest star is 250,000 times as far from the Earth as the sun is.

Although the sun is not a very large star, it is much larger than anything else in the solar system. It contains 99 percent of all the mass in the solar system. All matter attracts all other matter with a gravitational force. The size of the force depends on the mass and distance. It is the sun's great mass that keeps the bodies in the solar system orbiting around it.

Planets The solar system has nine major planets. They are not very big compared to the sun or to the vast, empty spaces in the solar system. If you wanted to build a model of the sun and the planets, you would need a very large, flat field. You would need such a large field that it is easier just to imagine it. At the middle of the field, imagine a ball four feet (1.2 m) high. This ball would represent the sun. Take a marble a half-inch (1 cm) across and put it 480 feet (146 m) from the "sun." This marble would represent the Earth. Another half-inch marble, 350 feet (107 m) from the sun, would represent Venus. A pea 185 feet (56 m) from the sun would represent Mercury. Going out from the Earth, Mars would be a slightly larger pea, 740 feet (226 m) from the sun.

Mercury, Venus, Earth, and Mars are the *terrestrial* (Earthlike) planets. They are all somewhat small and about as dense (hard and solid) as the Earth. They have thin *atmospheres*—layers of gas surrounding them. The air we breathe is part of the Earth's atmosphere. The terrestrial planets are almost perfect spheres (round balls), and they rotate (turn on their axes or poles).

The next four planets are called the giant planets. They are much larger than the terrestrial planets, but they are much less dense. You could represent these planets with balls of cotton. The balls should be a little wider than they are high, because the giant planets bulge in the middle. Jupiter, the largest planet, would be five and a half inches (14 cm) across and 2,500 feet (762 m) away from the sun. Saturn would be four and a half inches (11.4 cm) across and 4,600 feet (1,402 m) from the sun. Uranus and Neptune would each be a little less than two inches (5 cm) across. Uranus would be 9,000 feet (2,743 m) from the sun, and Neptune would be 14,500 feet (4,420 m) from the sun.

Pluto, the ninth planet, is so small and so far away that not very much is known about it. While orbits of the other planets are nearly circular, the orbit of Pluto is an ellipse—a flattened circle. Pluto swings in and out of the orbit of Neptune. On the model, Pluto would be a small pea slightly less than four miles (21,120 feet or 6.4 km) out from the sun.

Astronomers have observed some peculiarities or "wobbles" in the orbit of Neptune. These peculiarities have suggested that there might be a tenth planet beyond Pluto.

The planets are all cold bodies. We can see them only because they reflect the light of the sun. The planets also receive almost all of their heat from the sun. Because of this, the planets closer to the sun are generally warmer than those farther away. Also, planets with thicker atmospheres are warmer because an atmosphere holds in heat.

Only two planets, Venus and Mars, have even approximately the right atmosphere and temperature to support life as we know it on Earth. But Venus's atmosphere is mostly carbon dioxide, creating a very hot surface temperature of over 800° F (426° C), with a high atmospheric pressure (weight of the atmosphere). Contrasted to Venus's hot, dense atmosphere is Mars's cold, thin atmosphere. Carbon dioxide and nitrogen are the major gases in Mars's atmosphere. The planet has a cold surface temperature averaging about −80° F (−62° C) with a low atmospheric pressure. In 1976, U.S. Viking space probes landed on Mars to examine its soil for living or once-living organisms. No evidence of life has been found.

Satellites   Several of the major planets have *natural* satellites. A natural satellite orbits a major planet the same way a major planet orbits the sun. Natural satellites are small, solid bodies with usually little or no atmosphere. The moon is the only natural satellite of the Earth. A natural satellite is always smaller than the planet it orbits, but it does not have to be smaller than any planet. Jupiter and Saturn each have a number of satellites, some as large as Mercury.

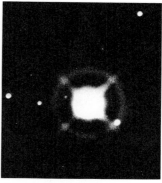

▲ *Uranus is one of the most remote planets. It has a ring system, like Saturn, and 15 satellites or moons. The five largest moons are shown in this photograph taken from Earth.*

Recent findings show that the outermost planet, Pluto, is smaller than astronomers thought—1,370 miles (2,200 km) across. The other surprising thing about this icy ball is that its single moon, Charon, is comparatively large—about 720 miles (1,160 km) across, more than half the size of Pluto itself.

▼ *Saturn is the second largest planet, after Jupiter. Its structure, as shown here, is similar to that of Jupiter. Rings A, B, and C are the main rings, beyond which lie two fainter rings. The rings are made of ice or dust.*

Core

Metallic hydrogen

Liquid hydrogen

Ring A

Cassini's division

Ring B

Ring C (Crepe ring)

SUN   Mercury   Venus   Earth   Mars   Jupiter

▲ *The planets of the solar system move in orbits around the fiery sun. The orbits are shown here as blue loops around a tiny orange ball (the sun). The hazy blue belt between the orbits of Jupiter and Mars marks the orbits of the asteroids. The long orange loop shows the orbit of a comet swinging far out into the solar system. The major satellites, or moons, of the planets are also shown. Some are small: Uranus, for example, has five main moons (illustrated) and ten smaller ones, discovered by the Voyager 2 spacecraft in 1986.*

▶ *The most distant planets (not to scale). From left to right: Uranus with its faint rings and five satellites, Neptune, and Pluto with its satellite called Charon, about half its own diameter.*

Saturn   Uranus   Neptune   Pluto

FACTS ABOUT THE SOLAR SYSTEM

Name	Average distance from sun (millions of miles)	(km)	Diameter at equator miles	(km)	Circles sun in:	Turns on axis in:
Sun	—	—	865,000	(1,392,000)	—	25⅓ days
Moon	—	—	2,160	(3,476)	—	27⅓ days
Mercury	36	(58)	3,015	(4,850)	88 days	59 days
Venus	67	(108)	7,545	(12,140)	224 days	244 days
Earth	93	(150)	7,926	(12,756)	365¼ days	23:56 hours
Mars	142	(228)	4,220	(6,790)	687 days	24:37 hours
Jupiter	483	(778)	88,600	(142,600)	11.9 years	9:50 hours
Saturn	887	(1,427)	74,700	(120,200)	29.5 years	10:14 hours
Uranus	1,783	(2,870)	30,500	(49,000)	84 years	15:48 hours
Neptune	2,794	(4,497)	31,200	(50,000)	164.8 years	15:48 hours
Pluto	3,666	(5,900)	1,800	(1,370)	247.7 years	153 hours

▲ *The dusty, rock-strewn surface of Mars, visited in 1976 by Viking space probes.*

Saturn's surface is a most unpleasant place. Winds blow at speeds of over 1,000 mph (1,600 km/hr).

▼ *Mercury is the planet nearest to the sun. Its surface is pockmarked with craters and, like our moon, also has mountains and valleys.*

The Earth also has several hundred *artificial* (man-made) satellites. And several satellites and space probes launched from Earth have gone into orbit around other planets and around the sun.

Asteroids and Visitors The orbits of about 2,000 asteroids have been mapped, and more asteroids are being discovered all the time. The total number is probably much larger. Most of these asteroids move in nearly circular orbits between the orbits of Mars and Jupiter. A few have more elliptical orbits, swinging toward the sun and then far out.

The largest asteroid, Ceres, is only about one-third the size of the moon and one-fifth the size of the smallest planet, Mercury. Asteroids are too small to have much gravitational pull, so they are too small to hold an atmosphere. Only one, Vesta, can be seen without a telescope.

The exact make-up of a comet is uncertain. Comets are probably collections of frozen gases and dust particles. A comet has a head and, when near the sun, a tail. The tail is probably formed by particles and gases driven off from the head of the comet by the solar wind.

While most planets, satellites, and asteroids have nearly circular orbits, most comets have orbits that look like

▲ *The cloudy atmosphere of Venus hides a mysterious planet.*

flattened circles or open curves. Some comets pass near the Earth at regular intervals, every so many years. Other comets pass by once and are not seen again.

Meteoroids are small, hard bodies flying through space. Most of them are made of stone, but a few are iron. It is not certain exactly where meteoroids come from or how they are formed. Some may be fragments of asteroids.

When a meteoroid enters the Earth's atmosphere, it begins to burn up. From the Earth it looks like a streak of light—a meteor or "shooting star."

"Dust" particles and gases are given off by the sun, by comets, and by the atmospheres of the planets. (Some dust may come from space.) They are scattered around the solar system, between and beyond the planets. Some masses of interplanetary dust can be seen in the reflected light of the sun as the *zodiacal light*.

The largest thing in the solar system, in volume, is not the dust, the planets, or even the sun, but space. In building your imaginary model of the planets, you got some idea of how little space is taken up by the sun and the planets. But the solar system does not end with the planets. It extends outward to the limits of the sun's gravitational pull, or until that pull becomes weaker than the pull of another star. The solar system extends at least as far as the farthest point in the orbit of any known comet, and that would make it a thousand times larger than the area orbited by the planets. And most of that is empty space, without planets.

ALSO READ: ASTRONOMY; ATMOSPHERE; COMET; CONSTELLATION; COPERNICUS, NICOLAUS; DAY AND NIGHT; ECLIPSE; GALILEO; GRAVITY AND GRAVITATION; KEPLER, JOHANNES; METEOR; MILKY WAY; MOON; OBSERVATORY; RADIATION BELT; RADIO ASTRONOMY; SATELLITE; STAR; SUN; UNIVERSE.

SOLID A rock, a book, a baseball, and a nail all have one thing in common. They all are solids. A solid is a kind of matter that has a definite shape and volume (size). If you put a rock into a covered bowl, the rock will still have the same shape and volume. If you put liquid into a covered bowl, the liquid keeps its volume, but takes the shape of the bowl. Gas takes the volume and shape of the bowl.

The particles that make up almost all solids are arranged in an orderly pattern, and they keep this arrangement. The arrangement is called *crystalline*. The particles that make up some solids called *amorphous* solids, such as glass, are not arranged in a completely orderly pattern.

When we say that something is solid, we mean that it is solid at ordinary temperatures. If you heat a solid to a high enough temperature, it will melt and become a liquid.

ALSO READ: CRYSTAL, GAS, LIQUID, MATTER, TEMPERATURE SCALE.

SOLOMON ISLANDS see MELANESIA, PACIFIC ISLANDS.

SOLSTICE see SEASON.

SOLUTION see CHEMISTRY.

SOMALIA This easternmost nation of Africa covers an area often called the "Horn of Africa." Somalia, which is slightly smaller than Texas, juts out into the Indian Ocean. Its western neighbors are Kenya and Ethiopia. The small nation of Djibouti is to the northwest, and the Gulf of Aden to the north. (See the map with the article on AFRICA.)

Somalia is one of the poorest countries in Africa, and it receives economic aid from a number of foreign nations. If it were not for a little rainfall, the land would be a desert. In some regions, the soil looks like red dust. Temperatures sometimes go above 120° F (49° C). The seaport of Mogadishu is the capital.

The planet Mercury is so near the sun that the sun has slowed Mercury's rotation. It spins so slowly that one day on Mercury—from one sunrise to the next—takes 176 Earth days. Mercury goes around the sun in 88 Earth days, meaning, its year lasts 88 Earth days. On Mercury you would have four birthdays a year!

If the sun were the size of a basketball, the Earth would be the size of a pea 284 feet (87 m) away. The nearest star to our own sun would be 8,000 miles (13,000 km) away.

SOMALIA

Capital City: Mogadishu (700,000 people).
Area: 246,219 square miles (637,657 sq. km).
Population: 8,500,000.
Government: Republic.
Natural Resources: Iron ore, gypsum, uranium.
Export Products: Livestock, bananas.
Unit of Money: Somali shilling.
Official Language: Somali.

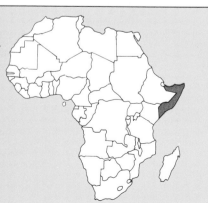

▲ *Somali people gathered for a Muslim celebration. Many are wearing traditional white Muslim caps.*

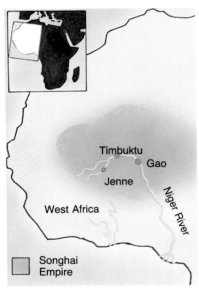

▲ *A map showing the extent of the powerful Songhai Empire in medieval Africa.*

Most of the people are nomadic, moving from place to place with their herds of camels, sheep, goats, and cattle. Agriculture is limited by the low rainfall to riverbanks, coastal regions, and the area between the Shebelle and Juba rivers. The main crops are bananas, sugarcane, sorghum, maize, peanuts, and cotton. Frankincense and myrrh (forest products used in making incense and perfume) are exported.

The Somali are an ancient, proud people who have lived in this region for more than a thousand years. During the A.D. 600's, the Qureishite kingdom was established by people from nearby Yemen. Arabs then settled along the coast of present-day Somali. The people of the region became Muslims. They passed down stories and traditions orally in Somali, a language that had no standard written form until 1973. Arabic, Italian, and English are also spoken.

In the 1500's, Portuguese explorers landed on the coasts and engaged in trade. Later, parts of the area were ruled by the Sultan of Zanzibar. In the last half of the 1800's, the Italians and the British gained footholds, the British establishing control over the northern portion of the country. The British army occupied all of Somalia during World War II. From 1950 until independence in 1960, Somalia was a U.N. Trust Territory, with Italy as the administering authority. The country (until then known as Italian Somaliland and British Somaliland) declared independence in 1960 and became a republic. In 1969, a military group seized power and renamed the country the Somali Democratic Republic. Somalia disputes ownership of the Ogaden desert region with Ethiopia which is peopled mainly by Somalis.

As with Ethiopia, drought is a serious problem which causes frequent and widespread famine.

ALSO READ: AFRICA, ETHIOPIA.

SONGHAI EMPIRE During the Middle Ages a rich empire flourished in West Africa. This was the empire of the Songhai people, who were soldiers, farmers, and traders.

The Songhai Empire included lands in the countries now named Mali, Niger, and Nigeria. Its chief towns were Gao, Jenne, and Timbuktu, which grew up on the Niger River, a main trade route for the peoples of West Africa. From about A.D. 800 the Songhai controlled not only river trade, but also the caravans that merchants sent northward. Salt and gold were prized goods carried by these caravans of camels and donkeys. The Songhai merchants and townspeople were Muslims, while country villagers mostly practiced local religions.

The Songhai grew rich on the salt and gold trades. Their kings challenged the rulers of the Mali Empire, another black empire that lay farther north. This led to war. There were also quarrels between Songhai princes, and these began to weaken the empire. In the 1500's, the Songhai were attacked by armies from Morocco. The Moroccans had firearms, unlike the Songhai, and these powerful new weapons helped lead them to victory. The last Songhai king, Issihak II, was defeated, and the Songhai Empire was taken into Morrocan control. With its towns and rich trade routes captured, the Songhai Empire was no more.

ALSO READ: AFRICA.

SOUND Hook one end of a rubber band to something solid. Stretch the rubber band with one hand and pluck it with your other hand. See how the rubber band vibrates—moves back and forth very quickly. As the rubber band vibrates, you can hear a humming sound.

If you can find many different sizes

of rubber bands, you can try them out. You will discover that each kind of rubber band makes a different humming sound. Thin, short rubber bands make a high-sounding hum. Thick, long rubber bands make a low-sounding hum.

All sounds are made by vibrations. Make a humming sound with your mouth and put your fingers lightly on your "Adam's apple." You can feel your "Adam's apple" vibrate. If you have a guitar or a piano in your house, you can try the same experiment. Pluck a guitar string or strike one of the piano keys. Let your fingers touch the guitar or piano very lightly. You will feel the vibrations with your fingers.

If you have a tuning fork, you can even see these vibrations. Strike one of the tines (prongs) of the tuning fork. Carefully touch the tine to a soup plate filled with water. You can see how the water vibrates. As the humming sound dies away, the water also stops vibrating.

How Sounds Travel Sounds need something to travel through. Most

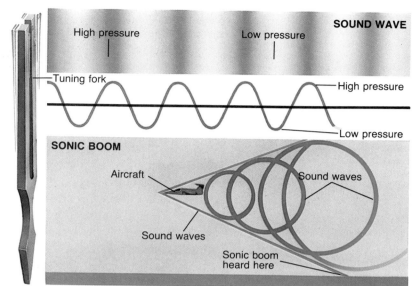

SOUND WAVE
High pressure
Low pressure
Tuning fork
High pressure
Low pressure

SONIC BOOM
Aircraft
Sound waves
Sound waves
Sonic boom heard here

▼ *When a column of air vibrates, it gives out a musical note. As its length changes, so does the note. Putting fingers over the holes of a wind instrument in different combinations changes the notes.*

sounds travel through the air. Air is made up of molecules of gas. These molecules are extremely small. Billions of molecules will fill a thimble.

Go back to the vibrating rubber band. Imagine that you can see the molecules of air. Imagine also that the rubber band vibrates back and forth very slowly. When the rubber band is moving in one direction, it presses against the molecules of air next to it. The molecules of air are pushed together. These molecules of air then push the molecules of air that are next to them.

If you have ever tipped over a row of dominoes by making the first domino fall, you can imagine how the molecules of air gradually push against molecules that are farther and farther away from the rubber band. This pushing of molecules away from the rubber band is similar to how a wave of water travels away from a stone falling into a pond.

What happens when the rubber band moves in the other direction? The rubber band sucks the molecules of air after it. This leaves some vacant space next to the molecules. Nearby molecules are then sucked into the empty space. It is as if a row of dominoes you had tipped over all stood up again, one by one, when you raised the first domino.

Every time the rubber band moves

▲ *Sound is a form of energy. When a tuning fork is struck, it gives out waves. The waves consist of alternate bands of high and low pressure (top diagram). A supersonic aircraft flies faster than sound (lower diagram). The speed of sound is greater at sea level than high in the air, but at any height it is known as Mach 1. Twice the speed of sound is Mach 2, and so on. A supersonic aircraft reaches any point before its sound does. The sound arrives in a strong shock wave, formed by the bands of pressure traveling together. On the ground people hear this shock wave as a bang or "sonic boom."*

The loudest noise ever created in a laboratory— about 400,000 decibels— was produced by NASA at Huntsville, Alabama, in 1965. Extremely loud sounds such as this can destroy solid materials.

SOUND

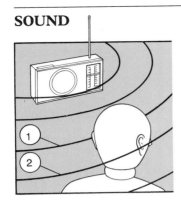

▲ *Sound waves from the radio reach the left ear (1) only one-hundred-thousandth of a second before they reach the right ear (2). But the brain detects the difference and tells you that the radio is to the left of your head.*

Sound from climber

Sound returns to climber

▲ *When you hear an echo of a sound, you hear the sound two or more times. The sound bounces off a wall or some other surface. After you hear the first sound wave directly, you may hear further echoes as the sound goes backward and forward. The climber in this picture hears the sound of his voice reflected from a mountain.*

back and forth, the molecules of air make waves in the air, something like the waves that are made in water when you drop a stone in the water. When these waves of squeezed-together molecules strike your ear, you hear the sound made by the rubber band.

The Speed of Sound Whenever a sound is made, the sound travels through the air at a speed of over 700 miles (1,100 km) an hour. Putting it another way, it takes about five seconds for a sound to travel one mile through the air.

Light travels through the air almost instantaneously. Because light travels so fast, you can tell how far away a flash of lightning is from you. The flash of lightning reaches you in an instant. The clap of thunder takes five seconds to travel one mile. Therefore, when you see the lightning, immediately start counting, "One and . . . two and . . . three and . . . four and . . . five and," and so on until you hear the thunder. Now divide the number of seconds by five. The answer is the distance of the lightning in miles. (To get the answer in kilometers, multiply the figure by 1.61 on a calculator.)

Sound travels faster through liquids or solids than through gases, such as air. In fact, sound travels four times as fast in water as it does in air. Sound travels faster in water because the molecules of water are packed closer together than the molecules of air are. Sound also travels about 16 times faster through iron than it does through air.

Echoes Sound can bounce off walls and cliffs and other straight, hard surfaces. The sound waves will bounce off a wall just as a rubber ball does.

Sounds reflect even better under water. The next time you are in a noisy swimming pool, hold your breath and duck your head under

water. Then listen. You will be surprised how loud the sounds are and how strong the echoes are. If you are at the seaside, listen underwater to the sounds made by people playing on the beach and swimming. They will sound very loud. The *sonar* equipment used by navies can listen for enemy submarines. The sonar picks up the faint sounds a submarine makes when it travels under water.

Music and Noise What is the difference between music and noise? When you pluck a stretched rubber band, the humming sound you hear is *music*. It is musiclike because the back-and-forth vibrations of the rubber band are very regular. When you knock a stick against a wall, you make *noise* because the back-and-forth vibrations of the stick are very irregular. The vibrations of the stick hap-

▼ *Acoustic engineers work out how to stop sound waves bouncing off concert-hall walls and ceilings and producing distracting echoes. This is a model hall with seats and blocks to take the place of people.*

INTENSITY LEVELS OF SOME COMMON SOUNDS
(measured in decibels)

Threshold of hearing	0
Whisper	10 to 15
Light music	30
Conversation	60
(average speaking voice)	
Subway train	100
Thunder	110
Threshold of pain	120
(the level at which sound may hurt the ears)	

pen every which way. The study of the nature and the characteristics of musical sound is called *harmonics*.

Musical instruments make sounds in one of three ways. In a guitar, a violin, or a piano, you make a string vibrate. You make it vibrate by plucking the string on the guitar, by striking the string inside the piano via a piano key, or by drawing a bow across the string on the violin. The continued vibration of the strings causes the sound box of the instrument to vibrate. These secondary vibrations form the sound quality, or *resonance*, of the instrument.

Another kind of musical instrument depends on making a solid surface vibrate. A xylophone, for example, is made up of different-sized bars of wood. When you strike one of these bars of wood with a soft hammer, the bar of wood vibrates.

The third kind of musical instrument makes a sound when the air inside of it vibrates. Instruments of this kind—tubas, bugles, trumpets, and trombones—are wind instruments. So are reed instruments like flutes and clarinets.

■ LEARN BY DOING
You can make a wind instrument out of a drinking straw. Flatten one end of the straw. Cut the corners off the sides of the flattened end of the straw. Now put the flattened end of the straw in your mouth and blow. You may have to practice blowing in

different ways before you get a humming sound from the straw.

Then, take a deep breath and play a long note through the straw. As you blow, cut a short piece from the end of the straw with a pair of scissors. You will notice how the sound becomes higher. Quickly cut another short piece from the end of the straw, and then another short piece. Every time you snip a piece off the straw, the sound gets higher. ■

The kind of sound that comes from the straw depends on how long the inside of the straw is. When you blow into the straw, the air inside the straw is made to vibrate back and forth. The longer the straw, the longer the vibrations of air. And the longer the vibrations, the lower the sound. On the other hand, the shorter the vibrations of air, the higher the sound. These vibrations are waves, and like water waves, they have crests (high points) and valleys (low points). The distance from one crest to another is the *wavelength* of the wave. The *frequency* of a wave is the number of crests that pass by in a second. Because all sound waves travel through air at the same speed, a long wavelength means a low frequency, and a short wavelength means a high frequency.

We hear frequency as *pitch*. A high frequency has a high pitch, and a low frequency has a low pitch. A flute has a higher pitch than a drum has.

Sound is also measured by intensity or loudness. The measure of intensity is the *decibel*. A sound that is just loud enough to be heard has an intensity of one decibel. A sound of 120 decibels is so loud it is painful.

ALSO READ: EAR, HEARING, MUSIC, SPEECH, WAVE.

SOUSA, JOHN PHILIP (1854–1932)
The American composer and band conductor, John Philip Sousa, is

▲ *Sound is absorbed by soft materials such as cloth or plastic foam. To make recording studios soundproof, the walls have no windows (sound can travel through glass). The walls and ceilings are lined with sound-absorbing materials.*

The brass instrument called the sousaphone was designed by John Philip Sousa and first made in 1899. It is a kind of tuba with a very deep sound and a bell-shaped end. The sousaphone gives a resounding bass rhythm in a marching band.

▲ *John Philip Sousa, American bandmaster and composer.*

The deepest mine in the world is Western Deep Gold Mine in South Africa. It is 12,600 feet (3,840 m) deep and could hold eight Empire State buildings, one on top of the other.

often called the "March King." He wrote many stirring marches, including the well-known "Stars and Stripes Forever."

Sousa was born in Washington, D.C. His father was Portuguese and his mother Bavarian. At the age of 13, Sousa became an apprentice (learner) musician with the United States Marine Corps Band. He learned to play several band instruments, including the trombone. Sousa also took violin lessons and studied musical composition.

Sousa stayed with the Marines for five years. He then worked as conductor and musician with several orchestras in the United States. He began to write music and showed his interest in musical theater by composing several operettas (light musical dramas). The most successful of these was *El Capitan*, which contained a march by the same name.

In 1880, Sousa accepted an offer to become the conductor of the Marine Corps Band. He wrote "Semper Fidelis," which became the official march of the band. In 1892, Sousa organized his own professional band, which gave concerts all over the world. Among the most familiar of his marches are the "Washington Post March," "High School Cadets," and "Liberty Bell."

ALSO READ: BRASS INSTRUMENTS, OPERA, ORCHESTRAS AND BANDS.

SOUTH AFRICA The Republic of South Africa occupies the southernmost part of Africa. The country is about three times the size of California. South Africa is divided into four provinces—the Cape of Good Hope (also called Cape Province), Natal, the Orange Free State, and the Transvaal. The black homelands of Transkei, Bophuthatswana, Ciskei, and Venda exist within the country. Bordering South Africa on the north are Botswana and Zimbabwe. Mozambique and Swaziland are to the northeast and Namibia to the northwest. The small country of Lesotho is completely surrounded by South Africa. (See the map with the article on AFRICA.)

On the eastern coast along the Indian Ocean, the weather is hot and humid. Along the western coast, there is a cold current (Benguela) of water flowing up from the Antarctic. The country's average year-round temperature is about 60° F (15.5° C).

In the northwest central area of the Transvaal and the Orange Free State lies a region of high plains called the *veldt* (or *veld*). Good farmlands are found there, along with huge deposits of diamonds and gold. Coal, iron ore, uranium, platinum, asbestos, manganese, and many other minerals are found in South Africa, too. The country has many industries, chief of which are chemicals, clothing, iron and steel, and processed foods.

SOUTH AFRICA

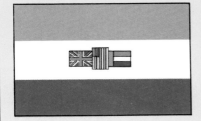

Capital cities: Cape Town (legislative, 1,900,000 people), Pretoria (administrative, 822,000 people), Bloemfontein (judicial, 231,000 people).

Area: 471,479 sq. miles (1,221,037 sq. km).

Population: 35,600,000.

Government: Republic.

Natural Resources: Coal, iron ore, manganese, chrome, copper, gold, silver.

Export Products: Gold, diamonds, fruit, vegetables.

Unit of Money: Rand.

Official Languages: Afrikaans, English.

▲ *A worker pouring molten gold into ingots (molded blocks). South Africa is a leading world producer of gold.*

Johannesburg is the largest city, followed by Cape Town (the legislative capital), Durban, Pretoria (the administrative capital), Port Elizabeth, and Bloemfontein (the judicial capital). On the Transvaal's eastern border is Kruger National Park, a protected wild animal reserve visited by tourists.

The original inhabitants of the area were Hottentots and Bushmen. Dutch settlers were the first Europeans in the area. The British occupied the cape at the end of the 1700's. After fighting a war with the descendants of the Dutch called the Boers (farmers), the British established the Union of South Africa in 1910. Britain granted the country full independence as a member of the Commonwealth of Nations in 1931. After World War II, the Afrikaners (descendants of the Boers) gained political control. Their policies led to the founding of the Republic of South Africa, a totally independent nation, in 1961. In that year, South Africa also ended its membership in the Commonwealth.

South Africa is governed by a president, a prime minister, and a parliament. The National Party of the white-dominated government believes in *apartheid*, or separation of the races. The Africans, Coloreds (persons of mixed race), and Asians (primarily Indians) outnumber the whites by more than four to one, but their civil and political rights are severely limited. For example, black South Africans have no vote. South Africa is strongly criticized by other nations for its racial policies.

ALSO READ: AFRICA, BOER WAR, NAMIBIA, TRANSKEI.

SOUTH AMERICA South America stretches from the warm waters of the Caribbean Sea in the north to the icy waters near the Antarctic Circle, where the Pacific and Atlantic waters join. Chile has many islands, but only a few islands are scattered along the rest of the continent. A narrow strip of land, the Isthmus of Panama, connects North and South America.

The continent of South America is smaller than Eurasia, Africa, or North America, but larger than Australia or Antarctica. South America consists of 12 independent nations. Brazil is the largest, with almost half of the continent's land area. The other countries in order of size are Argentina, Peru, Colombia, Bolivia, Venezuela, Chile, Paraguay, Ecuador, Guyana, Uruguay, and Suriname (or Surinam). French Guiana is a territory belonging to France. South America is part of the larger area called Latin America, which includes Mexico, Central America, and some Caribbean islands.

Even though South America is about twice as large as the United States, it has a smaller population. Most of the people live near the coast, but a few large and very modern cities are in the mountains and interior plains. Some primitive Indian tribes still live in forest villages, remote from civilization.

▲ *The blacks of South Africa include the Zulus, a people who first settled in what is now northern Natal, South Africa, in the 1600's. By the 1800's, the Zulus controlled an empire, which they held by the skillful use of their armies. Eventually, the Zulus were defeated by the British.*

The population of South America has increased by a staggering 100,000,000 in the last 20 years.

▲ *Patagonia is the name of the upland plain in the south of Argentina. This wild region has deposits of oil, coal, and other minerals.*

SOUTH AMERICA

Total Population: 273,000,000.

Highest Point: Mount Aconcagua in Argentina, 22,834 feet (6,960 m).

Lowest Point: Valdes Peninsula in Argentina, 131 feet (40 m) below sea level.

Longest River: Amazon River, 3,900 miles (6,276 km).

Biggest Lake: Lake Maracaibo in Venezuela, 5,000 square miles (12,950 sq. km).

Largest City: São Paulo (15,000,000 people in metropolitan area).

Geography South America is a continent with one of the world's most barren deserts—the Atacama in northern Chile—and also the high, cold Andes Mountains. These great mountains are like a backbone for South America. They follow the coastline in the west, from the Caribbean Sea to the tip of the continent at Cape Horn. The Andes is the longest mountain range in the world. It is about 4,500 miles (7,242 km) long and, in some places, over 400 miles (640 km) wide. About 50 peaks in the Andes are over 20,000 feet (6,000 m) high. Mount Aconcagua in Argentina is the highest at 22,834 feet (6,960 m). The Andes range contains high plateaus and deep gorges. On one of the plateaus is the highest large lake in the world, Lake Titicaca, between Bolivia and Peru. West of the lake are many volcanic mountain peaks.

The Guiana Highlands, the Brazilian Highlands, and Patagonia are other major regions in South America. They include plateaus, hills, and low mountains. In the Venezuelan part of the Guiana Highlands is the world's highest waterfall, Angel Falls, which drops 3,212 feet (979 m). The Brazilian Highlands stretch about 2,000 miles (3,200 km) along the Atlantic coast and many hundreds of miles into the interior. Patagonia, in the extreme south of the continent, is a cool, dry plateau.

The Amazon Basin is a vast plain that extends from the Andes Mountains to the Atlantic Ocean. Here, the largest river system in the world, the Amazon, flows through the dense tropical forest. North of the basin between the Andes and the Guiana highlands are the Orinoco *llanos*, vast, flat grasslands with low hills and almost no people. South of the Brazilian plateaus, another lowland is drained by three great rivers, the Paraguay, the Paraná, and the Uruguay. They flow into the large estuary called the Río de la Plata. The northern part of this lowland is called the Gran Chaco. In the south, fertile grasslands known as the *pampas* form a large part of Argentina.

Climate Most of the continent lies south of the equator, where the seasons are just the opposite of those in the north. The cold winds of winter blow in July and August, while people swelter in the heat of January and February. The shortest day of the year is in June, and the longest day is in December.

The Amazon Basin, lying just south of the equator, has a hot, tropical climate year-round, because here the sun's rays shine almost directly down with great intensity. Some places on the equator, however, are at higher altitudes, which keep them from being so hot. Quito, the capital

	SOUTH AMERICAN NATIONS			
Country	Area (sq. miles)	Area (sq. km)	Population	Capital
Argentina	1,068,379	2,766,889	32,600,000	Buenos Aires
Bolivia	422,265	1,093,581	6,570,000	La Paz and Sucre
Brazil	3,286,727	8,511,965	154,000,000	Brasília
Chile	295,754	765,945	12,866,000	Santiago
Colombia	439,769	1,138,914	31,820,000	Bogotá
Ecuador	109,491	283,561	10,500,000	Quito
French Guiana (French Territory)	35,138	91,000	92,000	Cayenne
Guyana	82,632	214,000	800,000	Georgetown
Paraguay	157,059	406,752	4,500,000	Asuncíon
Peru	496,260	1,285,216	21,800,000	Lima
Suriname	63,042	163,265	400,000	Paramaribo
Uruguay	68,042	176,216	3,000,000	Montevideo
Venezuela	352,170	912,050	19,250,000	Caracas

Barranquilla• •Maracaibo Caracas■

Orinoco

VENEZUELA

•Medellin

Georgetown■
Paramaribo
•Cayenne

GUYANA SURINAM FRENCH GUIANA

Llanos

■Bogotá

•Cali COLOMBIA

Equator

•Quito

ECUADOR

Guayaquil•

•Belém

Manáus•

Amazon

Fortaleza•

PERU Selvas BRAZIL

Chiclayo•

Trujillo•

Recife•

São Francisco

•Salvador

Callão• •Lima

A
N
D
E
S

•Cuzco

BOLIVIA

•La Paz

■Brasília

•Cochabamba

PACIFIC
OCEAN

Oruro•

M
O
U
N
T
A
I
N
S

•Sucre

Brazilian
Highlands

Paraná

PARAGUAY

Rio de
Janeiro•

São Paulo•

Gran Chaco

•Asunción

Atacama Desert

CHILE

•Pôrto Alegre

Córdoba•

Rosario•

URUGUAY

Valparaiso• ▲Mt.Aconcagua
■ Santiago

Buenos Aires• •Montevideo
■ ■
La Plata

ARGENTINA

P
a
m
p
a
s

•Bahia Blanca

Colorado

ATLANTIC
OCEAN

Chubut

SOUTH AMERICA

Patagonia

**Falkland
Is.**

**Tierra del
Fuego**

**Cape
Horn**

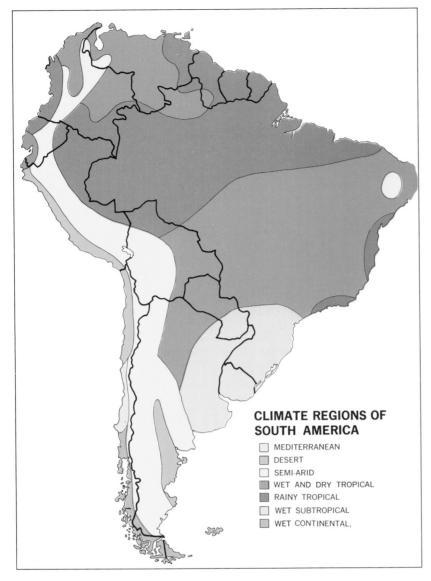

CLIMATE REGIONS OF SOUTH AMERICA

☐ MEDITERRANEAN
☐ DESERT
☐ SEMI-ARID
☐ WET AND DRY TROPICAL
☐ RAINY TROPICAL
☐ WET SUBTROPICAL
☐ WET CONTINENTAL,

of Ecuador, has cool weather all year because it lies nestled in the Andes Mountains at over 9,000 feet (2,700 m). The Amazon Basin has areas with some of the heaviest rainfall in the world. There is rich farmland in many places and rocky, scorched earth in others.

Natural Resources Rich mineral deposits in South America furnish raw materials for industries. There are thick forests of valuable timber and great rivers that can provide waterpower for electricity.

The most important oil deposits are in Venezuela, one of the largest oil producers in the world. Colombia, Ecuador, and Peru also have oil fields. Bolivia, high in the Andes, has tin, and Chile has copper and nitrate. Guyana and Suriname have bauxite from which aluminum is made. There are also large deposits of iron ore, manganese, lead, zinc, gold, and silver.

Brazil has the largest tropical forest in the world, in the Amazon Basin. Its trees provide lumber, rubber, Brazil nuts, oils, waxes, and medicines. The importance of this rain forest to the Earth's ecology is of even greater value.

Since the end of World War II, South America has built many factories to make use of its raw materials. Textiles, processed foods, chemicals, automobiles, machinery, electrical appliances, and paper are among the principal manufactured products. Today, more than half of the people earn their living by working in factories. However, many goods must be imported through the sale of farm products, such as bananas, beef, coffee, cotton, sugar, wheat, hides, furs, and wool.

Plants and Animals Many crops first grown by the Indians in South

◄ *A Peruvian woman sells traditional and modern knitwear at a market in Luzco.*

America are now grown on other continents. These crops include peanuts, potatoes, tomatoes, cacao, tobacco, and cassava.

The rain forests are the living places of many animals. Giant anteaters, monkeys, sloths, jaguars, and many colorful toucans, macaws, and other kinds of parrots live in the forests. The tapir and armadillo are South American animals. Crocodiles and fierce little piranha fish live in some of the rivers.

People Although the climate and landscape and people differ from country to country, there are ways in which the South American countries are somewhat alike. Almost all of them were settled by Spanish or Portuguese colonists. As a result, most people speak Spanish and follow the Catholic religion. Portuguese is spoken in Brazil. Dutch is the language of Suriname, and French is spoken in French Guiana. Large numbers of Indians speak their tribal languages. Every country has many festivals, many of which are connected with the church. People all over South America love music and dancing. Instruments such as marimbas and maracas originated here, as well as dances such as the tango.

Much of the art in the colonial days of South America was influenced by the Catholic faith of the Spanish and Portuguese. After independence was won, artists began to integrate the art of the native Indians into original paintings, sculpture, and other arts. South American Indians have always been expert weavers and potters.

All of the South American countries won their independence from Spain or Portugal in the 1800's. They are republics, with constitutions much like that of the United States, although not all have had stable democratic governments.

The first people to live on the South American continent were the Indians. Some of their descendants

still live in the forests and mountains in much the same way their ancestors did hundreds of years ago. They live in small villages, sometimes in very crude homes made of mud or stone. Most of them are very poor and work hard to raise enough food for their families. Almost all of them make their living by farming or herding, but most do not own the land where they work. Many of these people cannot read or write. They live far from schools and the children are needed to work in the fields. They speak Indian languages.

In the tropical lowlands and rain forest, a few groups of Indians still live much as people did in the Stone Age. They hunt and fish and raise simple crops. Many collect wild fruits and other plants for food. In Ecuador, the Jivaro Indians use blowguns with poison darts while hunting in the forest.

Many South Americans, however, live in the great cities of the continent.

South America has no really large animals. The biggest wild animal in the continent is the hog-like tapir. It is only about three feet (a meter) high at the shoulder.

▼ The llama is the most useful native South American draft animal. It carries loads in the high Andes Mountains, and its wool is used to make warm clothing.

▲ *These reed boats are made by the people of Peru and Bolivia for use on Lake Titicaca, the world's highest navigable lake.*

▲ *Many South Americans carry their babies in slings on their backs. Fast-growing populations are a common feature of the continent's countries.*

Some of them live in elegant old homes with patios and iron grillwork balconies. Many live in apartments or in shanty towns (slums) on the edge of the cities. Away from the cities, some people live on large estates or ranches where coffee and other crops and cattle are raised. Some of the estates have been owned by the same family since the first settlers arrived. The families are very close, and sometimes many members live together. They are usually well educated. The landowners often provide the officers in the army or important officials, and so control the government and protect their land.

In colonial times, the Spanish and Portuguese brought in black slaves from Africa to work on the plantations. Many people in South America are mixtures of European, black, and Indian ancestry. This mixture of people has added much to the literature, art, music, dance, and folklore of the continent.

All over South America are found people with ancestors of different races. They are called *mestizos* if they are part European and part Indian, and *mulattos* if they are part European and part black. About one-half of the South American population is of mixed ancestry.

During the past century, other people have migrated to South America. Shepherds in Patagonia have come from England, Scotland, and Wales. Japanese have settled in Brazil. Ger-

mans, Italians, Poles, Jews, and others have come in great numbers, many to escape from Europe after World War II.

Although much of South America's land is not suitable for farming because of the mountains, deserts, and jungles, agriculture is very important. Many of the people make their living from the land. In the Andes are scattered fertile valleys where livestock is raised and crops are grown, some on terraced hillsides. More than half the world's coffee is grown in South America, most of it in Colombia and Brazil. In some areas fruits, vegetables and grain are harvested. Sugarcane and cacao grow well in the low-lying tropical areas. Cattle, sheep, llamas, and alpacas graze where it is too cold or dry to raise crops. In Argentina, *gauchos* (cowboys) care for great herds of cattle on the plains.

The waters off the coasts of Peru and Ecuador, in western South America, are rich fishing areas. Fish caught here range in size from the small anchovy to the large tuna.

History South American civilizations were well developed long before the first European explorers arrived in the early 1500's. The most advanced was the Inca Empire which domi-

▼ *Cape Horn lies at the most southerly tip of South America. It belongs to Chile. The seas here are very stormy and extremely hazardous to shipping.*

nated other Indian tribes in Bolivia, Peru, Ecuador and parts of Chile and Argentina. South America was settled by Europeans before North America. As early as the 1530's, explorers were traveling up the Río de la Plata, and in 1537, they established a fort at Asunción, Paraguay. In Peru, Francisco Pizarro with only a small number of fellow Spaniards conquered the Inca Indians. In many places, the Indians had developed a high degree of civilization, with organized governments and magnificent cities. But they were treated cruelly by the conquerors, who thought only of riches. Only a few priests who served as missionaries treated the Indians well. They brought them education, a new religion, and a new language.

By the end of the 1500's, the control of South America by Spain and Portugal was well under way. They ruled their South American colonies for 290 years, while the North American colonies belonged to England for just 174 years. By 1607, the date of the first settlement in Virginia, there were already towns in many parts of South America. Each was governed by officials appointed by the kings of Spain and Portugal. The Catholic Church was responsible for much of the life in the early days. Because much of the wealth was sent back to Europe, trade and industry did not develop very fast.

There was much unrest in South America during these years. Some of the *creoles* (people born in South America of Spanish parents) were angry because they were not allowed to take part in the government. They wanted to rebel and form independent nations. One of the creoles was Simón Bolívar, who helped many South American countries win their independence in the early 1800's when Spain's power in Europe was declining.

The leaders of the newly formed South American republics called themselves presidents, but actually many were dictators. This is still true for some countries, for although they are republics, there are few democratic elections. Abuses of civil rights occur, and guerrilla rebels disrupt life in some states. In some of the countries, a *junta*, or group of military officers, holds power. Poverty, unemployment, and disease are serious problems in parts of South America. However, some South American nations, such as Brazil, are emerging as major regional powers.

For further information on:
Cities, *see* BUENOS AIRES, RIO DE JANEIRO, SÃO PAULO.
History, *see* BOLÍVAR, SIMÓN; COLUMBUS, CHRISTOPHER; CONQUISTADOR; MAGELLAN, FERDINAND; ORGANIZATION OF AMERICAN STATES; PIZARRO, FRANCISCO; PORTUGAL; SPAIN; SPANISH HISTORY; ROMANCE LANGUAGES.
Indians, *see* INCA; INDIANS, AMERICAN.
Physical Features, *see* AMAZON RIVER, ANDES MOUNTAINS, ATLANTIC OCEAN, CARIBBEAN SEA, DESERT, EQUATOR, JUNGLE, PACIFIC OCEAN, PANAMA CANAL.
For individual countries, see Index at name.

The tallest South American tree is the Brazil-nut tree of the Amazon River forests. It grows to a height of 150 feet (45 m).

▼ *In 1960, Brasília replaced Rio de Janeiro as the capital of Brazil. Like Washington, D.C., it is a planned city with government buildings, parks, and a large artificial lake. Other South American cities are busy, chaotic (unplanned) and crowded places compared to this.*

▲ *Two children gaze out from this jetty at the sunset over South Carolina's Low Country, near the Atlantic Ocean coastline.*

SOUTH CAROLINA Parts of the city of Charleston, South Carolina, look the way they did in colonial days. Many of the old houses are examples of the finest early American architecture. On Rainbow Row along the waterfront, each house is painted a different color. But modern Charleston is also the chief seaport of the state, and before the American Revolution, it was the capital.

The Land and Climate South Carolina, on the Atlantic coast, is shaped like a piece of pie wedged between North Carolina and Georgia. The state is divided into two parts. One is the Up Country. The other, nearer the ocean, is the Low Country. These two parts are separated by the Fall Line (rivers that cross this line have falls along it). The line, running a little east of the capital, Columbia, crosses the state from the Georgia border to North Carolina.

Northwest of the Fall Line is the Up Country. Most of it is the hilly Piedmont Plateau. But the short northwestern border of the state is in the Blue Ridge, which is part of the Appalachian Mountains.

Southeast of the Fall Line is the Low Country, which covers about two-thirds of the state. The Low Country is part of the long Atlantic Coastal Plain. Much of it is gently rolling hills, but near the coast it is almost level. It drains poorly. The rivers flow slowly and there are many marshes, cypress trees, and reeds growing in the swamp water.

Over half of South Carolina is covered with woods, mostly pine. The Low Country has oak and gum, too. Poplar, sycamore, and black walnut grow in Up Country forests.

Summers in the Low Country are very warm. Near the coast, however, ocean breezes make summer days pleasant. Winters are mild in all parts of the state, with little snow. There is plenty of rain for crops everywhere.

History This land of hills and plains, with its gentle climate, is a good place for people. Many Indian tribes lived here. On the coast were small tribes, which together were called the Cusabo. Their special enemy was the warlike Westo tribe. In the Piedmont, the Cherokee were the most powerful Indians.

The first Europeans to reach South Carolina were Spaniards. For 20 years, they had a fort on Parris Island in the south. (U.S. Marines train there today.) In 1586, the Spaniards withdrew to Florida.

The English were the first to build a lasting settlement. In 1670, the English colony of Carolina was founded. Later on, it became two colonies, North Carolina and South Carolina. In 1670, English and Irish settlers sailed up the Ashley River and built a settlement named Charles Towne in honor of King Charles II. (It is called Charleston today.) French Huguenots (Protestants) also arrived.

Ten years later, the colonists moved to the point where the Cooper River meets the Ashley. A big harbor lies here. Soon ships from England were tying up at Charles Towne wharves. They loaded on furs that Indians had brought down the rivers

▼ *Charleston, in southern South Carolina, is a historic city. The houses, many built in the 1700's and 1800's, are a major attraction for visitors. Palm trees, which do not grow much further north, add to the beauty of the city.*

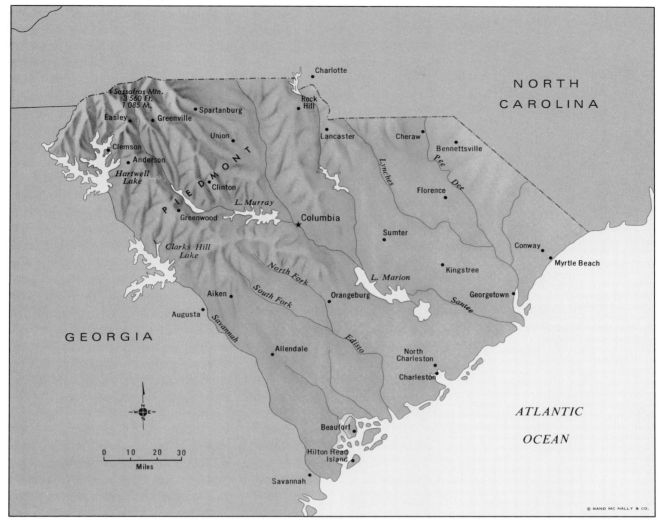

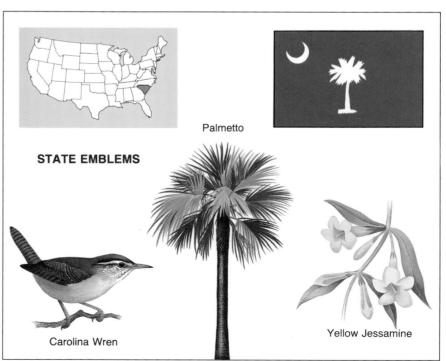

SOUTH CAROLINA

Capital and largest city
Columbia (101,000 people)

Area
31,055 square miles (80,426 sq. km). Rank: 40th

Population
3,470,000 people. Rank: 25th

Statehood
May 23, 1788 (eighth to ratify the Constitution)

Principal rivers
Pee Dee River, Edisto River

Highest point
Sassafras Mountain; 3,560 feet (1,085 m) in the Blue Ridge

Motto
Dum spiro spero ("While I Breathe, I Hope")

Song
"Carolina"

Famous people
John Caldwell Calhoun, Robert Young Hayne, Andrew Jackson

STATE EMBLEMS

Palmetto

Carolina Wren

Yellow Jessamine

▲ *Traditional Scottish customs such as playing the bagpipes and wearing tartan kilts are kept alive in Up Country, South Carolina, where there were many Scottish settlers.*

Bull Island, one of South Carolina's Sea Islands, is part of a wildlife refuge. Giant sea turtles swim about. Herons, egrets, and graceful ibis live on the island. Alligators are often seen lying on the mud flats.

in canoes. They also took on rice and indigo grown on nearby coastal plantations. (Indigo was used in making blue dye.)

The colonists faced dangers. In 1686, Spaniards from Florida attacked the colony. French warships threatened Charles Towne in 1706. Later, there were Indian wars. Pirates often captured ships nearby. Thousands of black slaves were brought from Africa to work on the plantations. By 1700, there were many more blacks than whites in South Carolina.

Living in the Low Country were the English plantation owners and their slaves. Here also was Charleston. It was the home of craftworkers, and of rich merchants who traded with England. Charleston was the first city in the American colonies to have many of the refinements of European cities. Charleston had the first museum, the first municipal college, the first landscape gardens, and the first prescription drugstore of any city in the American colonies.

The Up Country was very different. It had been settled by Scotch-Irish and German farmers. Their farms were small. Most of them had no slaves. Up Country farmers resented the colony being run by Low Country landowners and merchants. They demanded a voice in the colony's government. Shortly before the American Revolution, they won a voice. In the Revolution, some South

Carolinians took the king's side. Others fought for independence.

After the Revolution, cotton became the main crop. More slaves were brought in for the cotton plantations. White South Carolinians feared that the nation would decide to abolish slavery. In December 1860, the state's leaders voted to secede (withdraw) from the Union. The next year, South Carolina and other Southern states formed the Confederate States of America. The Civil War began at Fort Sumter in Charleston Harbor, when the Confederates bombarded the fort and the Northern troops surrendered.

The war ruined South Carolina. United States troops occupied the state after the war until 1877. White South Carolinians then used force to gain control of state and local governments. Laws that discriminated against blacks were passed.

Today, South Carolina's blacks enjoy the same rights as the whites do. Blacks have won election to local boards and state offices. The state's once-segregated public school system is now integrated, but some schools have been slow to change.

South Carolinians at Work The manufacturing of textiles is the state's leading industry. Other important manufactured products are chemicals, machinery, electrical equipment, paper, and furniture. South Carolina has ample electric power for industry. The large Lake Wylie power plant, completed in 1981, produces electricity from nuclear energy. The Atomic Energy Commission's Savannah River power plant, completed in 1963, produces plutonium and other nuclear materials. Agriculture is a major business in South Carolina. Tobacco, soybeans, cotton, peaches, and corn are the leading crops. Beef cattle, hogs, and chickens are raised.

Many tourists come to South Carolina. The seaside resort of Myrtle

Beach has crowds of visitors each summer. People also visit the Sea Islands, which lie along the coast south of the Santee River.

ALSO READ: APPALACHIAN MOUNTAINS, CONFEDERATE STATES OF AMERICA, FORT SUMTER, NORTH CAROLINA.

SOUTH DAKOTA The state of South Dakota received its name from the Sioux Indians, who call themselves the Dakota. South Dakota's nicknames are the "Coyote State" and the "Sunshine State" (the state is known for its comfortable sunny climate).

Each year, millions of tourists visit South Dakota, especially the Black Hills in the western part. These hills are mountains and they are not really black; their pine forests give them a dark green color. But the Sioux Indians called them the Black Hills. Mount Rushmore in the hills is famous for its huge sculpture of the faces of Presidents Washington, Jefferson, Lincoln, and Theodore Roosevelt. Near Mount Rushmore is Harney Peak, the highest mountain east of the Rockies.

The Land and Climate The state is shaped like a rectangle. In length and width, it nearly matches its northern and southern neighbors, North Dakota and Nebraska. The state is made up mostly of two kinds of plains. Much of western South Dakota is in the Great Plains, where the land is rolling and has few trees. Its grass needs little water. East of the James River, South Dakota has plains of a different kind. Instead of belonging to the Great Plains, they belong to the plains region near the Great Lakes.

A great river, the Missouri, flows through the state from north to south. The land west of the river is very different from the land east of it. Long ago, a great glacier covered the eastern part of the state. When it melted, the deposits of clay and sand it left formed rich land for farming. The west is mostly cattle country.

Rainfall is fairly light all over the state. But the west—except in the Black Hills—receives less rain than the east. South Dakota lies in the heart of the North American continent. Its climate is of the kind known as *continental*. Such a climate has hot summers and cold winters. Oceans are too far away to influence these seasons.

History In the 1600's, the Arikara Indians were the most powerful in South Dakota. Their villages stood along the Missouri. Around each village were patches of corn, beans, and squash. Women tended them. Warriors hunted bison for meat and hides. About 1750, the Sioux tribes began coming into the region. They drove the Arikara Indians slowly northward.

Few white people entered the region before 1700. South Dakota became part of France's Louisiana Territory. In 1743, French explorers reached the spot where the town of Fort Pierre is today. They buried a lead plate to prove they had been there and to back up France's claim to the area. In 1913, youngsters found the plate. It is now in the South

▼ *The Mount Rushmore sculptures of (from left to right): Presidents Washington, Jefferson, Theodore Roosevelt, and Lincoln, in the Black Hills of South Dakota. The busts are 60 feet (18 m) high.*

One of South Dakota's most historic places is Deadwood, the little town that sprang up when gold was discovered in the Black Hills in 1874. The town became famous for the making of quick fortunes and gun law. Wild Bill Hickok was shot dead in Deadwood while playing cards in a saloon.

Dakota Historical Museum across the Missouri River in the state capital, Pierre. (Note: In South Dakota, "Pierre" is pronounced "peer.")

In 1803, the United States acquired the area as part of the Louisiana Purchase. The American exploring expedition led by Meriwether Lewis and William Clark passed through South Dakota on its journey west. Lewis and Clark had little trouble with the Sioux. Captain Lewis wrapped an American flag around a newborn Sioux infant. He told the parents that their child was now an American. When the young Indian grew up, he became a chief. Unlike many Sioux, he was friendly to white Americans.

The fur trade was South Dakota's earliest business. In 1817, a French-Indian fur trader started the first settlement that lasted. It was on the Missouri at the point where the Bad River joins it. This was the settlement that became Fort Pierre. After 1800, the town of Pierre grew up on the Missouri's opposite bank.

Early in the 1870's, gold was discovered in the Black Hills, which was Indian country. White people had been forbidden to enter the area, but thousands poured into the area to search for gold. The Sioux were angry. Although the white people were there unlawfully, the army moved in to protect them. War resulted. The Sioux fought hard and had some success, but in the end they were defeated. The Sioux now live on eight reservations in South Dakota.

On November 2, 1889, both North Dakota and South Dakota were admitted to the Union. Which became a state first? No one knows. President Benjamin Harrison took care that no one saw which paper was signed first. On lists of states, North Dakota has number 39 and South Dakota number 40. Why? Because "N" comes before "S."

In the early 1900's, after a severe drought, more settlers came to South Dakota and agriculture developed.

Farm land and products were the main economy except from 1930–40 when another bad drought, together with a grasshopper plague and great dust storms, hit the state. World War II saw a booming farming industry. After the war, many public projects were undertaken.

South Dakotans at Work Agriculture is the leading business of South Dakota. Livestock raising earns much more money than crops do. Beef cattle graze on the state's western plains. Many are sold to farmers in the southeastern corner. Here they are fattened on corn. Other cattle are sold to farmers in corn-raising sections outside the state. Corn is South Dakota's biggest crop. Another important feed crop is hay. Wheat is grown in the northern part of eastern South Dakota.

Meat processing and packing is the state's main manufacturing industry. Dairy processing and flour milling are big industries, too.

Much gold is mined in South Dakota. The Homestake Mine at Lead (pronounced "leed") is the largest gold-producing mine in the United States.

South Dakota also has much lignite. This soft brown coal is a low-grade fuel. A large gasification plant south of Rapid City turns lignite into fuel gas.

Tourism is also an important business in South Dakota. The eastern part of the state has beautiful lakes for boating and swimming. But most visitors go west to the Black Hills. The Mount Rushmore Presidential heads are not the only big rock sculptures here. Another is the huge figure of a Sioux warrior chief, Crazy Horse. It is the work of Korczak Ziolkowski. At Wind Caves National Park, there are herds of elk, bison, and antelope. The famous old mining town of Deadwood also draws tourists.

ALSO READ: GREAT PLAINS, LEWIS AND CLARK EXPEDITION, SIOUX INDIANS, SITTING BULL.

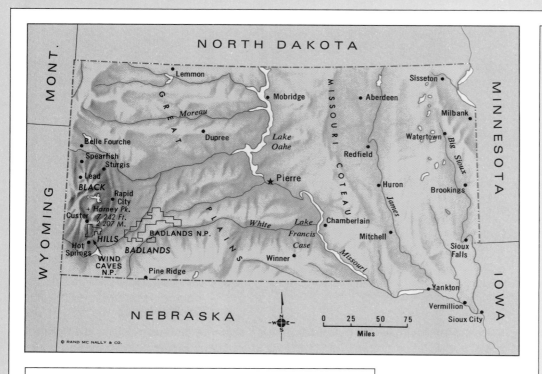

Capital
Pierre (12,000 people)

Area
77,047 square miles
(199,536 sq. km)
Rank: 16th

Population
713,000 people
Rank: 45th

Statehood
November 2, 1889

Principal river
Missouri River

Highest point
Harney Peak; 7,242
feet (2,207 m)

Largest city
Sioux Falls (81,000
people)

Motto
"Under God the People
Rule"

Song
"Hail, South Dakota"

Famous people
Calamity Jane, Sitting
Bull, Crazy Horse,
George McGovern,
Laura Ingalls Wilder

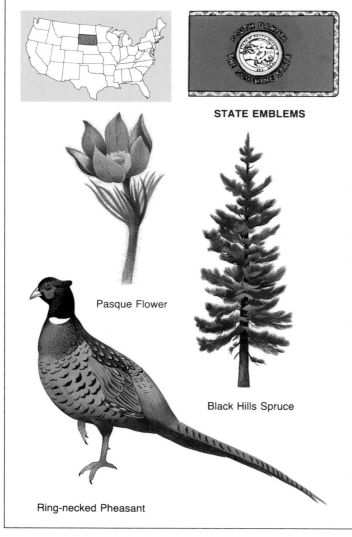

STATE EMBLEMS

Pasque Flower

Black Hills Spruce

Ring-necked Pheasant

▼ *Badlands is a region
in southwestern South
Dakota. It is a land of
unusual rock shapes
created by erosion.*

SOUTHEAST ASIA

▼ *In Southeast Asia, all available land must be cultivated to feed the vast population. Besides farming the river valleys, the people also cut terraces into the hillsides to make extra fields. Here, they grow crops such as rice.*

SOUTHEAST ASIA lies to the south of China and to the east of India. It includes the region known as Indochina, which occupies the eastern portion of the rounded Southeast Asia peninsula. Here are found the nations of Burma, Thailand, Malaysia, Singapore, Kampuchea (formerly Cambodia), Vietnam, and Laos. Farther south, the peninsula gives way to a chain of islands, forming the countries of Indonesia, Brunei, Papua New Guinea, and the Philippines.

Southeast Asia is mainly mountainous. It has a tropical climate, with heavy rainfall in the wet season. Thick forests cover the mountains, through which flow several important rivers. These rivers include the Irrawaddy, Chao Phraya, Mekong, Red, and Salween.

Most of the people farm for a living. They live along the rich rice-growing valleys and river deltas. Besides rice, the people grow corn, rubber, sugarcane, and tea. Lumber is an important industry, and mineral resources include tin, petroleum, and bauxite (aluminum ore). Although many Southeast Asian people live in rural villages, there are also great and busy cities, such as Bangkok (Thailand), Kuala Lumpur (Malaysia), Ho Chi Minh City (formerly Saigon, Vietnam), and Singapore, one of the greatest trade ports of the world.

From the A.D. 900's to the 1400's,

much of Southeast Asia was under the influence of the Khmers, who built a powerful empire. The temple of Angkor Wat in Kampuchea is a reminder of this period of history. Europeans arrived in the 1500's, searching for spices, for which Malacca was an important trade center. Spain occupied the Philippines; Indonesia was taken by the Dutch; Burma and Malaysia by Britain; and Indochina by France. French Indochina consisted of five states: Laos, Cambodia, Cochin China, Annam, and Tonkin. Cochin China, Annam, and Tonkin were joined as Vietnam in 1945. The struggle for control of Vietnam brought about the end of French rule in Indochina, and the involvement of the United States in the Vietnam War.

Southeast Asia has great potential riches. Indonesia, for example, is the fifth most populous country in the world, with vast untapped mineral resources. Given political stability, the peoples of Southeast Asia are able to make their region a powerful force in Asian, and world, affairs.

ALSO READ: ASIA, BRUNEI, BURMA, INDONESIA, KAMPUCHEA, LAOS, MALAYSIA, PAPUA NEW GUINEA, PHILIPPINES, THAILAND, VIETNAM, VIETNAM WAR.

SOUTH KOREA see KOREA.

SOUTH POLE see ANTARCTICA.

SOUTH WEST AFRICA see NAMIBIA.

SOUTH YEMEN see ARABIA.

SOVIET UNION The Soviet Union is the largest country in the world. It extends for more than 6,500 miles (10,400 km) over most of eastern Europe and northern Asia. The country is almost two and a half times the size of the United States. The official name of the Soviet Union is the Union of Soviet Socialist Republics (U.S.S.R.). This Communist state was established in 1922. The Soviet Union, often called Russia, consists mainly of the lands of the old Russian Empire, which was overthrown during the Russian Revolution in 1917.

The Soviet Union is a federation (union) of 15 republics, called union republics. The largest of these is the Russian Soviet Federated Socialist Republic, which stretches from eastern Europe to the Pacific Ocean. Moscow, the capital city of the Soviet Union, is in the western part of this republic. Other union republics include the Kazakh Soviet Socialist Republic (S.S.R.), in west central Asia; the Ukrainian S.S.R., north of the Black Sea; and the Estonian S.S.R., the Latvian S.S.R., and the Lithuanian S.S.R. along the Baltic Sea.

The Soviet Union is bordered on the north by the Arctic Ocean and on the east by the Pacific Ocean. To the northwest are Norway, Finland, and the Baltic Sea. On the western border of the Soviet Union are the nations of Poland, Czechoslovakia, Hungary, and Romania. To the southwest are the Black Sea and the nations of Turkey, Iran, and Afghanistan. To the southeast are China, Mongolia, and North Korea.

The Land and Climate A vast area of flat plains stretches from west to east across the Soviet Union. About one-third of the way across, the plains are cut from north to south by the low, wooded Ural Mountains. The Urals divide the Soviet Union into European and Asian sections. West of the Urals is the eastern part of the Great European Plain. Several great rivers run southward over this plain. One of these rivers, the Volga, is the longest river in Europe. South of the plain, the Soviet border runs along the north coast of the Black Sea and

▲ *A bridge crosses the Razdan River on the western border of Armenia in the Soviet Union. Part of the river forms the border between the Soviet Union and Turkey.*

About 20 percent of the world's rail passenger traffic is carried in the Soviet Union. The country also accounts for over 50 percent of the world's rail freight. Every day Soviet trains carry about 11 million passengers.

SOVIET UNION

Capital City: Moscow (8,800,000 people)

Area: 8,650,166 square miles (22,402,200 sq. km).

Population: 287,000,000.

Government: Communist federated union.

Natural Resources: Lumber, petroleum, gold, uranium, coal, waterpower.

Export Products: Manufactured goods, electrical and engineering products, transport equipment, textiles, chemicals, plastics.

Unit of Money: Ruble.

Official Language: Russian.

CLIMATE

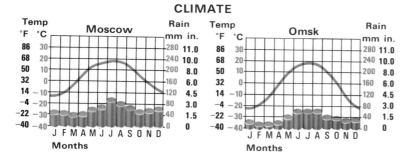

▲ *Moscow in the western part of the Soviet Union is cold, but Omsk, farther east in Siberia, is even colder, as these temperature graphs show. Because Omsk lies far from the sea, however, it has only half as much rain and snow as Moscow.*

The heaviest bell in the world is the Tsar Kolokol in Moscow. It weighs 793 tons (806 metric tons) and measures 19 feet 4¼ inches (5.9 m) in diameter. At one part the metal is 2 feet (60 cm) thick. The bell is cracked and stands on a platform in the Kremlin.

the south shore of the Caspian Sea. These seas are divided by the Caucasus Mountains. The Caspian Sea is actually a huge saltwater lake. Another large saltwater lake, the Aral Sea, lies to the east of the Caspian.

East of the Ural Mountains is the Siberian Plain, which stretches as far as the great Yenisei River and the Altai (or Altay) Mountains in central Asia. Still farther east is a mountainous region that stretches to the Pacific coast. A series of mountain ranges in the south divides the Soviet Union from the rest of Asia. These include the Pamir Mountains, which contain Mount Communism, the highest mountain in the Soviet Union. A short distance north of the border with Mongolia is Lake Baikal (or Baykal), the largest freshwater lake in Eurasia (Europe and Asia).

The great plainlands of the Soviet Union can be divided into four main types. In the extreme north, an area of rocky, treeless land, called *tundra*, borders the Arctic Ocean. The soil in the tundra region is permanently fro-

zen. Farther south lies the *taiga*, a vast area of forest that covers more than half of the nation. South of the forest is a belt of grassland, called the *steppes*, that stretches from the western borders of the Soviet Union to the Altai Mountains. Most of the steppe region has very rich soil used for farming. In the southern part of the Soviet Union east of the Caspian Sea is a dry, hot region of desert. Most northern areas of the Soviet Union have long and very cold winters. Freezing winds blow across the open plains from the Arctic.

The People The immense Soviet nation contains more than 100 different peoples, all with their own languages and traditions. The largest group of people is the *Slavs*. This group includes the original Russian people, sometimes called the Great Russians. The Slavic peoples live mainly in the European part of the Soviet Union. The second largest group of peoples are the *Turko-Tatars*, who live on the southern steppelands. These people are mainly descended from the Tatar warriors who invaded Russia from Mongolia in the A.D. 1200's. Other groups include the *Armenian* and *Georgian* peoples, who live in the Caucasus mountain region, and the *Finno-Ugrians* in the northern Soviet Union. Russian, the language of the Great Russians, is the official language for the whole nation.

REPUBLICS OF THE SOVIET UNION

Republic	Capital	Area (sq. mi.)	Area (sq. km)	Population (Estimate, 1988)
Armenian S.S.R.	Yerevan	11,306	29,283	3,459,000
Azerbaijan S.S.R.	Baku	33,436	86,599	6,920,000
Belorussian S.S.R.	Minsk	80,154	207,599	10,140,000
Estonian S.S.R.	Tallinn	17,400	45,100	1,570,000
Georgian S.S.R.	Tbilisi	26,911	69,699	5,290,000
Kazakh S.S.R.	Alma-Ata	1,064,092	2,755,998	16,470,000
Kirghiz S.S.R.	Frunze	76,642	198,503	4,240,000
Latvian S.S.R.	Riga	24,600	63,700	2,700,000
Lithuanian S.S.R.	Vilnius	25,200	65,200	3,700,000
Moldavian S.S.R.	Kishinev	13,012	33,701	4,230,000
Russian S.F.S.R.	Moscow	6,593,391	17,076,882	284,000,000
Tadzhik S.S.R.	Dushanbe	54,019	139,909	5,000,000
Turkmen S.S.R.	Ashkhabad	188,417	488,000	3,500,000
Ukrainian S.S.R.	Kiev	232,046	600,999	51,400,000
Uzbek S.S.R.	Tashkent	158,069	409,399	20,000,000

Alaska Peninsula

BERING SEA

Bering Strait

Chukchi Peninsula

EAST SIBERIAN SEA

180°

150°

New Siberian Is.

120°

LAPTEV SEA

Kolyma R.

Indigirka R.

Yakutsk

CENTRAL SIBERIAN PLATEAU

Taymyr Peninsula

Severnaya Zemlya

90°

KARA SEA

Novaya Zemlya

60°

ARCTIC OCEAN

North Pole

Lena R.

Angara R.

Krasnoyarsk

YABLONOVYY RANGE

Lake Baykal

Irkutsk

MONGOLIA

REPUBLICS

SOCIALIST

SOVIET

Yenisei R.

WEST SIBERIAN PLAIN

Ob R.

Irtysh R.

Omsk

Novosibirsk

ALTAY MTS.

OF

Franz Josef Land

75°

BARENTS SEA

UNION

URAL MTS.

Ob R.

Sverdlovsk

Chelyabinsk

KAZAKH S.S.R.

Lake Balkhash

TIEN SHAN MTS.

Alma-Ata

Frunze

KIRGHIZ S.S.R.

Kola Peninsula

WHITE SEA

N. Dvina R.

Perm

Kama R.

Syr Darya R.

Tashkent

TADZHIK S.S.R.

ALAY RANGE

Communism Peak (24,590 ft.)

Arctic Circle

SWEDEN

FINLAND

Lake Onega

L. Ladoga

Kuybyshev

ARAL SEA

UZBEK S.S.R.

Amu Darya

Dushanbe

Gorky

Volga R.

Ural R.

TURKMEN S.S.R.

NORWAY

60°

Leningrad

L. Peipus

Moscow

Volgograd

Ashkhabad

AFGHANISTAN

BALTIC SEA

ESTONIA

LATVIA

LITHUANIA

Minsk

BYELORUSSIAN S.S.R.

Kharkov

Don R.

Astrakhan

CASPIAN SEA

GREAT BRITAIN

DENMARK

R.S.F.S.R.

POLAND

Kiev

Dnieper

Dnepropetrovsk

R

AZOV SEA

CAUCASUS MTS.

GEORGIAN S.S.R.

AZERBAIJAN S.S.R.

Baku

IRAN

E. GERMANY

Lvov

UKRAINIAN S.S.R.

Odessa

Tiflis

ARMENIAN S.S.R.

Erivan

JAPAN

SEA OF JAPAN

Vladivostok

Lake Khanka

NORTH KOREA

SOUTH KOREA

SEA OF OKHOTSK

Kamchatka Peninsula

Sakhalin I.

Amur R.

45°

BELOW SEA LEVEL
PLAINS
HIGHLANDS
MOUNTAINS

▲ *An open-air market in Tbilisi, in the Georgian S.S.R. Even in a communist state like the Soviet Union, market places have become an important feature of local trade.*

▲ *The Soviet Union is a land of great variety. These factory workers in Baku, the capital of the republic of Azerbaijan, are dressed in regional folk costume. Folk festivals are popular throughout the Soviet Union.*

Most property in the Soviet Union, including land, housing, factories, and farms, is owned by the state. Workers in factories and on farms are paid wages by the government. Communities, or collectives of people, rent some farms from the state and work the land. They turn over their produce to the government, which sells it and returns a certain profit back to the collective. Other farmland is worked by the government directly, through *state farms*.

The Soviet Union is one of the leading industrial nations of the world. Most of the factories are on the Great European Plain near the largest Soviet cities—Moscow, Leningrad, and Kiev. New factories and power plants are being built in Siberia, in the east. Chief Soviet products are steel, foodstuffs, textiles, chemicals, and machinery.

The Soviet Union grows much of the food needed to feed its people. The main crops are wheat, rye, oats, sugar beets, potatoes, and corn. Lumbering is an important industry for people who live in the great northern forests. Fishing for cod, haddock, and herring is done in the surrounding seas. Sturgeon are caught in the Caspian Sea. Sturgeon eggs, or roe, are salted and made into black caviar, a luxury food, which is exported.

The Soviet Union produces most of the raw materials needed for industry. Coal is mined in Siberia and on the Great European Plain. Petroleum and natural gas are plentiful in the Caucasus region. Iron ore is mined in the Ukraine and Siberia. Waterpower from the great Soviet rivers and lakes produces electricity. There are a number of nuclear power plants.

Education Schools and universities in the Soviet Union are run by the government. Education is free and compulsory for all children between the ages of seven and 17. Young people are encouraged to specialize in technical and scientific subjects, to give the country the skilled workers it needs.

Recreation Each Soviet city and town has its own *house of culture*, where people can get together for various events—ballet performances, concerts, lectures, movies, classes, workshops, plays, and other kinds of entertainment or educational projects. In spite of government restrictions on freedom in the arts, the Soviet Union has had many great artists. Sergei Prokofiev, Dmitri Shostakovich, and Aram Khachaturian were famous composers; Boris Pasternak and Ilya Ehrenburg, famous writers; Sergei Eisenstein, a noted film director; and David Oistrakh, a violin virtuoso (his son, Igor Oistrakh, is also a great violinist). Other Russian artists include the novelist, Mikhail Sholokhov, and the poet, Yevgeny Yevtushenko. The writer, Aleksandr Solzhenitsyn, was deported from the Soviet Union in 1974 and settled in the United States. Other artists, such as the composer-cellist, Mstislav Rostropovich, also defected (left). The Bolshoi Ballet is known worldwide for its excellence.

Government Each Union Republic of the Soviet Union has its own *supreme soviet, the legislative (law-making) council that is elected by the people. Within each republic are soviets of working people's deputies. These are local councils in towns, cities, or country districts. Each Union Republic sends representatives to the Supreme Soviet of the U.S.S.R. in Moscow. The Supreme Soviet elects the Presidium. The Presidium consists of a president, who is head of state, and several deputies. The Supreme Soviet also appoints the Council of Ministers, which is the highest governing body in the Soviet Union. The presiding officer of the Council of Ministers is the premier, or chief government official of the nation.

The Communist Party is the only political party in the Soviet Union. The General Secretary of the Communist Party is the party chief and political leader of the nation. Any Soviet citizen over the age of 18 can become a member of the Communist Party although fewer than one-fourth are accepted. The party organization directs political affairs at every level of Soviet life—in schools, community groups, factories, businesses, farms, vacation resorts, camps, and in many other areas. The Komsomol, or Communist Youth League, runs educational, sports, and social projects to prepare young people for future membership in the Communist Party.

History At the outbreak of World War I in 1914, the Russian Empire was in a state of dangerous crisis. The common people had very little food or money. For almost 100 years, secret revolutionary organizations had been active. People wanted reforms in the government and in the hard conditions under which citizens had to live. But the czars, who had complete power, were surrounded by incompetent advisers and corrupt government officials. Czar Nicholas II was afraid to allow democracy because he feared this would encourage revolution.

In March 1917, revolution broke out in the capital city of St. Petersburg (now Leningrad). Revolutionaries forced the czar to resign and set up a provisional government headed by Alexander Kerensky and Prince Lvov. The provisional government promised reforms, but it was too late. More radical groups wanted a complete change. The Bolshevik (Communist) Party, headed by Nikolai Lenin, overthrew the provisional government in November 1917. Lenin became head of the first Communist government. He moved the capital to Moscow, declared all land to be the property of the government, and got the nation out of World War I by quickly making peace with Germany. Czar Nicholas and his family were executed the following year.

Many Russians were against Com-

Perfectly preserved mammoths have been found frozen into the ground of Siberia. The flesh could still be eaten by dogs after a period of 10,000 years.

▼ *Onion-shaped domes are a familiar feature of historic Russian orthodox churches. These onion domes are inside the Kremlin fortress in Moscow—now the seat of the Soviet government.*

The Soviet Union's MIL Mi-26 helicopter set an official record by lifting 125,153 pounds (56,768 kg) to a height of 6,561 feet (2,000 m) in 1982. This is roughly equal to the total weight of 30 fully equiped, four-door, U.S. automobiles.

munist rule, and a bitter civil war broke out that lasted until 1922. In that year, the Mensheviks (anti-Communist forces) were defeated and the Imperial Russian State officially became the Union of Soviet Socialist Republics.

Lenin died in 1924. A struggle for power developed among the leaders of the Communist Party. In 1929, Joseph Stalin was declared premier and head of the Communist Party. Stalin started vast new programs for improving agriculture and industry. Peasants were forced to give up their land to huge collective and state farms. Millions of peasants were killed when they refused to turn over their lands.

From 1928 to 1932, the Communist Party gained complete control. From 1934 to 1938, a series of trials took place because Stalin suspected anti-Communist plots against the government. Many people, including a number of generals and government officials, were executed or imprisoned.

In 1940 during World War II, Germany invaded the Soviet Union and came almost within sight of Moscow. The Soviet people suffered great hardships. But eventually the Soviet Army drove back the Germans and defeated them in Romania, Hungary, Czechoslovakia, Poland, and the eastern part of Germany. After the war, Communist governments closely tied to the Soviet Union were set up in those countries.

▲ Moscow's largest department store, GUM, has three vast covered galleries full of small shops.

The United States and nations of Western Europe began to fear Soviet power. The Soviets were fearful of Western power. A situation of distrust and hostility, called the Cold War, developed. After Stalin's death in 1953, Nikita Khrushchev served as Soviet premier and head of the Communist Party. In 1964, he was replaced as premier by Aleksei Kosygin and as Communist Party head by Leonid Brezhnev (upon Kosygin's death in 1980, Brezhnev also became premier).

Brezhnev died in 1982. His successors were Yury Andropov (died 1984) and Konstantin Chernenko (died 1985), followed by Mikhail Gorbachov. Gorbachov introduced a new vigor into Soviet affairs, seeking a less rigid economic system at home, and actively seeking nuclear arms agreements with the United States.

ALSO READ: AFGHANISTAN; ARAL SEA; BLACK SEA; CASPIAN SEA; CAUCASUS MOUNTAINS; COMMUNISM; GORBACHOV, MIKHAIL; KHRUSHCHEV, NIKITA; KREMLIN; MOSCOW; RUSSIAN; RUSSIAN HISTORY; STALIN, JOSEPH; URAL MOUNTAINS.

▼ Red flags and pictures of Communist theorist Karl Marx are always prominent at important Soviet parades. This annual event celebrates the Revolution of 1917 that brought the Communists to power.

SOYA Cooking oil, the savory sauce used in Chinese food, imitation meat, and hay for animals seem an unlikely combination. But they are all made from the same vegetable, the soybean.

Soya has been grown in China for thousands of years. It is a sturdy plant with thick leaves and pods containing the beans. It is remarkably free from attacks by insects. Farmers cut the leaves for hay or make them into silage—a winter feed for animals.

Soybeans are used for both human and animal food. They are squeezed to extract the oil, which is used as a cooking oil and to make margarine and paint. The remaining part is used for animal feed. The beans can be ground to make flour and are sold dried for cooking. Because they are rich in fat and protein and low in starch, vegetarians use soya in one form or another as one of their main foodstuffs.

SPACE Space is everywhere. Some space is filled up by matter, and some space is empty. Most of the universe is empty. Only a very small part of it is taken up by planets, stars, and other matter.

When we speak of "outer space," or sometimes just "space," we usually mean all of the universe outside the Earth and its atmosphere (layer of air and gases). Sometimes the word "space" is used to mean only empty space, not the bodies in it.

Earth is only one planet orbiting around one ordinary star—the sun. The sun is only one of over 100 billion stars in our galaxy, or group of stars—the Milky Way. The Milky Way is only one of over 100 billion galaxies in the known universe. So you can see that we are not very big or important. In fact, it is amazing that astronomers have managed to see so far into space.

Distant objects cannot be examined in the laboratory, so scientists have to study the heat-rays, light, X rays, and other radiation these objects send out. These observations show that the space between the stars, and especially between the galaxies, is very "empty" indeed, with about one atom in each cubic inch (16 cm^3), compared with a million million atoms in the period at the end of this sentence.

The strange fact is that "empty" space can bend the path of light rays or anything else traveling through it. If you are going through a tunnel in a train, you cannot tell if the track is straight or curved just by looking at the tunnel walls. The same thing is true of space; if you were an astronaut and could set off in a spacecraft for a distant part of the universe, you would really travel in a curve. Eventually you would end up back at your starting-point, convinced that you had really traveled in a straight line!

ALSO READ: ASTRONOMY, OBSERVATORY, RELATIVITY, SOLAR SYSTEM, SPACE RESEARCH, SPACE TRAVEL, STAR, UNIVERSE.

SPACE RESEARCH Space research is a broad field of scientific activity. It includes research on space, whether conducted from the Earth or from other points in space. It also includes research on the Earth conducted from space.

Until recently, people could learn about space only by studying the radiation, such as light and radio waves, given off by the bodies in space. All bodies give off some radiation, but only a little of this radiation reaches the Earth, and even less penetrates the Earth's thick atmosphere. So what people could learn with even the most powerful telescopes was limited.

But, with the launching of the first satellites, people's view of space was greatly widened. Three major new possibilities arose. One was the possibility of studying space from above

▲ *The Earth, seen here from a spacecraft, is one of millions of bodies traveling through space.*

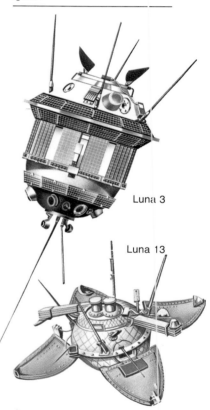

Luna 3

Luna 13

▲ *These two early Soviet probes flew to the moon. Luna 3 went around the moon in 1959 and sent back the first photographs of the moon's far side (which always faces away from us). Luna 13 soft-landed on the moon in 1966 and sent back to Earth photographs of the moon's surface.*

IMPORTANT UNMANNED SATELLITES AND SPACE PROBES

Name	Launching Date	Country	Achievements
Sputnik 1	October 4, 1957	Soviet Union	First artificial satellite.
Sputnik 2	November 3, 1957	Soviet Union	Carried dog, "Laika," into space.
Explorer 1	February 1, 1958	United States	First American satellite.
Vanguard 1	March 17, 1958	United States	Oldest satellite still in orbit.
Luna 1	January 2, 1959	Soviet Union	First lunar probe, missed moon and went into orbit around sun.
Pioneer 4	March 3, 1959	United States	First American lunar probe, went into solar orbit
Luna 2	September 12, 1959	Soviet Union	Lunar probe, struck the moon.
Luna 3	October 4, 1959	Soviet Union	Took pictures of far side of the moon.
Pioneer 5	March 11, 1960	United States	Interplanetary probe, transmitted information from over 22 million miles in space.
Tiros 1	April 1, 1960	United States	First weather satellite.
Echo 1	August 12, 1960	United States	First communications satellite.
Oscar 1	December 12, 1961	United States	Amateur radio satellite.
OSO 1	March 7, 1962	United States	First orbiting solar observatory.
Telstar 1	July 10, 1962	United States	Transmitted first television picture across the Atlantic.
Mariner 2	August 27, 1962	United States	First successful Venus probe; in solar orbit.
Ranger 7	July 28, 1964	United States	Lunar probe, sent back 4,300 pictures before striking moon.
OGO 1	September 4, 1964	United States	First orbiting geophysical observatory.
Mariner 4	November 28, 1964	United States	First successful Mars probe; in solar orbit.
Venera 3	November 16, 1965	Soviet Union	Struck Venus; first probe to hit another planet.
Luna 9	January 31, 1966	Soviet Union	Landed on moon; sent back first pictures taken from moon's surface.
Luna 10	March 31, 1966	Soviet Union	First artificial satellite to orbit the moon.
OAO 1	April 8, 1966	United States	First orbiting astronomical observatory. Batteries died shortly after launching.
Surveyor 1	May 30, 1966	United States	Landed on moon; sent back over 11,000 pictures of moon's surface.
Biosatellite 1	December 14, 1966	United States	Carried living cells into space for scientific study.
Biosatellite 2	September 7, 1967	United States	Carried living cells into space. The cells were recovered.
Zond 5	September 14, 1968	Soviet Union	First probe to orbit the moon and return to Earth.
OAO 2	December 7, 1968	United States	First orbiting astronomical observatory to function successfully.
Luna 16	September 12, 1970	Soviet Union	Brought back soil from moon's surface.
Luna 17	November 10, 1970	Soviet Union	Landed wheeled roving vehicle, *Lunokhod 1*, on moon's surface.
Mariner 9	May 17, 1971	United States	Reached Mars, becoming first craft to orbit it. Relayed data and photos.
Pioneer 10	March 2, 1972	United States	Flew by Jupiter and Saturn. Became first artificial object to escape the solar system.
Pioneer 11	April 6, 1973	United States	Flew by Jupiter and Saturn.
Mariner 10	November 3, 1973	United States	Flew by Venus. Arrived at Mercury for first close-up of that planet.
Venera 9	June 8, 1975	Soviet Union	Landed on Venus. Relayed photos of planet's surface.
Venera 10	June 14, 1975	Soviet Union	Landed on Venus. Relayed photos of planet's surface.
Viking 1	August 11, 1975	United States	Both landed on Mars, carrying life-detection laboratories.
Viking 2	August 21, 1975	United States	Relayed data and photos.
Voyager 1	August 20, 1977	United States	Flew by Jupiter and Saturn. Voyager 2 also passed Uranus and flew
Voyager 2	September 5, 1977	United States	on toward Neptune.
Pioneer Venus 1	May 20, 1978	United States	Orbited Venus. Relayed photos.
Pioneer Venus 2	August 8, 1978	United States	Landed on Venus.
Venera 11	September 9, 1978	Soviet Union	Both landed on Venus. Relayed data.
Venera 12	September 14, 1978	Soviet Union	
Einstein	November 13, 1978	United States	Studied X rays coming from space. Discovered very remote galaxies or quasars.
Solar Max	February 14, 1980	United States	Satellite to study the sun. Repaired by Shuttle crew on April 8, 1984.
Venera 13	October 30, 1981	Soviet Union	Both landed on Venus. Took photographs and sampled surface.
Venera 14	November 4, 1981	Soviet Union	
IRAS	January 25, 1983	USA-Europe	Observed heat radiation from 200,000 objects in the Milky Way galaxy. Discovered five new comets.
Vega 1	December 15, 1984	Soviet Union	Venus flyby. Sent landers to surface. Continued to rendezvous with
Vega 2	December 21, 1984	Soviet Union	Halley's Comet, March 1986.
Giotto	February 7, 1985	Europe	Passed close to Halley's Comet, March 14, 1986.

the filter of the Earth's atmosphere. Many, perhaps most, of the satellites have carried some means of detecting radiation. The United States' first satellite, Explorer I, made the important discovery that two doughnut-shaped belts of radiation, named the Van Allen Belts, circle the Earth. Later satellites have enabled people to see farther and more clearly into space than they had seen before. A satellite named IRAS, launched in 1983, discovered about 200,000 stars that could not be seen from Earth.

The second possibility was for studying the Earth from space, and for serving human needs from space. This has been met primarily in two areas—weather satellites and communications satellites. Weather satellites have greatly increased the area of the Earth's surface that can be watched by meteorologists and have sharpened their ability to predict storms and other disturbances and understand the dynamics of the atmosphere.

The third great possibility in space research is direct exploration of space, both manned and unmanned. And, like the other two possibilities, it is becoming a reality. Manned spacecraft have explored the moon, and unmanned space probes have explored the planets.

▼ Two Viking spacecraft like this touched down on Mars in 1976. They searched for signs of life in the soil, but found none.

Space Probes Space probes are equipment packages powered by rockets. They are similar to satellites, but they are designed to travel through space, rather than to go into orbit about the Earth. Some probes have gone into orbit about the sun. Probes have been used to explore planets and the space between planets.

The United States launched a series of Mariner probes to study Mercury, Venus, and Mars. The Soviet Union has also sent probes to the latter two planets. In 1971, U.S. Mariner 9 orbited Mars and sent back to Earth valuable photographs about that planet, helping pave the way for the landings of Viking 1 and Viking 2 in 1976. These latter two American probes have provided scientists with important information on the chemical make-up, temperature, and atmosphere of Mars. Also, the thousands of photographs from probes have been used in producing maps of the surfaces of Mercury and Mars. Pictures have revealed huge volcanoes and giant canyons on Mars. Mercury has craters similar to those on the moon.

Interplanetary probes are designed to collect information about the space between planets. These probes may gather data on radiation, magnetic fields, and solar wind. The first interplanetary probes of the United States were called Pioneer. Early Pioneer probes sent back valuable data in the 1960's. Pioneer 10, launched in 1972, flew through the asteroid belt and reached Jupiter in 1973. Pioneer 11 flew past Jupiter in 1974 and reached Saturn in 1979, sending back photographs. Voyager 1 and 2, both launched in 1977, passed Jupiter in 1979. Voyager 1 flew by Saturn in 1980, and Voyager 2 passed Saturn in 1981, sending back magnificent color pictures of Saturn and its rings and moons. Voyager 2 picked up velocity and sped toward Uranus, which it flew by in 1986, sending back pic-

▲ Skylab in orbit above the Earth (top). One of the craft's solar panels was torn off during launch. You can see the remaining panel sticking out at the top right of the space station. The panels provided electric power for Skylab's scientific instruments. This is the Skylab emblem (above).

One of the most surprising discoveries made by the Soviet cosmonauts during their long stays in space was that the human body grows in weightless conditions. Valeri Ryumin, who remained in space for six months, grew more than an inch (2.5 cm) during that time.

2289

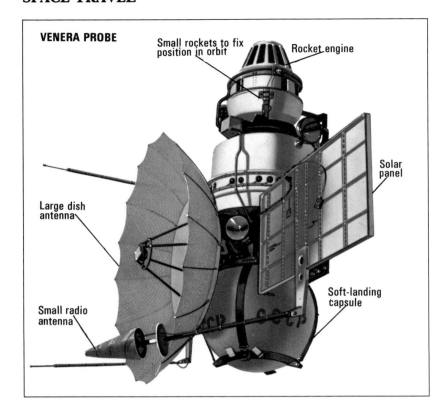

VENERA PROBE

Small rockets to fix position in orbit

Rocket engine

Large dish antenna

Solar panel

Small radio antenna

Soft-landing capsule

▲ *The Soviet Union made the first landing on Venus with its Venera probe. The larger part of the probe stayed in orbit around Venus, while the smaller soft-landing capsule floated down by parachute through the acid vapor clouds of the planet.*

The loneliest place anyone has ever been to is the far side of the moon. During the moon landings, one astronaut remained in space orbiting the moon. When he was on the far side of the moon he was about 3,500 miles (5,600 km) away from all his fellow human beings. No one had ever before been this far away from other people.

tures of that planet's rings and moons. It then traveled on toward Neptune (arrival date 1989).

Flights to the Moon The first successful lunar probe, the Soviet Union's Luna 2, struck the moon in 1959. The United States Surveyor spacecraft landed on the moon, examined samples of the soil, tested the surface for landings, and sent thousands of moon pictures back to Earth. These and numerous other probes prepared the way for manned flight to the moon. In 1969, the American astronaut, Neil Armstrong, became the first person to walk on the moon followed by Edwin Aldrin. They spent some two and a half hours on the surface, collecting samples of moon rock and soil to take back to Earth for scientific study. No landings on the moon have taken place since 1972.

ALSO READ: AEROSPACE; ARMSTRONG, NEIL; ASTRONOMY; COMMUNICATIONS SATELLITE; OBSERVATORY; ORBIT; ROCKET; SATELLITE; SOLAR SYSTEM; SPACE; SPACE TRAVEL.

SPACE TRAVEL The story of space travel is a mixture of dreams, genius, courage, and even tragedy. But most of all it is a triumph of people's urge to explore and their ability to solve problems in an orderly, scientific manner, using the knowledge and the mistakes of the past to build for the future.

The knowledge that made space travel possible was gathered over hundreds of years. As early as 1687, Isaac Newton calculated the velocity an object would need in order to escape the Earth's gravitational pull and travel into space. That velocity is seven miles a second, more than 25,000 miles (40,000 km) an hour. In Newton's time, people had little hope of ever going that fast. It was only with the development of the liquid-fuel, multiple-stage rocket in this century that "escape" velocities could be achieved. Almost all major spaceflights to date have been launched and powered by rockets of this type.

The problem of getting into space is only part of the overall problem of traveling in space. A human being in space faces a number of dangers. Some of these are known dangers—an unprotected person alone in space would not be able to breathe, would be poisoned by radiation, and the blood would boil. For the first space travelers, there was also the possibility of unforeseen danger. No one could be completely certain what effect extended weightlessness might have on people. And although some of the known harmful radiation could be blocked by shields, no one could be certain that a person in space would not be bombarded by even more harmful unknown radiation.

History of Space Travel The first spaceflights in 1957 (Soviet Union) and 1958 (United States) were unmanned. These flights provided information that helped in the planning of manned flights.

Then, on April 12, 1961, the Soviet cosmonaut, Yuri Gagarin, became the first person in space. A month later the American astronaut, Alan Shepard, made a suborbital flight. On February 20, 1962, John Glenn became the first American to orbit the Earth.

Shepard and Glenn rode in Mercury space capsules. These small, cone-shaped vehicles were barely large enough to carry one person. The first Mercury flights showed that the designs of the spacecraft and spacesuit were adequate for space travel.

After six successful Mercury flights, the United States began its series of Gemini flights. The Gemini space capsule was larger than the Mercury. It could carry two persons on longer flights. The Gemini program also allowed the astronauts still greater control over their spacecraft. The pilot could actually fly a Gemini spacecraft. An astronaut could leave the Gemini capsule and take a walk in space, called an EVA—extravehicular activity. The first EVA was performed from a Russian Voskhod spacecraft by the cosmonaut, Alexei Leonov, on March 18, 1965. In June 1965, Edward White emerged from the Gemini 4 capsule to become the first American to walk in space.

On later Gemini flights, the astronauts attempted to work during their EVAs. On the last Gemini flight,

▼ *The Mercury capsule carried the first U.S. astronauts into orbit.*

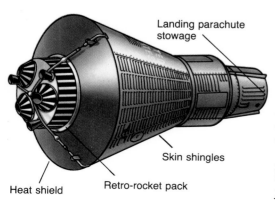

Landing parachute stowage

Skin shingles

Heat shield Retro-rocket pack

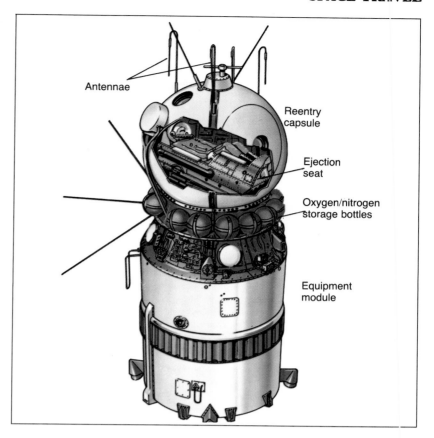

Antennae

Reentry capsule

Ejection seat

Oxygen/nitrogen storage bottles

Equipment module

Gemini 12, Edwin Aldrin performed 19 different tasks during a two-hour EVA.

Two other important achievements of the Gemini flights were the first space rendezvous (meeting) and the first docking (joining together) of two vehicles in space. The first rendezvous took place on December 15, 1965. Gemini 6 and Gemini 7 maneuvered to within one foot of each other and flew in formation for several hours. Gemini 7 remained in orbit for two weeks, the longest flight up to that time. On March 16, Gemini 8 hooked up to an Agena target vehicle to accomplish the first successful docking procedures and pave the way for the Apollo flights.

The Apollo Program While the Mercury and Gemini flights had been confined to orbits about the Earth, the Apollo program had a very dif-

▶ *The two-man Gemini spacecraft followed the Mercury program.*

▲ *The Soviet Vostok ("East") spacecraft was the world's first manned space vehicle. On April 12, 1961, Soviet cosmonaut Yuri Gagarin became the first person to orbit the Earth, in a Vostok spacecraft.*

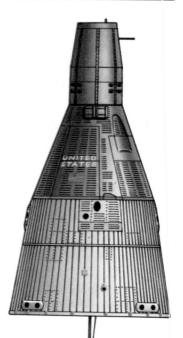

▲ *Edward White was the first American astronaut to carry out EVA (extravehicular activity) or "space walk." He did this in 1965.*

▲ *The first rendezvous in space between two spacecraft was in 1965, when the Gemini 6 and Gemini 7 spacecraft met in orbit.*

ferent goal—the moon. For this flight a larger, three-person spacecraft, launched by more powerful rockets, was needed. The Apollo spacecraft had three different sections—a command module, a lunar module, and a service module. The command module housed the main controls and was home for the astronauts during most of the flight. The lunar module was the vehicle that carried two of the astronauts down to the moon's surface. The service module contained the fuel, oxygen, water, and electrical equipment. At the base of the service module was the rocket engine that put the spacecraft in and out of moon orbit.

The start of the Apollo program was delayed by tragedy. A fire broke out in an Apollo capsule while three astronauts were undergoing a simulated flight. The astronauts—Virgil Grissom, Edward White, and Roger Chaffee—were killed. As a result, several changes were made in the design of the spacecraft.

The first few Apollo flights were unmanned. These flights tested the performance of the Apollo spacecraft and of the rockets used to launch it. The first manned Apollo flight was Apollo 7, launched on October 11, 1968. This flight only orbited the Earth. It did not include a lunar module. The next flight, Apollo 8, was the first manned flight to orbit the moon. Apollo 9 tested the lunar module in Earth orbit, and Apollo 10 tested it in lunar orbit.

Everything worked. Everything was ready for the most remarkable human exploration to date—the first trip to the moon. On July 16, 1969, Apollo 11 was launched. Four days later, Neil Armstrong crawled through the hatch of the lunar module, backed down a small ladder, and became the first person to set foot on the moon.

The knowledge gained in the development of the Apollo program was then put to use in Skylab—the Apollo

applications program. This program launched a manned scientific workshop into an orbit about the Earth in 1973. This workshop was used by three crews to study the Earth, sun, moon, space, and the influence of space on living organisms.

In 1975, an American and a Soviet spacecraft met and docked in space. Scientists, as well as trained astronauts, have made trips into orbit and carried out experiments to study the Earth's resources, the sun, and deep space. They used the scientific laboratory, Spacelab, fitted inside the Space Shuttle's cargo hold. The advent of the Space Shuttle, the world's first reusable orbital spacecraft, in 1981 was an important advance. Four orbiters were built, but one, *Challenger*, was lost in a tragic accident in January 1986. The seven people on board *Challenger* were killed when the spacecraft exploded shortly after takeoff. There was no further space shuttle flights until September 1988, when *Discovery* made a successful round trip.

Manned Spacecraft All spacecraft must protect people from the dangers of space and must fulfill people's essential needs.

Providing the air, water, and food

▼ *The Apollo spacecraft were launched on top of the mighty Saturn 5 rocket, first fired in 1967.*

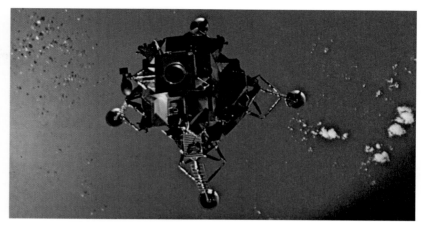

◀ *The Apollo 11 lunar module on the moon, with Neil Armstrong conducting one of the many scientific experiments beside it.*

▼ *The Apollo moon craft was in two sections; the crew traveled in the command module on the way to the moon*

▲ *A lunar module in space during an Apollo moon mission. The flimsy-looking module was the section of the Apollo craft designed to land on and take off from the moon's surface.*

APOLLO MOON CRAFT

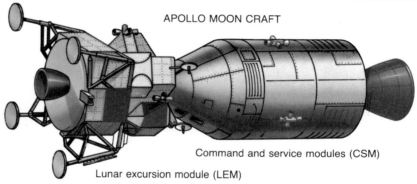

Command and service modules (CSM)

Lunar excursion module (LEM)

▼ *This diagram shows how the Apollo moon missions were carried out, from lift-off to final splashdown at sea.*

Parking orbit engine fires to boost CSM toward Earth

Return journey to Earth

Splashdown in Pacific

Parking orbit

LEM lifts off moon, rejoins CSM

Launch rocket third stage reignites to boost Apollo towards moon

LEM separates from CSM, lands on moon

Lift-off from Cape Canaveral (Kennedy)

Rocket engines fire to slow spacecraft and bring it into moon orbit

Outward journey to moon

U.S. MANNED SPACE FLIGHTS TO FIRST SHUTTLE ORBIT, 1981

Spacecraft	Launching Date	Astronauts	Flight Time	Achievements
Mercury-Freedom 7	May 5, 1961	Alan B. Shepard, Jr.	0 hrs. 15 mins.	First American manned space flight.
Mercury-Liberty Bell 7	July 21, 1961	Virgil I. Grissom	0 hrs. 16 mins.	Completed preparations for orbital flight.
Mercury-Friendship 7	Feb. 20, 1962	John H. Glenn	4 hrs. 55 mins.	First American in orbit.
Mercury-Aurora 7	May 24, 1962	M. Scott Carpenter	4 hrs. 56 mins.	Showed that a person could adapt to drifting in space.
Mercury-Sigma 7	Oct. 3, 1962	Walter M. Schirra, Jr.	9 hrs. 13 mins.	Made six orbits of the Earth.
Mercury-Faith 7	May 15, 1963	L. Gordon Cooper, Jr.	34 hrs. 20 mins.	First long American flight.
Gemini 3	Mar. 23, 1965	Virgil I. Grissom John W. Young	4 hrs. 53 mins.	First manned spacecraft to change its orbit.
Gemini 4	June 3, 1965	James A. McDivitt Edward H. White, II	97 hrs. 48 mins.	White became first American to walk in space.
Gemini 5	Aug. 21, 1965	L. Gordon Cooper, Jr. Charles Conrad, Jr.	190 hrs. 56 mins.	Studied effects of four days of weightlessness.
Gemini 7	Dec. 4, 1965	Frank Borman James A. Lovell, Jr.	330 hrs. 35 mins.	Longest manned flight at the time.
Gemini 6	Dec. 15, 1965	Walter M. Schirra, Jr. Thomas P. Stafford	25 hrs. 52 mins.	First space rendezvous. Came within one foot of Gemini 7.
Gemini 8	Mar. 16, 1966	Neil A. Armstrong David R. Scott	10 hrs. 42 mins.	First docking in space.
Gemini 9	June 3, 1966	Thomas P. Stafford Eugene A. Cernan	72 hrs. 21 mins.	Most precise landing of any Gemini spacecraft.
Gemini 10	July 18, 1966	John W. Young Michael Collins	70 hrs. 47 mins.	Rendezvous with two targets.
Gemini 11	Sept. 12, 1966	Charles Conrad, Jr. Richard F. Gordon, Jr.	71 hrs. 17 mins.	Rendezvous and docking.
Gemini 12	Nov. 11, 1966	James A. Lovell, Jr. Edwin E. Aldrin, Jr.	94 hrs. 33 mins.	Three successful space walks.
Apollo 7	Oct. 11, 1968	Walter M. Schirra, Jr. Donn F. Eisele R. Walter Cunningham	260 hrs. 9 mins.	First manned flight in Apollo capsule (Earth orbit). First live TV transmissions from orbit.
Apollo 8	Dec. 21, 1968	Frank Borman James A. Lovell, Jr. William A. Anders	147 hrs.	First manned flight around moon.
Apollo 9	Mar. 3, 1969	James A. McDivitt David R. Scott Russell L. Schweickart	241 hrs. 1 min.	Simulated lunar landing in Earth orbit.
Apollo 10	May 18, 1969	Thomas P. Stafford Eugene A. Cernan John W. Young	192 hrs. 3 mins.	Lunar module separated from command module and descended to within nine miles (14.4 km) of moon.
Apollo 11	July 16, 1969	Neil A. Armstrong Edwin E. Aldrin, Jr. Michael Collins	195 hrs. 18 mins.	Armstrong and Aldrin became first persons to walk on the moon.
Apollo 12	Nov. 14, 1969	Charles Conrad, Jr. Alan L. Bean Richard F. Gordon, Jr.	244 hrs. 36 mins.	Conrad and Bean landed on the moon.
Apollo 13	April 11, 1970	James A. Lovell, Jr. Fred. W. Haise, Jr. John L. Swigert, Jr.	142 hrs. 55 mins.	An explosion on way to moon canceled lunar landing. Astronauts returned safely.
Apollo 14	Jan. 31, 1971	Alan B. Shepard, Jr. Stuart A. Roosa Edgar D. Mitchell	216 hrs. 42 mins.	First mission to land in a lunar upland area. Performed many scientific experiments.
Apollo 15	July 26, 1971	David R. Scott Alfred M. Worden James B. Irwin	295 hrs. 12 mins.	Carried first wheeled vehicle to the moon. Scott and Irwin drove the lunar rover for over 17 miles (27 km) on moon's surface.
Apollo 16	April 16, 1972	John W. Young Charles M. Duke, Jr. Thomas K. Mattingly, II	265 hrs. 51 mins.	Collected more lunar samples than any previous flight. Performed ultraviolet camera experiment to study concentrations of hydrogen and other gases.
Apollo 17	Dec. 7, 1972	Eugene A. Cernan Ronald E. Evans Harrison H. Schmitt	301 hrs. 51 mins.	Last Apollo manned lunar landing. Schmitt became first scientist to travel to moon. Samples collected.
Skylab 2	May 25, 1973	Charles Conrad, Jr. Joseph P. Kerwin Paul J. Weitz	672 hrs. 50 mins.	First manned flight to Skylab space station. Conducted experiments about long-duration manned space flight.
Skylab 3	July 28, 1973	Alan L. Bean, Jr. Jack R. Lousma Owen K. Garriott	1427 hrs. 9 mins.	Continued scientific and medical experiments and made Earth observations from orbit.
Skylab 4	Nov. 16, 1973	Gerald P. Carr Edward G. Gibson William R. Pogue	2017 hrs. 17 mins.	Obtained medical data on crew for use in extending the duration of spaceflight. Longest flight to date.
Apollo/Soyuz	July 15, 1975	Thomas P. Stafford Vance D. Brand Donald K. Slayton A. A. Leonov (U.S.S.R.) V. N. Kubasov (U.S.S.R.)	217 hrs. 28 mins. (U.S.) 142 hrs. 31 mins. (U.S.S.R.)	First manned rendezvous and docking in space. Aimed at developing a space rescue capability.
Columbia	April 12, 1981	John W. Young Robert L. Crippen	54 hrs. 20 mins.	First orbital flight of shuttle.

for a short flight is a relatively simple problem. Tanks of compressed oxygen, a supply of water, and packages of dried foods can be fitted into the spacecraft. Wastes can be stored and thrown away back on Earth.

But for longer trips, such as to Mars, new solutions must be found. Wastes will have to be converted and reused. Since there is no oxygen in space, a productive source of oxygen must be found. One suggestion for converting waste gases to oxygen is to put living green plants in the spacecraft. The plants would take in waste carbon dioxide and give off oxygen. They could also break down other wastes.

Various kinds of radiation are given off by the sun and other bodies in space. Many of these can destroy living tissue, so people in space must be protected from them. The shields of spacecraft are designed to block most harmful radiation. However, the heavy radiation particles given off by solar flares on the sun are too powerful to be blocked by anything but a thick carbon shield. Such a shield would be too heavy to carry on a spacecraft, so flights must not be scheduled at times of possible heavy solar flare activity.

Since space has no atmosphere, it has no atmospheric pressure. When there is no pressure on a liquid, the liquid evaporates, or boils. In space, all the fluids in a person's body would boil if they were not kept under an artificial pressure. The spacecraft and spacesuit must provide this pressure. The spacecraft must be tightly constructed with double doors and hatches to prevent loss of air. Spacesuits must carry their own air supply to maintain pressure during space walks. Because of the need to maintain pressure, any leak or tear in a spacecraft or spacesuit is very dangerous.

The lack of atmospheric pressure has other effects on a spaceflight. All the liquids and lubricants (greases)

that are not pressurized must be carefully selected so that they will not evaporate in space. Even the paint on the outside of the spacecraft may evaporate.

When a spacecraft reenters the Earth's atmosphere, or any atmosphere, it faces new problems. The worst problem is heat—the friction of reentry can create temperatures of 9,000° F (almost 5,000° C) or higher. Spacecraft are protected by special heat shields that melt quickly during reentry. The heat is carried away by the melted material, leaving the main part of the spacecraft undamaged.

People in Space Weightlessness and acceleration do not seem to have any short-term ill effects on people, but no one can be certain of their long-term effects.

Weightlessness results from the lack of gravitational pull in space. It may put a strain on the heart. When a person is at rest in a weightless state, the heart does not have to pump very hard. But when the person begins working, the heart suddenly has to pump much harder. Long-term weightlessness may also damage the bones, tissues, and functions of the body. Soviet cosmonauts, after long periods of weightlessness, had difficulty regaining their sense of balance on Earth.

Acceleration is an increase in velocity. Deceleration is the opposite—a

▲ *Unlike Soviet spacecraft, which after reentry were parachuted down onto dry land, all U.S. manned spacecraft before the space Shuttle "splashed down" into the sea. The cone-shaped reentry vehicle floated until Navy personnel could recover it and the astronauts inside.*

▲ *After people had successfully landed on the moon with the Apollo missions, they needed a vehicle to help explore its surface. On the later Apollo missions, astronauts used wheeled lunar rovers.*

▶ The instrument panel of the Shuttle is similar to that of an airliner, but it has even more computerized instruments. Here, Columbia astronauts John Young (left) and Robert Crippen carry out a preflight check.

▲ The Space Shuttle is launched on the back of its huge fuel tank, powered by two long booster rockets as well as by the main engines. The boosters fall off when spent and are recovered for use on a future flight.

▼ The first Shuttle flight was by Columbia in April 1981. The Shuttle can carry satellites in its loading bay, for launch in orbit.

decrease in velocity. If you are in a car that is accelerating rapidly, you feel a force pressing you against the back of the seat. If the car decelerates suddenly, you may be thrown forward.

These forces are also produced when a spacecraft takes off and lands. A spacecraft may accelerate from 0 to 17,000 miles an hour (27,000 km/hr) in only 12 minutes. The forces of acceleration and deceleration at these velocities can be as much as 12 G's (12 times the force of the Earth's gravity). If the force is too strong, or lasts too long, it may cause permanent physical damage.

Space travel can have effects that are not easily explained. For instance, Apollo astronauts working on the

moon showed irregularities in their heartbeats. When they came back to Earth, it was found that the level of potassium in their bodies was very low. On a later flight, astronauts were given doses of potassium. Their heartbeats remained regular.

Planning Space Travel Computers on the ground and on board the spacecraft ensure that the craft keeps on the right course. Otherwise, if the craft were just aimed at a target in space, it would miss wildly. This is because bodies in nearby space are moving in orbit around the sun, and also exert a gravitational pull on the other bodies passing by. A rocket or a spacecraft traveling through space will be pulled off course when it passes near the moon, the Earth, other planets, or stars. Also, the gravitational pull of the planets attracts an atmosphere, a layer of gases, that can alter the course of a spaceflight.

The atmosphere of the Earth places tight limits on the angle at which a spacecraft can reenter the atmosphere. If the angle is too shallow, the spacecraft may bounce back out into space. If the angle is too deep, the spacecraft may burn up.

Future of Space Travel Just as space has no known limits, so the extent of space travel has no known limits. Trips to Mars may be possible in the not very distant future. Trips to even more distant planets, and perhaps other planetary systems, are not impossible. It may be that some day people will set out on voyages to other solar systems that will last for generations, giving birth, growing, and dying in spaceships and space stations, and knowing the Earth only as a bright speck in the sky.

ALSO READ: AEROSPACE; ALDRIN, EDWIN; ARMSTRONG, NEIL; ASTRONAUT; ATMOSPHERE; CAPE CANAVERAL; COLLINS, MICHAEL; COMMUNICATIONS SATELLITE; GAGARIN, YURI; GLENN, JOHN; GODDARD, ROBERT H.; ORBIT; ROCKET; SATELLITE; SOLAR SYSTEM; SPACE; SPACE RESEARCH; VON BRAUN, WERNHER.

SPACE WEAPONS The age of space weapons dawned in the 1940's with the invention of the first long-range guided missiles. These rocket weapons flew in space too high and too fast to be shot down. Today's intercontinental ballistic missiles (ICBM's) can travel thousands of miles carrying nuclear warheads.

For defense against such weapons, some experts suggest a space defense system. Spy satellites in orbit around the Earth can detect a missile launch. It could then be intercepted and destroyed, either by missiles fired from the ground or by missiles, lasers, and energy-beam weapons fired from satellite "battle-stations." In 1984 the U.S. Army successfully destroyed a warhead launched from a Minuteman ICBM. They tracked the ICBM and fired a second missile that released a large metal "umbrella" in front of the warhead.

The U.S. government is investigating a space defense system, known as the Strategic Defense Initiative. Already experts believe there are armed satellites in orbit. These "hunter

satellites" could track and destroy spy and communications satellites.

ALSO READ: MISSILE, SPACE RESEARCH.

SPAIN The Iberian Peninsula in southwestern Europe is made up of Spain and Portugal. Spain occupies about 85 percent of the peninsula and is about twice as large as the state of Wyoming. The Bay of Biscay lies to the north, the Atlantic Ocean to the west, and the Mediterranean Sea to the south and east. The Pyrenees separate Spain from France in the north. Africa lies only a few miles south.

▲ *The U.S. space defense system would use powerful lasers, mounted on satellites, to knock out enemy nuclear missiles in space before they could re-enter the Earth's atmosphere and cause massive devastation.*

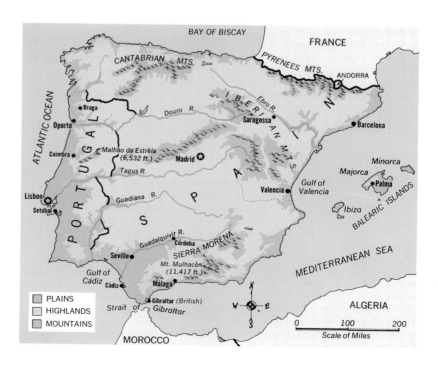

▲ *Spain's sunny beaches are popular with tourists particularly from the colder northern European countries. This is a resort in Majorca, an island off the Mediterranean coast of Spain.*

A huge, dry plateau, called the *Meseta*, covers central Spain. Near the center of the Meseta is Madrid, the capital and largest city. The Tagus and other rivers have cut deep canyons into the Meseta, whose reddish-brown soil is not good for farming. Many farmers along the Guadalquivir River valley in southern Spain depend on irrigation to water their crops. Ships travel more than 50 miles (80 km) up this river to the inland port of Seville.

Many Spanish people are farmers. They grow wheat, olives, grapes, and citrus fruits. Valencia, in southeast Spain, is the center of an area where lemons, oranges, melons, dates, and figs are grown. Cork trees also grow in Spain, and their bark is exported. Spanish fishermen catch cod, tuna, and sardines.

In nothern Spain, people mine iron ore for export. Spain has rich mineral resources, including coal, iron, copper, mercury, and many others. The iron and steel industry has been developed in recent years. The seaport of Barcelona is a textile-manufacturing center.

The Basque people, who live in northern Spain by the Bay of Biscay, are a people whose origin is unknown. They have their own language and customs. Through the years, many Basques have fought for independence. In 1980, the Spanish government granted self-government to the Basque region.

Tourists can see fine works of art in

▲ *Roman walls surround an ancient city in Castile, a region in central Spain.*

the museums, which include the Prado National Museum in Madrid. Bullfights, with colorfully dressed *matadors*, attract tourists, and are popular with the Spanish people.

Spain was part of the Roman Empire. In the A.D. 700's, the Moors (Muslims) from northern Africa conquered the country. Madrid grew out of a Moorish fortress built in the A.D. 900's. The Moors lived in Spain for about 700 years until they were defeated by the armies of the Spanish kings and queens. Spain then acquired an enormous overseas empire, most of which lasted until the 1800's. Today, Spain owns only the Canary Islands in the Atlantic, the Balearic Islands in the Mediterranean, and Ceuta and Melilla in North Africa.

Bullfighting is no longer the great spectator sport of the Spanish. For a long time now, soccer has been the number one sport. Over 100,000 people can crowd into the Santiago Bernabeu stadium to watch Real Madrid play soccer.

SPAIN

Capital City: Madrid (3,500,000 people).

Area: 194,912 square miles (504,782 sq. km).

Population: 39,800,000.

Government: Constitutional monarchy.

Natural Resources: Lignite, mercury, iron, lead, zinc.

Export Products: Manufactured goods, chemicals, textiles, leather goods, fish, wine, fruit and vegetables, olive oil.

Unit of Money: Peseta.

Official Language: Spanish.

General Francisco Franco, a dictator, ruled Spain from 1939 to 1975. He was succeeded by Prince Juan Carlos, who became king and chief of state. The new constitution of 1978 created a new, democratic *Cortes*, or parliament.

ALSO READ: CANARY ISLANDS; FRANCO, FRANCISCO; GIBRALTAR; SPANISH HISTORY.

SPANISH see ROMANCE LANGUAGES.

SPANISH - AMERICAN WAR

The Spanish-American War was fought between the United States and Spain. The war lasted only during the spring and summer of 1898. However, though it was a short war, it was important for the United States. Through its victory in the war, the United States gained new territory and became a world power.

The Spanish-American War was fought over the island of Cuba in the Caribbean Sea. Cuba was a Spanish colony. The Cubans had been fighting for many years for their independence. Many Americans felt that the island should be free from Spanish rule.

In January 1898, the United States battleship *Maine* was anchored in Havana harbor to protect U.S. citizens in Cuba. On February 15, the ship was sunk by an explosion, and 260 sailors were killed. Nobody ever proved that Spain was responsible for the sinking. But Spain was thought by many Americans to be responsible, and newspapers in the United States printed large headlines saying, "Remember the *Maine*." U.S. President William McKinley sent a message to Spain, demanding Spanish withdrawal from Cuba. American ships began a blockade of Cuban ports. On April 25, Spain declared war.

The first battle of the war was fought off the Philippine Islands in the Pacific Ocean. The islands belonged to Spain. On May 1, six American warships under Commodore George Dewey sailed into Manila Bay and destroyed the Spanish Pacific fleet. Not a single American life was lost.

American troops began landing in Cuba on June 22. By July 1, they had surrounded the port of Santiago where the Spanish fleet was anchored. They captured the fort of El Caney and stormed San Juan Hill, above the city. A hero during the Battle of San Juan Hill was the future U.S. President Theodore Roosevelt, who commanded a brave attack by the Rough Riders, a volunteer cavalry regiment. On July 3, the Spanish fleet tried to escape from Santiago and was destroyed by American warships. Spain surrendered on August 12, 1898. The following day, the American commander in the Philippines, not knowing of the surrender, captured the city of Manila.

On December 10, 1898, the United States and Spain signed a peace treaty. Cuba became an independent territory under U.S. protection. Spain ceded (gave) the Caribbean island of Puerto Rico and the Pacific island of Guam to the United States. Spain also surrendered the Philippine Islands to the United States for a payment of $20 million. (The Philippines became an independent country in 1946.)

The Spanish-American War had a significant effect on the U.S. role as a world power. Since the war, the United States has played an important role in Far Eastern and Caribbean affairs. The war also highlighted the need for a canal to cut through the isthmus separating the Caribbean Sea from the Pacific Ocean. U.S. warships would soon benefit from the building of the Panama Canal.

ALSO READ: CUBA; MCKINLEY, WILLIAM; PHILIPPINES; PUERTO RICO.

▲ *Colonel Theodore Roosevelt led the Rough Riders regiment in the charge up Kettle Hill during the Battle of San Juan Hill in the Spanish-American War.*

▲ *A contemporary painting showing the fight between the Spanish Armada and the English fleet (left). The English chased the Spanish ships into Calais harbor (France) and sent in fire ships to create panic and confusion. This caused the Spanish to scatter, and the English guns and violent storms completed the rout of the Spanish fleet.*

▲ *This Roman aqueduct in Segovia, in north-central Spain, was built during the time of the Roman Emperor Trajan, about A.D.100. It is the largest Roman construction still standing in Spain.*

SPANISH ARMADA In 1588, a mighty fleet of 130 Spanish warships, which the Spaniards called an *armada*, set sail from Spain. The Armada was going to take part in an invasion of England. The warships would engage the English fleet while the Spanish army was shipped across the English Channel from France.

Queen Elizabeth I of England and King Philip II of Spain had long been enemies. They were champions of rival Christian faiths, the Church of England and the Catholic Church. Philip had supported the claims of the Catholic Mary, Queen of Scots, to Elizabeth's throne. Elizabeth had helped Protestant Netherlands to rebel against Spain. In 1587, Elizabeth had Mary executed.

The Spaniards called their fleet the Invincible (unbeatable) Armada. But the English were tough and confident sailors. Tradition tells that Sir Francis Drake, a commander of the English fleet, was playing a game of bowls at the English port of Plymouth when the Armada was first sighted. Drake calmly finished his game before setting sail. The English fleet consisted of 197 ships, most of which were smaller than the Spanish warships.

As the Armada sailed through the channel, the English followed behind, firing from a distance and scurrying away before the Spaniards

could turn their heavy ships. Many Spanish galleons were sunk. The remaining Spanish ships took refuge in the French port of Calais. Under cover of darkness, the English sailed several burning ships into the harbor. The Spaniards fled from the harbor in confusion, and the English attacked them again. Battered and weary, the Spaniards tried to escape back to Spain around the north of Scotland. But most of their ships were wrecked in storms at sea. Only 76 battered ships got back to Spain.

ALSO READ: DRAKE, SIR FRANCIS; ELIZABETH I; ENGLISH HISTORY; PHILIP, KINGS OF SPAIN; SPANISH HISTORY.

SPANISH HISTORY The Iberian Peninsula, which contains the present-day nations of Spain and Portugal, is cut off from the rest of Europe by the Pyrenees Mountains. But Spain has always played an important part in the history of Europe.

Early Spain Stone Age hunters were living in Spain about 15,000 years ago. They painted colorful pictures of animals on the walls of their caves, which can still be seen today. About 3000 B.C., most of Spain was settled by small, dark-haired horsemen and women from northern Africa. Ancient writers called these people Iberians. The Iberian Peninsula became known as a rich source of copper, tin, and gold. Greeks and Phoenicians from the eastern Mediterranean set up trading colonies along the coast. In the 400's B.C., the Carthaginians from northern Africa captured most of Spain.

The Romans defeated the Carthaginians in the 200's B.C., and Spain became a part of the Roman Empire. The Romans made Spain one of the richest and most peaceful provinces. They built roads and towns. They mined the precious metals in the Spanish mountains. Roman emperors, Trajan and Hadrian, were born in Spain.

Barbarian peoples from northeastern Europe began to invade the Roman Empire in the A.D. 400's. The Visigoths overran Spain and set up a powerful kingdom. In the A.D. 500's, the Visigothic king became a Christian. Gradually Christianity became the religion of most of the people.

A people from northern Africa, called the Moors, invaded Spain in the early A.D. 700's. Some of the Moors were Berbers, a native people of northern Africa. Others were Arabs, who had conquered the Berbers. The Moors conquered the whole of Spain and then settled in the south. The Moors were industrious traders and business people. They built several beautiful cities and founded schools and universities. They set up an irrigation system, which Spanish farmers still use, to bring water to the dry lands of southern Spain.

The Moors were Muslims, but they allowed the Christian Spaniards to keep their religion. By the A.D. 1000's, the Moorish state had been weakened by quarrels among its governors. Christian leaders in the north began to win back some of their lands.

The Great Years By the 1400's, two Christian kingdoms, Aragon and Castile, had reconquered most of Spain. In 1492, King Ferdinand of Aragon and Queen Isabella of Castile were married. Spain was united as one nation. Ferdinand and Isabella set up the Inquisition, a court that tried and punished any person who questioned the laws of the Catholic Church. Many people were tortured and put to death. The Inquisition was closely controlled by the Spanish monarchs. It helped to strengthen the power of the government over the people. Most of the Jews in Spain fled to other countries during the time of the Inquisition.

Ferdinand and Isabella gave money

to the Italian explorer, Christopher Columbus, for his expeditions to the New World. Spanish explorers and *conquistadors* (conquerors) followed Columbus, and the Spaniards colonized several regions of Central and South America. Spain grew rich from the gold and silver of its American colonies. The Spaniards also took control of the Philippine Islands in the Pacific Ocean.

King Ferdinand's daughter, Joanna, married Philip, the son of the Holy Roman Emperor. Their son became King Charles I of Spain and Holy Roman Emperor. In 1556, Charles left the Spanish kingdom and parts of the empire, including the Netherlands and most of Italy, to his son King Philip II. In 1580, Philip II also conquered the kingdom of Portugal. He became the most powerful ruler in Europe. During the Protestant Reformation, several nations of Europe had broken away from the Catholic Church. Philip thought of himself as the champion of the Church. In 1588, he went to war with the Protestant country of England. But Philip suffered a bad defeat when his great fleet, the Spanish Armada, was destroyed by the English.

Spain Becomes Weaker Spain's great power did not last. Philip's successors were weak and extravagant rulers. Gold still poured in from the American colonies. But the Spanish people lived in poverty and hunger. In 1640, Portugal broke away from Spain. Eight years later, Spain was forced to grant the people of the

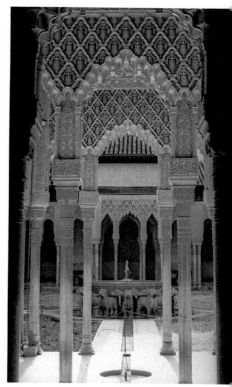

▲ *The Court of the Lions in the palace of the Alhambra at Granada in Spain. It was built in the late 1300's. Around the courtyard, with its fountain guarded by stone lions, are columns holding up arches in the Moorish (North African) style.*

▼ *The Escorial, built near Madrid in the late 1500's, was both a palace and a monastery.*

▲ *Charles I was king of Spain from 1516 until 1556.*

Netherlands their independence.

In 1700, King Charles II of Spain died without a successor. The powerful King Louis XIV of France supported the claim of his grandson, Philip of Anjou, to the throne of Spain. Other nations in Europe feared that the kingdoms of France and Spain would be united. The War of the Spanish Succession broke out. By the end of the war, Spain had lost its territories in Italy. Philip of Anjou became king. He was the first king of the Bourbon family.

In the early 1800's, the Bourbon king, Charles IV, supported Emperor Napoleon I of France in a war against Great Britain. A French and Spanish fleet was defeated by the British at the Battle of Trafalgar in 1805. Napoleon then invaded Spain and took over the kingdom. The Spaniards rebelled in 1808 and, with the help of the British, drove out Napoleon's troops.

Spain was forced to grant independence to most of its American colonies during the 1800's. The remaining colonies in the Americas and the Pacific were lost to the United States in 1898 at the end of the Spanish-American War. Spanish workers began to form trade unions, and revolts broke out. In 1931, King Alfonso XIII was forced to leave the country. Spain became a republic, and the Spanish people elected a president.

Modern Spain Many army leaders, clergy, and wealthy landowners refused to support the new government. In 1936, civil war broke out. The rebels, or Nationalists, who fought against the government were commanded by General Francisco Franco. The people who supported the government were called Loyalists. Many people from the United States, the Soviet Union, and France went to Spain to fight with the Loyalists. Germany and Italy sent arms and military advisers to the Nationalists. By 1939, Franco had won the war.

Franco set up a fascist dictatorship

More than a million people died in the Spanish Civil War (1936–1939). This war was one of the most violent and bloody in history. Both sides killed civilians and massacred prisoners.

▲ *Republican volunteers during the Spanish Civil War (1936–1939). The lawful government was overthrown by Franco's rebel forces.*

in Spain. Under his rule, the people were allowed little freedom. The army and the secret police enforced the laws of the government. Franco was succeeded in 1975 by Juan Carlos (who became king). Democracy was restored, and Spain joined the European Community in 1981.

ALSO READ: CARTHAGE; CHARLES, HOLY ROMAN EMPERORS; CID, THE; COLUMBUS, CHRISTOPHER; CONQUISTADOR; DICTATOR; EUROPEAN COMMUNITY; EXPLORATION; FASCISM; FRANCO, FRANCISCO; HOLY ROMAN EMPIRE; ISABELLA AND FERDINAND; NAPOLEON BONAPARTE; PHILIP, KINGS OF SPAIN; PORTUGAL; SOUTH AMERICA; SPAIN; SPANISH-AMERICAN WAR; SPANISH ARMADA.

SPANISH MAIN The words "Spanish Main" once referred to the mainland of Spanish America—that coastal region of South America from the Isthmus of Panama to the mouth of the Orinoco River in eastern Venezuela.

When Spanish *galleons* (large wooden ships) sailed home from the

New World, they were loaded with treasure, such as gold and silver. The galleons passed through the Caribbean Sea, north of the "Main." From the 1500's to the 1800's, many English *buccaneers* (pirates) attacked and captured the treasure ships, taking the valuable cargo for themselves. Other pirates came from France, the Netherlands, and America to prey along the Spanish coasts.

Later, the Spanish Main was expanded to include the West Indies and the entire Caribbean Sea, as well as the northern coast of South America. The term has become identified with pirate adventures and legends.

ALSO READ: PIRATES AND PRIVATEERS.

SPARTA see GREECE, ANCIENT.

SPARTACUS (died 71 B.C.)
Spartacus was the leader of a slave revolt, known as the Gladiators' War, against the ancient Romans in Italy. Spartacus was born in Thrace (an ancient country, now part of Greece and Turkey). He served as a soldier in the Roman army. But he was later sold as a slave by the Romans, probably because he deserted from the army.

Spartacus was sent to Capua in southern Italy to train as a *gladiator* to fight wild animals and people for entertainment. With about 70 other gladiators, he escaped from the training school in 73 B.C. and fled to nearby Mount Vesuvius. He was soon joined by other gladiators and runaway slaves. Spartacus and his followers defeated two Roman armies and marched through Italy burning towns.

Spartacus wanted to lead his army of several thousand strong over the Alps and out of Italy. But his followers preferred to stay and plunder (take by force). Spartacus turned southward, hoping to cross over to

Sicily. In 72 B.C., a Roman army pushed his forces into the narrow peninsula of Rhegium, but Spartacus managed to break through the Roman *cordon* (encircling line). At Brundisium (now Brindisi) in 71 B.C., a Roman army under Marcus Licinius Crassus defeated the slaves and gladiators. Spartacus was killed in the battle. The Romans then crucified (put to death by nailing to a cross) about 6,000 captured slaves.

ALSO READ: GLADIATOR, SLAVERY.

SPECIAL EDUCATION
Handicapped children and adults have the same basic needs as other individuals. Special education programs have been set up in schools, hospitals, and clinics to help handicapped people in a number of different ways, but especially to help people gain a feeling of self-worth.

Personnel workers, school psychologists, counselors, therapists, and teachers, as well as doctors, work with handicapped people and their families. Together they identify the people's problems and plan for their education and *rehabilitation* (preparation for normal, active living).

Handicapped people do not want to be burdens to others. The major part of their training involves learning to be as independent as they possibly can. The more they can do on their

▲ *Spartacus is remembered as a gladiator who attempted to lead Rome's slaves in rebellion. This still comes from the motion picture* Spartacus *starring Kirk Douglas (center).*

▼ *Modern hearing-aid equipment and traditional toys, such as this doll, are combined to help this young deaf girl's education.*

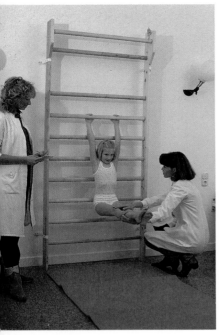

▲ *Young people with physical handicaps, such as this young girl who cannot walk, are given therapy to restore the use of their joints and muscles. They also study normal school subjects.*

own, the more they can be a help to others, and the more worthwhile they will feel.

Types of Special Education The needs of each individual person determine the kind of special education he or she receives. Programs are designed for people with *mental retardation,* whose mentality (ability to reason and learn) has developed more slowly and not as far as that of most people. People with crippling or chronic (always present) health conditions, such as heart trouble, muscular dystrophy, and multiple sclerosis, are provided with special training programs. People with specific learning disabilities or handicaps, such as the inability to understand printed words, are helped through special education. Severe hearing disorders, such as complete or partial deafness, require special education. Speech problems, such as stuttering, lisping, and stammering, are helped with special training. Visual handicaps, such as blindness, tunnel vision, and mirror vision, can also be aided with special training.

MENTAL RETARDATION. There are generally two types of mental retardation. The *educable mentally retarded* person is one who is capable of some learning, but progresses about one-fourth to one-half more slowly than the average person does. The special education program is prepared carefully with a person's abilities in mind. It aims toward developing the person's social relationships, preparing him or her to handle a job, and providing the person with various experiences that will help him or her gain skills needed to manage life alone.

The *trainable mentally retarded* person is much more limited in learning ability. He or she can, however, be helped to learn a little bit about him or herself as a person. This person can also be trained in simple household and job skills that help him or her contribute to family and community.

The special education program for the trainable retarded person stresses relationships with others, training in the tasks of daily living, and safety.

CRIPPLING AND CHRONIC HEALTH CONDITIONS. The special programs for the physically handicapped include physical training as well as education. Handicapped persons are taught school subjects, but they are also given therapy (health-improving treatments) to help them develop the skills and attitudes (ways of thinking) that they will need throughout life. Kinds of therapy may include squeezing and shaping putty or clay to strengthen hand muscles or lifting dumbbells to develop arm and shoulder muscles.

SPECIFIC LEARNING DISABILITIES. Problems of visual perception, such as seeing the word "soon" as "noos," or eye-hand coordination, such as being unable to position the hands to catch a thrown ball, are examples of specific learning disabilities. Another type of disability is *hyperactivity.* The person is unusually active, energetic, or excitable and seems unable to stay calm.

SEVERE HEARING DISORDERS. The auditorily handicapped person is one with a very serious and complicated hearing problem. He or she may be totally or partially deaf. This person may be able to hear only certain sounds, such as t, d, p, or b, or may be able to hear only sounds of a certain volume (loudness) or pitch (highness and lowness). Deaf people need special education programs that teach them listening, speaking, reading, and writing skills. The deaf are taught a manual alphabet—a sign language in which they use finger positions to form words, phrases, and letters of the alphabet. With sign language, the deaf can speak to each other and to nondeaf people who know the signs. Lipreading (following a person's speech by watching mouth and lip movements) helps the deaf understand something of what people around them are saying. Deaf people learn to communicate with the nondeaf by being taught to speak themselves. It takes many hours of hard training for deaf people to learn to speak, because they cannot hear the sounds of speech. They must depend on feeling the vibrations in their throats and on learning ways to place their tongues and lips to form various sounds.

VISUAL HANDICAPS. People who are completely or partially blind are given special training in learning how to move about by themselves. The blind are taught to develop a keen sense of hearing. By listening to the sounds of their own footsteps, or the sounds made by other people or objects around them, the blind can tell how far away certain objects are. Many blind people are taught to use a white cane when walking outdoors. By tapping the cane in front of them as they walk, they can note changes in sound and so avoid bumping into objects or persons.

Many blind people own seeing-eye dogs. The dogs are specially trained to be their masters' "eyes." They guide the blind person across traffic intersections, through complicated building corridors, up and down stairways, onto buses and trains, or anywhere the blind person needs to go. The blind person and the dog go through many months of training together to become used to each other and to learn to communicate.

Blind people learn to read with the Braille alphabet—letters formed by combinations of raised bumps on paper. By moving their fingers along these bumps, the blind can read. Braille typewriters enable blind people to write in Braille.

SPECIAL HEALTH PROBLEMS. People whose health difficulties keep them at home or hospitalized for a long time need special education programs that will prevent their falling behind in their school studies or their work. They are given programs of

home teaching, training, and guidance. Workers who must be away from their jobs for a long time are encouraged to learn new skills and take on work that they can do while in bed or hospitalized. If students are away from school for a very long time, a home-to-school telephone service is sometimes set up to keep them in daily contact with their teachers and class.

ALSO READ: BRAILLE; DISEASE; EDUCATION; EXERCISE; GUIDANCE; HEALTH; HEARING; KELLER, HELEN; LEARNING; MENTAL HEALTH; PSYCHOLOGY; SCHOOL; SENSES; SIGHT; SIGN LANGUAGE; SPEECH; TEACHING.

SPECTRUM The colors in a rainbow run from red through orange, yellow, green, and blue to violet. This band of colors from red to violet is called a spectrum of colors.

Where do the colors in a rainbow come from? The answer was discovered by the famous English mathematician, Sir Isaac Newton, in 1666. Newton put a triangle-shaped piece of glass, called a *prism*, in front of a beam of light. The prism *refracted* (bent) the light and separated it into different colors. Newton then put another prism upside-down in the path of the spread-out colors. When the light came out of the second prism, the light had joined together into a beam of white sunlight again.

By these experiments Sir Isaac Newton showed that sunlight is made up of different colors. We believe that sunlight is "white" only because all the colors of the rainbow are mixed together.

Where The Spectrum Comes From If sunlight contains all the colors of the rainbow, where do all these different colors come from? They come from the atoms that are being made and broken apart inside the hot sun. Every different kind of

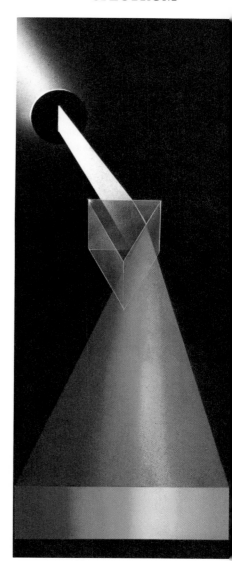

▲ *A glass prism slits up a beam of light so that we see a spectrum of the light's component colors.*

The wavelength of waves that make up the electromagnetic spectrum varies enormously. Radio waves can be ten miles (16 km) long; gamma rays are less than a billionth of an inch (a ten-billionth of a meter) long. But all these waves travel at the same speed—the speed of light—186,000 miles (300,000 km) per second.

SPECTRUM

The colors of the spectrum are the same as the colors of the rainbow. This is because the raindrops that make a rainbow each split sunlight up in the same way as a glass prism. A prism and raindrops split up white light because the rays of light bend as they pass into and out of the prism or raindrop. Each color mixed together in white light bends by a different amount. Red light bends least, violet light most.

The human eye is sensitive to electromagnetic wavelengths of between 4 and 7 ten-thousandths of a millimeter (below left). The whole range of electromagnetic radiation (below right) covers wavelengths from less than one millionth of a millimeter (gamma rays) to thousands of meters (radio waves).

atom in the sun gives off a particular set of colors. This happens on Earth also. If you make any substance hot enough its atoms will begin to give off colors of light. Each different kind of substance gives off its own special colors.

For example, ordinary salt is made up of a chemical called sodium chloride. The atoms of sodium in the salt give off a bright yellow color when they are very hot. Carefully shake some salt into the flame of a candle. You will see the flame turn yellow as the sodium heats.

A neon light is bright red because the inside of the glass tubing is filled with atoms of neon gas. When the atoms of neon are excited by electricity, they give a bright red glow.

The Spectroscope Scientists have invented an instrument that lets them look more closely at the light given off by atoms. This instrument is called a spectroscope. A spectroscope has a prism inside it to separate the colors of light. The spectroscope also has a magnifying glass or a telescope that lets the scientist look closely at the colors that come out of the prism.

Suppose a scientist were to look closely at the light given off by a piece of burning sodium. He or she would see two bright yellow lines. The other lines would be quite faint.

Every different substance gives off its own particular pattern of colors. These colors appear as bright lines of color inside a spectroscope. By looking at these lines of colors, a scientist can tell what atoms are in the substance. Whenever a scientist sees the two bright yellow lines of sodium, for

example, the scientist knows there are sodium atoms in that substance being tested.

The light given off by a substance is called a bright-line or *emission* spectrum. Each substance also absorbs light and can have a dark-line or *absorption* spectrum, too. For instance, if white light is passed through sodium vapor (gas), the sodium vapor absorbs two lines of bright yellow light. These are the same two lines the sodium would give off if it were burned. But while these appear as bright lines on the emission spectrum, they appear as dark lines on the absorption spectrum. The sun's spectrum is a dark-line spectrum. By using spectroscopes, scientists learned what the rocks of the moon are made of.

Scientists even know what kinds of atoms are in the stars that are billions of miles from Earth. All they have to do is connect a spectroscope to a telescope. When they look through the eyepiece of the spectroscope, all the colors of light given off by the stars are spread out before them.

The Electromagnetic Spectrum The spectrum of light is only one segment of the whole electromagnetic spectrum. The electromagnetic spectrum is arranged according to the *frequency* (number of waves each second) and *wavelength* (distance between waves) of the electromagnetic waves. *Gamma rays* have the highest frequency and the shortest wavelength. Then come *X rays*, ultraviolet radiation, and so on until we come to the low frequency end of the spectrum—*radio waves*.

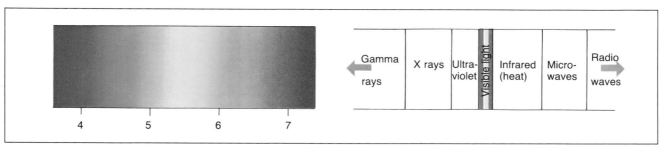

When you turn the dial on a radio, you hear different radio stations. Each radio station has its own radio signal. There is a whole spectrum of such signals, each with a different wavelength. When you select a station, it is as if you pick out one particular color in a spectrum of colors.

ALSO READ: COLOR, LIGHT, MUSIC, RADIATION, RADIO, WAVE.

SPEECH When you speak, you make certain regular, controlled sounds with your voice in order to communicate with another person. The combination of these vocal sounds is called speech. The different kinds of speech people use are called languages.

How Speech Is Made Your *speech mechanism* is all the parts of your body that you use to make speech sounds. A mechanism is a combination of things that makes something work. Your speech mechanism has three main sections—the power source, the voice box, and the articulators.

POWER SOURCE. Speaking takes energy because you must make your vocal cords vibrate to produce sound. The source of power for your speech is your two lungs and the muscles that operate them. Your lungs, controlled by these muscles, expel air up and between your vocal cords to make them vibrate. If your lungs are weak, your voice will sound weak. The lungs also control the flow of air in and out of your body so that you won't run out of breath when speaking.

VOICE BOX. The scientific term for voice box is *larynx*. The larynx is not really a box but an air valve in your throat that helps control the flow of air in and out of the lungs. The larynx is made up of a pair of muscles side by side. These are your vocal cords. Air from your lungs passes between the

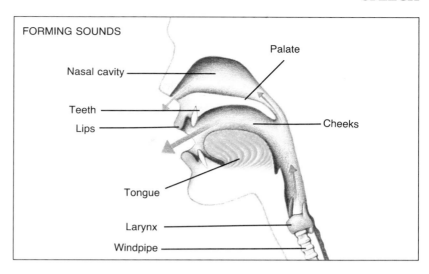

FORMING SOUNDS

Nasal cavity
Palate
Teeth
Lips
Cheeks
Tongue
Larynx
Windpipe

cords. This causes the cords to vibrate and send the air from your body in the form of sound waves that can be heard. When your vocal cords are completely relaxed, air can pass in and out of your body without causing them to vibrate. Since no vibration is produced, no voice sound can be heard. But if you tighten your vocal cords (which also shortens them), air from your lungs must be pushed with greater force to get through. This causes a vibration, and sounds can be heard.

The tighter you make your vocal cords, the higher will be the *pitch* of your voice. Women generally have higher-pitched voices than men do because their vocal cords are shorter. Shorter vocal cords vibrate faster and produce a higher pitch. Men can generally make their voices louder than women because their lungs are larger and their muscles are more powerful. Larger lungs can hold more air, and stronger muscles can exert greater force to push the air out.

ARTICULATORS. The word "articulate" means to put vocal sounds into language. When you articulate, you move your lips, tongue, and other organs to make words and sentences from the vocal sounds produced by your larynx.

Articulators are divided into two kinds—bony and fleshy. Bony articulators include your upper and lower

▲ *Speech is made by several parts of the mouth that help to form sounds. The cavity inside the nose is also important, as you will find if you try to speak while holding your nose.*

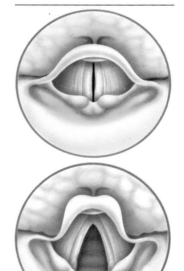

▲ *Two bands of elastic cartilage, the vocal cords, are stretched across the larynx. They can be opened or closed by muscles. Air from the lungs passes through the slit and makes the cords vibrate. This produces sounds. These pictures show the cords stretched (top) to produce a high-pitched sound, and relaxed (bottom) to produce a deeper sound.*

▲ *Your tongue, teeth, and lips work together to make sounds. At top, the lips are shown pushed out to make a hole for the sound "oo." At bottom, tongue, teeth, and lips combine to make the sound "th."*

Most people who speak English use 15 vowel and 23 consonant sounds. With these 38 different sounds we can say any of the half million words in the English language. However, most of us, in everyday speech, seldom use more than about 5,000 words.

teeth, jaws, and hard palate (roof of your mouth). Fleshy articulators include your lips, tongue, and soft palate (the upper back part of your mouth that leads to the throat).

■ LEARN BY DOING

To see how the articulators work, try this simple experiment. Begin humming, and continue to hum while changing your articulators in the following ways. (1) Drop your jaw so your mouth opens slightly. Notice the "AH" sound. (2) With your mouth in the "AH" position, place the tip of your tongue against the back of your upper teeth. Notice the "L" sound. (3) Put your tongue tip against the back of your lower teeth, raise your jaw a bit, and stretch your mouth a little at the corners. Notice the "EE" sound. (4) Go back to your original hum and simply open your lips and put your teeth together. That's the "N" sound. (5) With your mouth in the "N" position, force the air out between your front teeth to make the "Z" sound. (6) Now stop your vocal cords from vibrating and simply push air out between your teeth This makes an "S" sound. ■

Try forming other sounds and notice the various positions of your articulators. People have learned to produce all these sounds in thousands of different combinations to make words. And the amazing thing is that people have learned to produce the sounds automatically, without having to think about it. Babies make all sorts of sounds before they learn to talk, but the sounds make no sense because they are not in the right order to form words. Eventually, babies begin paying attention to and imitating the speech of people around them. If you have ever heard babies learning to talk, you know how hard they practice. They repeat words and phrases over and over and over again. They try them out on people to see if anyone can understand them. As ba-

bies become older, they learn more and more words, and their pronunciation gets better.

Speech Defects When a person is unable to form speech sounds in the normal way, he or she is said to have a speech defect. Speech defects can be caused by serious illness, emotional problems, or by being born with disorders (or *birth defects*) of muscles and organs of the speech mechanism

BIRTH DEFECTS. The most obvious birth defects affecting speech are the *cleft palate* and *cleft lip*. In these cases, a person's upper lip and the roof of the mouth are split down the middle, making it impossible to form speech sounds correctly. A cleft palate and lip can usually be corrected by surgery soon after birth so the person can speak normally.

A youngster born deaf cannot learn to speak in the usual way. You must be able to hear yourself and others speak, and deaf youngsters cannot do this. Special schools and clinics have been set up to teach deaf youngsters to speak. They learn to imitate speech sounds by feeling the changing vibrations in the throat and by watching and imitating the placement of the jaw, mouth, lips, and tongue.

OTHER CAUSES. Illnesses and injuries that damage the brain can cause speech defects by paralyzing part of the speech mechanism.

Some people have a speech disorder called *lisping*. Lisping can be the result of learning to pronounce incorrectly (substituting a "TH" sound for the "S" sound). Other types of lisping can be caused by too large a tongue, too narrow a jaw, too low a palate, or a number of other things. Corrective speech training helps young people overcome lisping.

Stammering and *stuttering* are speech defects that may be caused by physical or emotional problems, or a combination of both. Many psychologists and psychiatrists agree that people who stammer or stutter are greatly helped through programs of psychotherapy (which reduce people's emotional problems) and through various uses of learning theory. Stammering and stuttering often occur together. Stammering is a hesitation in starting or finishing a sound. A stammerer may have a hard time starting words that begin with certain sounds, such as M or T. Or a stammerer may find it difficult to finish certain kinds of words. Stuttering is repeating the first sound of a word over and over, seeming to be unable to get to the next sound. One simple way stammerers and stutterers can control their speech is by training themselves to speak slowly.

ALSO READ: ANIMAL VOICES, COMMUNICATION, LANGUAGES, PRONUNCIATION, PUBLIC SPEAKING, SINGING, SPECIAL EDUCATION.

SPELLING Language is one means that people have of communicating with each other. Spelling is the arrangement of letters to form the written words of a language. When a person wants to communicate with someone else in writing, the message must be in a form that others will understand. The uniform (unchanging) spelling of words in a language makes written communication understandable to everyone who reads the language.

You have probably noticed in reading that English spellings often do not correspond to pronunciations (ways words are said). The alphabet used in English contains only 26 letters, but there are many more sounds in the language. Many letters, particularly vowels, are used to spell several quite different sounds. For example, the words "cute," "cup," and "turn" all contain the letter "u," but that letter has a different sound in each word. And there are several groups of words in English that have the same pronunciation, but different spellings and meanings. "To," "too," and "two" are pronounced the same way, as are "be" and "bee." Many English spellings were once much closer to pronunciations. For example, in the Middle Ages, the final "e" on such words as "late" was pronounced. But since speech changes much faster than written langugages, many pronunciations have changed a great deal, while the accepted spellings remained the same.

Some general rules give clues to the correct spelling of certain words. However, since there are also exceptions to many rules, many spellings must be memorized. But you *can* improve your spelling. Listen to words as they are pronounced and try to pronounce the words accurately yourself. (Note the silent letters.) Study words in your reading. Observant reading is possibly the best way to improve your spelling ability. Learn to use spelling rules and their exceptions. Consulting a good dictionary will help you learn the correct spelling of words you want to use, by showing you the root, or derivation, of the word. If you are doubtful about the spelling of a word, look it up. Keep a list of difficult words and learn their correct spelling. When you *do* misspell words, make sure you then learn their correct spellings.

Many games can improve your spelling while they entertain you. Try playing charades with a variation—the person who guesses a word must spell it correctly. If that person cannot spell it correctly, he or she must act out the next word. Crossword puzzles also improve spelling. A spelling bee is a contest in which individuals, or teams, have to spell words first pronounced by a judge or moderator. The winner is the last person left in the game. This game shows how the pronunciation of a word can be very different from its spelling.

ALSO READ: CROSSWORD PUZZLE, ENGLISH LANGUAGE, PRONUNCIATION.

SOME SPELLING "BUGS"

RIGHT	WRONG
absence	abcense
all right	alright
answer	anser
Arctic	Artic
athlete	athalete
believe	beleive
bicycle	bycycle
breath (n.)	breathe
breathe (v.)	breath
coming	comeing
February	Febuary
forty	fourty
friend	freind
government	goverment
grammar	grammer
guess	geuss
interest	intrest
license	lisence
nuclear	nucular
occurred	occured
often	offen
piece	peice
principal (adj.)	principle
principle (n.)	principal
receive	recieve
separate	seperate
sincerely	sincerly
surprise	suprise
their (pron.)	there
there (adv.)	their
truly	truely
until	untill
weather (n.)	wether
Wednesday	Wenesday
weird	wierd
whether (conj.)	wether
would (v.)	woud
writing	writting

The spelling of words varied quite a lot in days gone by. Shakespeare spelled his surname in 11 different ways.

▲ *These spelunkers, or cavers, are inside a massive passageway of the Cantabrian mountains in northern Spain.*

▲ *Many herbs have long been used for medicinal purposes. This page from a book written during the 1700's shows some of them.*

SPELUNKING Have you ever been inside a cave? It's dark and quiet, and often cold and damp, too. Yet inside a cave there is much to see and learn. People who explore caves for fun and to discover more about them are called cavers or spelunkers.

Beginning cavers should first explore caves where there are guides and electric lights. This way they gain experience of being underground. Caves can be dangerous, and no caver should venture in alone. It is easy to get lost.

Cavers follow several safety rules. They wear strong boots with soles that won't slip on sharp or wet rocks. They wear tough, waterproof clothing and helmets (like those worn by miners). The hard helmet protects against bumps and falling stones and has a compact carbide lamp attached. Cavers carry flashlights and, for use in an emergency, some candles and matches. Did you know that matches can be made waterproof by dipping their heads in fingernail polish?

If you want to explore a cave, be sure it is safe. Always take one other person along, and carry a first-aid kit. Always make sure someone on the surface knows which cave you are in.

ALSO READ: CAVE.

SPHINX A sphinx is an imaginary creature found in the folk tales and art of many ancient peoples. In early Egypt, the sphinx usually had the head of a man and the body of a lion. The Egyptians carved many statues of sphinxes. The head was usually a portrait of the pharaoh (king) who was ruling at the time. One of the best known of all Egyptian sphinx statues is the Great Sphinx of Giza near the Great Pyramid. King Khafre (Chephren) is thought to have ordered it made around 2500 B.C. It is 240 feet (73 m) long and rises to about 66 feet (20 m) in height.

▲ *The sphinx stands near the Great Pyramid of Giza near Cairo, Egypt.*

In the legends of ancient Greece, the sphinx was often a frightening monster. The Sphinx of Thebes had the head of a woman, the body of a lion, and the wings of a bird. She lay in wait for passersby, who were each asked the riddle, "What walks on four legs in the morning, two at noon, and three at night?" If they could not solve the riddle, she ate them. A Greek hero named Oedipus gave the correct answer, "Man." A person crawls on all fours when a baby, walks on two feet in the middle years, and uses a cane in old age. The Sphinx was so angry that she killed herself.

ALSO READ: EGYPT, ANCIENT; RIDDLE.

SPICES AND HERBS Spices and herbs are food seasonings made from plants. Spices are fragrant flavorings made from plants grown mainly in the tropics. The term "spices" is also used for herbs, parts of certain plants that grow in the temperate zone. When plant parts are dried to make spices and herbs, they produce seasonings with many different strong tastes. Some sauces made from spices and herbs, such as mustard and ketchup, are *condiments*.

Spices may be made from any part of the plant. Ginger is the underground stem of an Asian plant. Cinnamon is the bark of a tree. Whole cloves are flower buds, and black pepper is the fruit, or berry, that grows on a woody vine. Herbs are usually the green, leafy parts of the plant. The leaves of some of the common herbs, such as bay and thyme, are dried before they are used as seasonings. Others, such as parsley and mint, are most often used fresh. The seeds of some herbs, such as mustard and sesame, are used as flavorings. The roots, or bulbs, of some herbs, such as garlic, are also popular seasonings. The seeds and fruits of herbs used as flavorings are called *aromatic seeds.*

Nearly all spices were first grown in

▼ *An Arab market seller, with a variety of spices. In the Middle Ages, Crusaders brought spices from the Holy Land back to Europe, where they were used in cooking.*

and exported from Asia. People have used spices at least since the time of ancient Egypt. Spices were first used as perfume and medicine. These uses remained popular after their use as flavoring was discovered.

■ LEARN BY DOING

It is fun to make your own herb garden and watch the plants grow. Find a warm place inside your house and decide how large a planter you can keep there. Then get potting soil from a dime store or seed store. For planters, use tiny clay pots, or small plastic pots—even small waxed or plastic-coated milk cartons will do. Use a shallow pan to stand your little planters in. This can be an old ice-cube tray or an aluminum tray for frozen food—just don't use an iron or a copper pan. Make sure you make small holes in the bottom of your planters. Then plant a separate kind of seed in each planter. Begin with seeds of herbs like dill, basil, summer savory, cooking thyme, and chive. These seeds should be planted just slightly beneath the top of the soil—not too deep. Place all the planters with seeds in the shallow pan. Water all the plants by pouring water into the base pan. In that way, water will go up into the soil. Keep these planters moist, but not wet. If you take care of your garden, you should eventually have a good crop of herbs. You would then also have your very own food seasonings for cooking. ■

ALSO READ: COOKING, FOOD, SEEDS AND FRUIT.

Nutmeg

Clove

Cinnamon

▲ *These useful spices for cooking are nutmeg, clove, and cinnamon. In cinnamon, the bark of the twig is peeled off and rolled up to form the spice.*

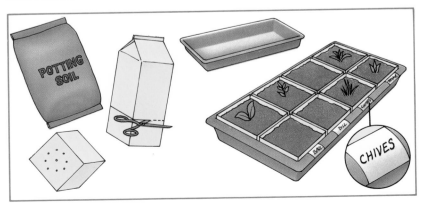

▲ *Baby spiders emerging from their egg cocoon. Each will make a silken thread and drift away on the breeze to find a new home. However, only a few of these baby spiders will survive to grow up and breed.*

▲ *A red-and-black jumping spider. Most spiders have four pairs of eyes, but jumping spiders have one enlarged pair that gives them better vision than other spiders.*

SPIDER A spider is a small animal with four pairs of legs and no wings. Spiders are commonly thought to be insects, but they actually belong to a group of small invertebrates (animals without backbones) called *arachnids*. Like other arachnids, a spider's body is divided into two main parts. (An insect has three pairs of legs and three body parts.) Spiders have two to four pairs of eyes. Sight and touch are their best-developed senses. Spiders range in size from some that can barely be seen to bird-catching spiders as big as your hand. Mites and ticks are also arachnids.

Spiders are hunters, catching insects and other small animals for food. The hunting instinct is so strong that during mating, many male spiders must take care the females do not eat them. Spiders have poison glands and fangs that enable them to kill their prey by biting. When a spider bites, poison passes through the fangs and enters the bite wound. The poison paralyzes, rather than kills immediately. The fangs of most spiders are not strong enough to penetrate human skin. A few spiders can give a person a bite that is painful but not serious. The bites of some spiders, such as the tarantula and the female black widow, can make a person very ill, but they seldom kill anyone if the bites are treated. Spiders are actually useful to people because they help control insect pests.

Most spiders have organs called spinnerets on the undersides of their abdomens. Through the spinnerets, spiders secrete a liquid that hardens to silk when it is exposed to air. They spin webs with their silk. Some spin complicated wheel-like webs. Others spin simple sheet webs. The silk is coated with droplets of a sticky liquid that helps the spider capture food. Insects that fly or walk into the web become stuck in it. The spider paralyzes its captives by biting them. Then the spider pumps its digestive

▲ *A web spider waits in its skillfully constructed trap for insects.*

juices into the victim's body. When the victim's body has softened enough, the spider eats it.

Female spiders also use their silk-making ability to spin protective coverings (cocoons) for their eggs. Eggs may be laid in groups of 1,000 or more, but some species lay only a few eggs. Larvae hatch inside the cocoon and develop into young spiderlings. Spiders have hard shells and molt (lose the old shell and grow another) until they are grown.

Trapdoor spiders dig burrows in the ground and line them with silk. These spiders also make silk doors to cover the burrow. They hide in the burrows and leap out at unsuspecting insects. They are among the rarest of spiders, found only in parts of Southeast Asia. The European water spider spins a dome of silk under water. Then it fills the dome with air by carrying down bubbles from the surface of the water. Bolas spiders make silk lassos with a gluey drop on the end. They swing the lassos to catch insects.

ALSO READ: INSECT, METAMORPHOSIS, SILK.

SPINNING AND WEAVING

Spinning is the process of twisting fibers into thread. Some kinds of thread are used for knitting, and some are used in weaving, the process of intertwining threads to make cloth. Most spinning and weaving is done in factories today, but for thousands of years, people spun their own thread and wove their own cloth. Spinning and weaving were considered domestic skills, just like sewing and cooking.

In 1620, when the Pilgrims came to America from England, most families brought a *distaff* and a *spindle*. The distaff was usually a forked stick. The spindle was a wooden block shaped like a carrot.

Wool, cotton, or flax was wrapped around the distaff. The person making the thread held the distaff under one arm and the spindle in the other hand. Then he or she pulled some of the fibers from the distaff and wound them around the point of the spindle. The spindle was kept turning constantly. This motion twisted the fibers into thread or yarn and wound them around the spindle.

In the 1500's, the *spinning wheel* was invented. It was simply a device for turning a spindle rapidly, so that thread could be made faster than by hand. The spinner pumped a pedal or used a crank to turn the wheel, which turned the spindle.

After the thread was spun, it was woven into cloth on *looms* that were operated by hand. Hand looms are wooden frames on which the lengthwise threads, called the *warp*, are stretched. Attachments on the loom separate the fibers of the warp and weave the crosswise threads, called the *weft* or *filling*, through the warp. Then the woven filling is pressed down to make tightly-woven fabric. The pattern used in intertwining the warp and the filling is called the weave. The plain weave consists of the regular alternation of the filling

over and under the threads of the warp. In the twill weave, the filling may go over two and under three warp threads, depending on the pattern chosen.

Cloth was woven much faster than thread could be spun, and weavers often had to wait for days to get more thread. But about 1764, an English weaver named James Hargreaves invented the *spinning jenny*, which made it possible for an operator to make eight times as much thread by using eight spindles at once, instead of just one. The spinning jenny had one defect—it could not twist thread as tightly as weavers wanted it, to make yarn. But in 1769, Richard Arkwright

▼ *Shown below are the machines that turned spinning and weaving from a handcraft to a mechanized factory operation.*

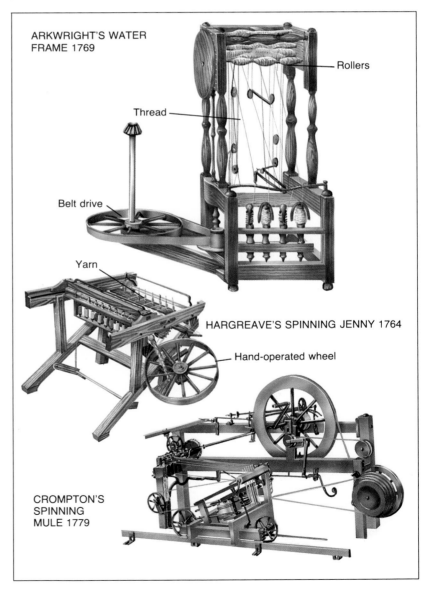

ARKWRIGHT'S WATER FRAME 1769

Rollers

Thread

Belt drive

Yarn

HARGREAVE'S SPINNING JENNY 1764

Hand-operated wheel

CROMPTON'S SPINNING MULE 1779

▲ *A power loom that worked in a New England mill in the 1840's. It wove cloth much faster than was possible on a hand loom.*

designed the water frame, a new machine that made tighter thread. In 1779, Samuel Crompton combined these two spinning machines, to make one that could spin several kinds of yarn.

The inventions of Hargreaves and Arkwright led to the building of a number of *textile mills* in England. These mills were factories for making woven fabrics, called textiles. The textile industry started the tremendous growth of business that is called the Industrial Revolution.

At first, textile machinery was run by waterpower, but in the 1770's the first practical steam engines appeared. Within a few years, steam engines were used to operate all kinds of machines in Britain and America.

Today, many operations are automated in textile manufacturing. Cloth was once made only of cotton, wool, flax (linen), or silk. In this century, many kinds of synthetic fiber, such as rayon, nylon, Orlon, and Dacron, have been invented. These fibers are made from chemicals.

■ LEARN BY DOING

With a small, square loom, you can weave place mats for your family. To make a loom, get four narrow sticks of wood about one inch (2.5 cm) wide and seven inches (18 cm) long. Make a square with the sticks so that the ends of the sticks overlap. Nail the four ends together so that the sticks

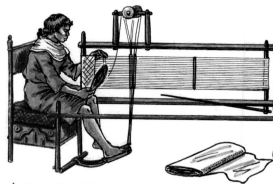

▲ *A medieval frame loom, worked by foot pedals that opened the "shed" to let the shuttle pass through.*

will not slip. (Instead, you may use a cigar box as a rectangular loom.) To make pegs to hold the warp and filling, you will need 80 small nails, one for each corner and 19 for each side. Use nails with a wide head to keep your work from slipping off. Ask a friend or parent to hold the loom while you tack the nails, evenly spaced, along each side.

You will need a darning needle (a long needle with a large eye) and a large quantity of wool or synthetic yarn. You might want to use two colors of yarn and alternate the colors of the squares. You will also need matching thread. Tie the yarn to a nail in one corner and stretch it around pairs of nails as shown, working back and forth. When all the nails on two opposite sides hold yarn, do the same at right angles, going over and under, over and under the yarn already in place. Repeat this process until yarn is wound around all the nails. Knot the end and cut the yarn, leaving about two inches hanging. Weave the two knotted ends into the square. Then remove the square from the loom. Weave five more squares the same way. When all the squares are made, arrange them so they are three squares wide and two long. Sew the squares together carefully, using the darning needle and thread to complete the job. ■

ALSO READ: KNITTING, TEXTILE.

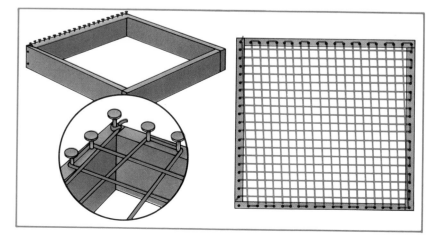

SPINY ANTEATER "Spiny anteater" is the nickname of a strange little animal whose real name is echidna. The spiny anteater and the platypus are both *monotremes*, the only mammals in the world that lay eggs. There are two species of spiny anteaters. One kind lives in New Guinea, and the other kind lives in Australia and Tasmania.

The spiny anteater has a broad body with a short tail. It may reach a length of from 18 to 31 inches (46 to 79 cm). Its head is small, and it has a long, pointed snout. The spiny anteater has no teeth, but it has a long, sticky tongue that it uses to catch ants, termites, and other small insects. Its back is covered with thick spines. If an enemy comes near, the spiny anteater rolls up into a tight little ball with its spines sticking out all over. If the spiny anteater has time, it will dig a hole in which to hide. It can dig very rapidly.

The mother spiny anteater lays one or two eggs. She then pushes the eggs into a pouch on the front of her body. This pouch develops only during the mating season. The eggs hatch inside the warm pouch. The baby spiny anteaters drink milk from milk ducts inside the pouch. They live in the pouch until they are old enough to walk. They may live from 30 to 50 years.

ALSO READ: ANTEATER, AUSTRALIAN MAMMALS, MAMMAL, PLATYPUS.

SPONGE Sponges are water animals that live in seas all over the world. They belong to a *phylum*, or zoological group, in the animal kingdom called the Porifera. There are about 5,000 different kinds of sponges. Most live in the ocean, but a few freshwater kinds exist. Some sponges are only about as big as your fingernail. Others grow up to six feet tall (1.8 m), with many branches.

A sponge is an extremely simple kind of animal. It has no legs, stomach, lungs, head, or brain. It has no fins for swimming. It cannot see or hear. Sponges hatch from eggs. The newly hatched *larva*, or baby sponge, can swim freely for a short time. Soon, it attaches itself to a firm surface under the water, like a rock, and begins to grow. For the rest of its life, it stays in the same place, something like a plant. A new sponge may also grow from an old one or from a piece cut off another sponge.

Sponges grow in many shapes. Some look like fingers. Others look like cups or vases. Certain kinds of sponges coat rocks like mats and are often brightly colored. The outer surface of a sponge is covered with tiny holes, or pores. Special cells inside the sponge have tiny whips, or *flagella*, whose beating causes water to be drawn into the sponge through the pores. Food particles and oxygen in the water are taken up by these cells. A sponge has a complicated skeleton designed to support the many chambers. The skeleton may be hard and brittle. Other sponge skeletons are like stiff fiber. Only a few special kinds of sponges have the kind of soft material that makes them useful to people for bathing and cleaning. These "sponges" are really the soft skeletons of sponges. Synthetic sponges are produced in very large

▲ *The spiny anteater, or echidna, is a primitive egg-laying mammal.*

▼ *Sponges are brought up from the seabed in nets and by divers. Over-exploitation of sponges for the tourist trade has made them rare in some parts of the world.*

▲ *Purple and orange sponges in the Caribbean Sea. The tiny pores, or holes, covering their body, give the sponges their scientific name of* Porifera *("pore-bearers"). Food and oxygen are taken in through the pores.*

▼ *One of the most testing of sporting events is the pentathlon, a five-part competition for athletes. Each contestant must take part in each event. The winner is the one with the highest total point score for the five events.*

numbers and are widely used now.

Sponge divers or fishermen collect sponges in the warm waters of the Mediterranean Sea, the Red Sea, in the Caribbean Sea in the West Indies, and off the coast of Florida and the Bahamas.

ALSO READ: ANIMAL KINGDOM, OCEAN, REGENERATION.

SPORTS Do you have a favorite sport? Is it baseball or football? Do you like acrobatics or gymnastics? What about running in races or swimming or skiing?

A sport is a physical activity that helps you develop strength, quickness, endurance, and skill. Usually a sport is a contest between individuals or teams. There are many kinds of sports. Some have been played for thousands of years by people in many different lands. Since prehistoric times, people have boxed, wrestled, and competed in foot races.

The ancient Greeks organized the Olympic Games about 776 B.C., in which the best athletes won prizes. Today, athletes from all over the world compete in the modern Olympic Games that are held every four years. The North American Indians played lacrosse, as well as a game much like modern-day field hockey. The Maya Indians in Mexico played a

▲ *Swimming is the oldest-known form of water sport. This stroke is the "crawl."*

game similar to both handball and basketball. Baseball, as we know it, began in 1845 when Alexander Cartwright laid out the first baseball diamond. The modern game of basketball was invented in 1891 by Dr. James Naismith, a teacher at Springfield College in Massachusetts.

There are *individual sports*, played by only one person in competition with another. Wrestling, boxing, archery, swimming, and weight lifting are examples of individual sports. *Team sports* are played by a group of people in competition with another group. Football, hockey, soccer, and softball are examples of team sports.

People who play a sport just for enjoyment are called *amateurs*. Athletes who play for money are called *professionals*. To become a professional, a sports player must be very skillful and have adequate experience in the particular sport. Usually, the person has played the sport as an amateur for several years before becoming a professional. As an amateur, he or she played only for fun and the joy of winning. The amateur may have won awards, such as medals or cups, but was not paid for playing.

Professional athletes often compete for prize money in sports such as bowling, golf, and tennis. They enter tournaments against other professionals and try to win. The better they do in a tournament, the more money they make. The winner of the tourna-

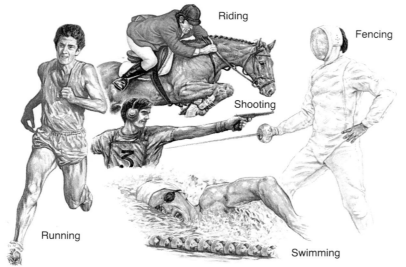

Riding

Fencing

Shooting

Running

Swimming

ment gets the most money. The player who finishes second gets more money than the one who finishes third, and so on. The more tournaments players enter, the more money they have a chance to win.

In sports such as baseball, basketball, football, and ice hockey, the professional athlete plays on a team. The teams that represent cities are almost always professional teams. Baseball has an American League and a National League. The pennant winners in each league meet in the World Series. Football has only one major league, the National Football League (NFL), which is split into two conferences. The winners of each conference meet in the Super Bowl. There is one league in basketball, the National Basketball Association (NBA), which is divided into two conferences.

▼ *A pole-vaulter comes to the moment of truth: Will he clear this height without knocking over the bar? This is one of many exciting track and field sports.*

Hockey also has one major league, the National Hockey League (NHL), which is made up of two conferences, each with two divisions. The division winners play against each other for the Stanley Cup. Professional soccer had one league, the North American Soccer League (NASL), broken into two conferences (but it was suspended in 1985).

Outstanding athletes in college often receive big contracts when they become professionals. Players who have earned much money and won fame include Hank Aaron, Willie Mays, George Brett, and Rod Carew in baseball; Joe Namath, O. J. Simpson, and Walter Payton in football; Wilt Chamberlain and Kareem Abdul-Jabbar in basketball; and Bobby Hull and Mike Bossy in hockey. Other U.S. athletes who have become famous and wealthy include John McEnroe, Jimmy Conners, Tracy Austin, and Chris Evert in tennis; and Jack Nicklaus, Tom Watson, Tom Weiskopf, Arnold Palmer, Nancy Lopez, and Kathy Whitworth in golf.

Perhaps one of the most important lessons an athlete can learn is *sportsmanship*. When you win, don't go around bragging about it, showing off, or making your opponents look bad. Just remember how you would feel if you were the loser. And when

▲ *Figure-skating on ice is one of the most graceful of sports.*

▲ *The world's top-ranking class of auto racing is the World Drivers' Championship, started in 1950. It involves many Grand Prix races held in various countries. Average speeds can be over 140 miles per hour (225 km/h).*

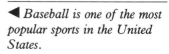

◄ *Baseball is one of the most popular sports in the United States.*

Kendo

Judo

Karate

▲ *Martial arts are methods of self-defense and combat. They began in ancient Asia and have become sports during the 20th century.*

▲ *Skiing is a sport that requires skill to master, so starting young is the best way. It is great fun at any age.*

you do lose a game, give the winner credit for success. Congratulate him or her and don't take your own loss too hard. Next time, you may be the winner.

For further information on:

Ball Games, *see* BASEBALL, BASKET-BALL, BILLIARD GAMES, BOWLING, CRICKET, CROQUET, FIELD HOCKEY, FOOTBALL, GOLF, HANDBALL, JAI ALAI, LACROSSE, POLO, RACQUETBALL, SOC-CER, SQUASH, TABLE TENNIS, TENNIS, VOLLEYBALL.

Ice and Snow Sports, *see* CURLING, ICE HOCKEY, ICE SKATING, SKIING, SLED, SNOWMOBILE.

Other Sports, *see* ARCHERY, BADMIN-TON, BOXING, EQUESTRIAN SPORTS, FENCING, GYMNASTICS, HANG GLID-ING, HORSEBACK RIDING, HUNTING, JUDO, KARATE, MARTIAL ARTS, MOUN-TAIN CLIMBING, ROLLER SKATING, ROWING, SHOOTING, TRACK AND FIELD, WEIGHT LIFTING, WRESTLING.

People in Sports, *see* GEHRIG, LOU; GIBSON, ALTHEA; OWENS, JESSE; ROBINSON, JACKIE; ROCKNE, KNUTE; RUTH, BABE; THORPE, JIM.

Sports Events, *see* AUTO RACING, HORSE RACING, MARATHON RACE, OLYMPIC GAMES.

Water Sports, *see* BOATS AND BOAT-ING, DIVING, FISHING, SAILING, SCUBA DIVING, SURFING, SWIMMING, WIND SURFING, WATER SKIING.

SPRING "The world's favorite sea-son is the spring. All things seem possible in May." Most people would agree with these words of the writer, Edwin Way Teale. Spring is the sea-son that follows the long, cold, sleepy months of winter. It is a time when the first warm days of the year give new life and energy to all living things.

Spring in the Northern Hemi-sphere begins around March 21. At this time, the sun is shining directly over the equator. The days have be-gun to grow longer and hotter as the northern half of the world tips closer to the sun. The Northern Hemi-sphere begins to tip away from the sun again around June 21. This date marks the end of spring and the be-ginning of summer. The Earth con-tinues its orbit, and the sun is again directly over the equator around Sep-tember 23. This is the beginning of fall (or autumn) in the Northern Hemisphere, and the beginning of spring in the Southern Hemisphere.

People in North America often consider the appearance of the robin as the first sign of spring. Robins, like many other North American birds, spend the winter in milder regions to the south. As the warm days return to the northern regions, robins fly north-ward to build their nests and hatch their eggs.

Some animals, such as ground squirrels, hedgehogs, and bears, hi-bernate during the winter. At the beginning of spring, they crawl out of their warm burrows and caves. Other animals shed their thick winter coats. The hare of North America grows a white coat in winter so that it cannot be seen against the snow. As the snows melt, its coat begins to darken. By the end of spring, the hare is a beautiful rust color. Insect eggs hatch out in the spring. Queen bumblebees wake up from their winter hibernation and build tiny nests. The queens then lay their thousands of eggs and a new bee colony is started.

Spring is the time when most baby animals are born or hatched. Birds and other animals are busy night and day building nests and shelters, finding food for their young, and protecting them from enemies. Even people feel a touch of excitement that they call "spring fever." When someone is really excited, people often say he or she is as "mad as a March hare." In spring, hares often rush about in a frenzy, leaping into the air and thumping their feet on the ground.

Spring is a very busy time for farmers. Seeds and seedlings must be planted. Baby animals must be cared for. Some farmers grow spring flowers such as daffodils and tulips, for the market. For many people, this season is the time for "spring cleaning"—cleaning the house from top to bottom.

Spring has long been a season for special festivals. In ancient times, the gods were often given gifts and sacrifices so that they would bless the farmers' crops and make them grow. Early calendars marked spring as the beginning of the year. In ancient Mesopotamia a great New Year festival was celebrated in March and April. The Romans worshiped two goddesses of spring—Flora and Proserpina. Their festival days were celebrated with huge garlands of flowers. Flowers are an important part of most spring festivals. For the ancient May Day festival in Europe, young girls gathered mayflowers, or hawthorn. Spring festivals held in the United States include the Daffodil Festival in Sumner, Washington; the Apple Blossom Festival in the Shenandoah Valley, Virginia; and the Cherry Blossom Festival in Washington, D.C. A special Bird Day is also celebrated in the United States every spring. On this day, youngsters are taught about the importance of protecting birds.

ALSO READ: APRIL, MARCH, MAY, JUNE, SEASON.

SPRUCE see CONIFER.

SPUTNIK see SATELLITE.

SPY A spy is a person who goes into enemy territory to collect secret information for his or her country or employer. Spies work for national governments both in peacetime and in wartime. Their job is usually to find out the military secrets of other countries, such as scientific research into new weapons or methods of defense. Governments frequently spy on their own citizens, too, whom they suspect of crime or disloyalty. Businesses occasionally hire people called industrial spies to find out the secrets of other companies in the same industry.

The work that a spy, or agent, carries out is called *espionage*. Most governments run espionage, or intelligence, agencies that send out spies and process the information they gather. Intelligence in spy work means information. This work is carried out in the United States mainly by the Central Intelligence Agency (CIA) and the Defense Intelligence Agency (DIA) of the armed forces. Each of the military services also has an intelligence section. Intelligence agencies also work to prevent enemy spies from gathering information. This is called *counterespionage*. Sometimes, a double agent will pretend to work as a spy for one country to make it easier for him or her to gain information for another country. One of the best-known double agents was the British intelligence officer, Kim Philby. He worked for the British intelligence service for many years before he was discovered to be a spy for the Soviet Union.

A spy must be completely familiar with the language and customs of the country in which he or she is working. In many cases, the spy is actually a citizen of the country. During

▲ *Spring flowers add welcome color after the long winter of northern climates. Here are wild daffodils growing in England.*

Spying played an important part in the American Civil War. The Confederate victory at the battle of Bull Run was largely the result of reports sent from Washington, D.C., by Mrs. Rose Greenhow to the Confederate general. Another woman spy, Miss Elizabeth Van Lew, spied for the Federal forces in the South. General Grant told her that her information was the most valuable received from Richmond during the war.

▲ *Mata Hari was one of the most notorious women spies, although some experts doubt that she really was a spy at all.*

▲ *Kim Philby worked for British intelligence but was secretly acting for the Soviet Union. His treachery remained undiscovered for many years, until he defected to Moscow in 1963.*

World War II, many spies parachuted into enemy territory.

Nowadays, spies have the most advanced scientific equipment to help them. Devices can be used for listening into conversations on the telephone ("wiretapping") or in another room ("bugging"). Spies can send information to their employers over tiny radio transmitters or in the form of *microfilm* (greatly reduced photographs). Enemy military bases can be photographed from planes or from "spy-in-the-sky" satellites operating at very great height. In 1960, an American U-2 or "high-altitude" spy plane was shot down over the Soviet Union. The pilot, Francis Gary Powers, was convicted of espionage and imprisoned. He was later released in exchange for Colonel Rudolf Abel. Colonel Abel was a Russian who had spied in the United States for the Soviet Union.

Several great military generals in the past have used spies to find out information about enemy armies. During the American Revolution, a young American schoolmaster called Nathan Hale was sent to spy on the British army. Hale was captured and hanged. One of the best-known spies of all time was a Dutch woman who called herself Mata Hari. During World War I, she posed as an Eastern dancer in Paris. She entertained many high-ranking Allied officers. Gossip that she learned she passed along to the Germans. Mata Hari was finally caught, put to trial, and executed by a firing squad.

ALSO READ: CRIME; HALE, NATHAN; TREASON.

SPYRI, JOHANNA (1827–1901)
The Swiss author, Johanna Spyri, wrote the delightful story of *Heidi*. Johanna was born in Hirzel, a small town in Switzerland, near the city of Zurich. Her father, Johann Jacob Heusser, was a doctor. Johanna grew up on the slopes of the Alps. She married Bernhard Spyri, a lawyer from Zurich. They had only one child, a son who died. Johanna Spyri wrote several books for children. She wrote of her own childhood memories—the murmur of wind in dark fir trees, the sound of cowbells merrily ringing, and sun shining on mountain meadows.

Heidi, translated into many languages, is loved by young people throughout the world. It is about a little girl who is sent to live with her crusty old grandfather. He lives in a tiny cottage high on the side of a mountain. Heidi grows to love her grandfather. She also finds a friend in Peter, the goatherd. But Heidi is soon taken away to be a companion to a young crippled girl. After many adventures, Heidi is reunited with her grandfather.

ALSO READ: CHILDREN'S LITERATURE, SWITZERLAND.

SQUARE DANCING
Square dancing is an American kind of folk dancing that developed in the middle and western parts of the United States in the early 1800's. After the country was settled, square dancing was performed in a few isolated areas until it was revived in the 1930's. Today, square dancing is popular in schools and clubs throughout the country.

Square dances developed out of the quadrilles or formal dances brought from France and England to New England, and the folk dances, such as the Kentucky Running Set, brought from England to the Appalachian Mountain areas.

The name "square dancing" comes from the dance pattern. Each of four couples in a set or group stands on one side of an imaginary square, moves from that spot to do various dance steps, and then returns. As many sets can dance at one time as will fit onto a dance floor.

▲ *Square dancing is a lively activity that is fun both for those who take part and for those who prefer to watch.*

Many different patterns of dance steps are used in square dancing. A *caller* either sings or speaks the instructions to the dancers as the music is playing. The caller does not dance but acts as a kind of director. He or she often chatters in a lively, joking way between actual dance instruction calls.

The best music for square dancing is played by an old-time fiddler with piano or accordion accompaniment, and a "strummer" playing a banjo or guitar. "Turkey in the Straw" and "Arkansas Traveler" are good square dance tunes. Round dances like the schottische, polka, and waltz are usually included in an evening of square dancing.

ALSO READ: FOLK DANCING.

SQUASH The British game of squash, or squash racquets, originated at the Harrow School near London, England, about 1850. It spread to the United States and Canada in the late 1800's. Later, the Americans created a slight variation of the game, called squash tennis.

It was not until 1907 that the first recognized champion from any country was established. In that year John Miskey of Philadelphia won the American Amateur Singles Championship.

World championships were started in 1926. The Pakistan player Jahangir Khan dominated the sport. He was undefeated from 1981 to 1987. In team events, Pakistan and Australia were the leading squash countries.

Squash racquets and squash tennis are played on a four-walled, indoor court. The court is usually 18½ feet (5.6 m) wide, 32 feet (9.7 m) long, and 16 feet (4.9 m) high on the frontwall. The players use strung rackets to hit a small hard rubber ball against the four walls (the squash tennis ball is larger, softer, and more bouncy than the squash racquets ball). The faster the ball travels the better the game is. The ball must hit the frontwall above the *telltale*, which is a strip of metal 17 inches (43 cm) above the floor.

To start a game, a player serves from a set area 22 feet (6.7 m) away from and parallel to the frontwall (a line divides the court into two equal service courts). The served ball must hit above the frontwall service line and drop into the opposite service court. The opponent must return the ball before it hits the floor or after one bounce, or he or she loses the point. The player who wins the point (two serves are allowed) earns the right to serve next. Usually 15 points wins a game of squash racquets.

▲ *Squash is a high-speed game that is enjoyed by enthusiasts in many countries. Spectators and TV cameras can now view the game through transparent court walls.*

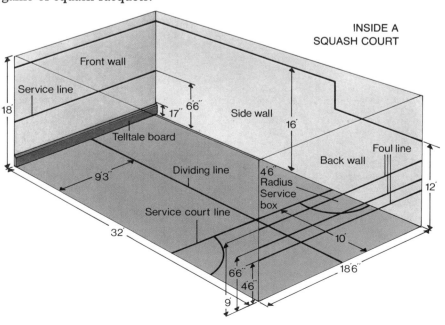

INSIDE A SQUASH COURT

Front wall
Service line
18'
17" 66"
Telltale board
93"
Dividing line
Side wall
16'
46"
Radius
Service box
Back wall
Foul line
12'
Service court line
10'
32'
66"
46"
9'
18'6"

Gray squirrel

Red squirrel

▲ *Squirrels are found all over the world in forest zones. The North American gray squirrel is also found in Europe and likes mixed woodland. The smaller red squirrel prefers coniferous woods.*

SQUIRREL More than 300 different kinds of squirrels live in forests, jungles, and city parks all over the world. Pygmy squirrels, no larger than mice, live in Africa and Borneo. The giant squirrels of India are as large as house cats. The most common squirrels in the United States are the red squirrel, the gray squirrel, and the fox squirrel. Chipmunks and prairie dogs are kinds of squirrels.

Squirrels are *rodents*. Rodents are small mammals with large front teeth or incisors. These incisors, two upper and two lower, never stop growing. A rodent must grind and chew food with its incisors to keep them worn down to usable size.

Most squirrels live in trees. Squirrels have long, sharp claws and strong hind legs that help them to climb trees and jump from branch to branch. Squirrels eat acorns, nuts, seeds, and the buds of leaves. They often collect more food than they need and store it away for the wintertime. Sometimes a squirrel is unlucky enough to forget where it has stored its food. Then the seeds may take root and grow into plants.

Most squirrels have thick, bushy tails. Such a tail is very useful, because it helps the squirrel keep its balance while climbing. If a squirrel should jump or fall out of a tree, the tail can be spread out like a small parachute to slow the squirrel down. In rainy weather, the squirrel can use its tail like an umbrella to keep itself

dry. When it sleeps, the squirrel can cover itself with its tail, like a blanket.

A squirrel will often have several nests. For warm weather, it will have an open nest like a bird's, built of sticks in the branches of a tree. In colder weather, it will live in a hollow in the tree or in a weatherproof nest built in the most protected part of the tree. Ground squirrels usually live in burrows all year-round.

Mother squirrels usually have babies twice a year. From three to six baby squirrels are born at the same time. The babies are helpless and blind. Sometimes a baby squirrel falls out of its nest. If you should ever find a baby squirrel on the ground, you can feed it milk through an eyedropper. When the squirrel is able to eat food on its own, you should release it.

ALSO READ: ANIMAL, FLYING MAMMALS, MAMMAL, PRAIRIE DOG, RODENT.

SRI LANKA Sri Lanka, formerly called Ceylon, is a pear-shaped island in the Indian Ocean about 30 miles (48 km) off the southeast coast of India. The island's coast is flat, and the central part is mountainous. The climate is hot but with cool ocean breezes.

Sri Lanka is famous for its fine tea and its many precious stones, such as sapphires, rubies, topazes, and cat's-eyes. Many gems come from the mines at Ratnapura. It is the world's

SRI LANKA

Capital City: Colombo (660,000 people).
Area: 25,334 square miles (65,610 sq. km).
Population: 17,500,000.
Government: Republic.
Natural Resources: Sapphires, rubies, garnets, graphite.
Export Products: Tea, rubber, coconut products, industrial goods.
Unit of Money: Sri Lanka rupee.
Official Languages: Sinhalese, Tamil, English.

leading producer of high-quality graphite. Exotic hardwoods, including teak, ebony, and mahogany, grow in Sri Lanka. Beautiful orchids and other flowers grow abundantly everywhere. Many tropical plants are displayed at the botanical garden at Peradeniya.

More than two-thirds of the people are Singhalese, whose ancestors came by sea from the northwest coast of India over 2,000 years ago. Others are Tamils, descendants of a later group of Indian invaders. The languages of these groups are different from one another. The Singhalese are Buddhists, while the Tamils are Hindus. Most Sri Lankans are farmers, growing tea, rice, and coconuts or working on rubber plantations. Fishing is also important.

The Portuguese took control of the island in the 1500's but were driven out by the Dutch about 1648. The British captured the island in 1796 and made it a crown colony two years later. The country became independent in 1948. A new constitution in 1972 changed the country's name from Ceylon to Sri Lanka. A new, strong presidential form of government was set up in 1978. Sri Lanka has a 168-member unicameral (one house) National State Assembly.

In recent years, Sri Lanka has been troubled by terrorism. Tamils in the northern part of the island have opposed the mostly Singhalese government and sought a separate Tamil state.

ALSO READ: ASIA, INDIA.

STAGE see THEATER.

STAINED GLASS The brightly colored glass used in the windows of many public and religious buildings is known as stained glass. This glass is also used to make decorative objects, such as screens and lampshades. Most stained glass is made by adding colored metal oxides to glass while it is still *molten* (hot and liquid). Another method is to paint over the surface of clear glass.

Stained glass is most often used for windows. Sunlight shining through the glass makes the jewel-like colors show up in brilliant hues. Stained-glass windows are usually decorated with colorful pictures and designs. Every patch of color in the original design is numbered. Pieces of colored glass are then cut to match each section. Fine details, such as facial features, are painted onto the glass with enamel paints. Enamel paint is made of molten glass and adheres to another glass surface without running or fading.

The pieces are then fired (baked at extremely high temperatures) so that the enamel fuses (joins) with the glass. The glass pieces are finally joined together with strips of lead. When the glass is completely leaded, the strips are soldered and spaces between the glass and the lead are filled in with putty. Most artists are careful to arrange the pieces so that the black lines of the leading follow the outlines of the main figures in the design.

Stained glass became popular in the United States during the 1800's. The artists, John La Farge and Louis Comfort Tiffany, made magnificent windows for public buildings. Tiffany also made lampshades of stained glass that have become popular again. More recently, the Russian-born artist Marc Chagall designed a large memorial window in tones of blue for the headquarters of the United Nations in New York City. He also did 12 windows depicting the 12 Tribes of Israel for the Hadassah-Hebrew University near Jerusalem.

ALSO READ: CATHEDRAL, GLASS.

STALACTITE see CAVE.

▲ *Elephants are used in the forests of Sri Lanka, as well as in other tropical countries, to move heavy lumber.*

▲ *The beautiful rose window in the cathedral at Amiens, France. Many Gothic cathedrals have windows set with stained glass.*

▲ *Joseph Stalin, dictator of the Soviet Union.*

STALIN, JOSEPH (1879–1953)

Joseph Stalin was a Communist leader who ruled the Soviet Union for almost 30 years. He played an important part in the Russian Revolution of 1917 and helped build the Soviet Union into one of the most powerful countries in the world.

Stalin was born Iosif Dzhugashvili in Georgia in southwestern Russia. As a young man, he studied for the priesthood in the Orthodox Church but later left the seminary and began to take part in revolutionary activities. During this time, he changed his name to Stalin to hide his identity from the police. After the revolution, Stalin was made a member of the Politburo, the decision-making body in the Communist Party's Central Committee. When Nikolai Lenin died in 1924, Stalin became the dominant leader of the Soviet Union. By 1929, he was the absolute dictator of the country.

Stalin wanted to build up the Soviet Union's economy. He stepped up the production of machinery and arms and began to *collectivize* farms. He took the land away from the peasants and put farms under government control. Many people opposed Stalin, but he used the secret police to find these people and eliminate them. At the outbreak of World War II, Stalin made a treaty with Hitler in which Germany and the Soviet Union agreed not to attack each other. When Hitler broke this treaty and invaded the Soviet Union, Stalin joined forces with the United States and Great Britain to fight against Germany. Stalin kept his position as dictator until his death. Stalin's daughter, Svetlana, emigrated to the United States. She married an American but later returned to the Soviet Union.

ALSO READ: COMMUNISM; LENIN, NIKOLAI; REVOLUTION; SOVIET UNION.

STAMP COLLECTING

Stamp collecting, or *philately*, is a popular hobby among people of all ages in many parts of the world. Some stamps are beautiful. Others show interesting facts about different nations. Many stamps are valuable, and so stamp collecting can be a profitable occupation.

People have been collecting stamps ever since they were first used. For many years, people paid for mail when they received it. In 1840, the British began to issue stamps, introducing the prepaid (paid by the sender) postal system. One of the first stamps was the "Penny Black." The United States issued its first stamps in 1847. Most nations of the world were printing stamps by 1860. The first stamp catalog for collectors was published in 1864. Rare stamps, which had been printed singly or in small quantities, became very valuable.

■ LEARN BY DOING

To start a stamp collection, you will need a large packet of about 500 different stamps, an album, paper mounting hinges, and a magnifying glass. Some albums have blank spaces for particular stamps that can be pasted in as they are collected. Stamp dealers and hobby shops sell all these supplies.

▼ *People all over the world collect stamps. Countries issue colorful and interesting sets of stamps. These issues from Zaire in West Africa illustrate famous old steam locomotives from Europe.*

You can collect more stamps by watching the mail coming into your home. You can ask your family and friends to save unusual stamps, especially foreign ones. You can save money for packets of stamps from particular countries. You can trade stamps with other collectors. A stamp guidebook or a subscription to a stamp magazine would make a fine Christmas or birthday present.

As your collection grows, you can enter exhibits, where stamp collections are judged on the basis of order, condition, rarity, and completeness. You might also join a stamp club. Most stamp magazines will give you the name of a local club. ■

ALSO READ: POSTAL SERVICE.

STANDISH, MILES   see PILGRIM SETTLERS.

STANLEY, SIR HENRY MORTON (1841–1904)

Adventurer, African explorer, and newspaper correspondent, Stanley was born in Denbigh, Wales. At age 18, he shipped as a cabin boy on a vessel to the United States. When the U.S. Civil War broke out, he joined the Confederate forces. He later joined and fought with the Union navy.

When the war ended, Stanley was hired as a newspaper correspondent for the *New York Herald*. The editors sent him overseas, first to Turkey and then to Spain, to send back news stories about the wars and political troubles in those countries. Stanley was a daredevil and a good reporter. In 1869, the editor of the *Herald* learned that a Scottish missionary and explorer, David Livingstone, had been missing in the wilds of the African jungles for two years. He sent Stanley to Africa to find Livingstone and bring back a good news story.

Stanley reached Zanzibar (part of Tanzania) in early 1871 and soon set out for the African interior. He and his bearers hacked their way through dense jungles. Eight months later, on November 10, Stanley found Livingstone, greeting him with the famous words, "Dr. Livingstone, I presume?" Stanley remained with Livingstone to explore the area around the north end of Lake Tanganyika.

In 1872, Stanley returned to Europe but set out the next year to explore more of Africa. He sailed around Lake Victoria and other lakes. After a journey of over 1,500 miles (2,400 km) on foot, he came out on Africa's Atlantic coast. He discovered that the Congo River was the same as the Lualaba River. Traveling more than 7,000 miles (11,000 km) in all, Stanley set up stations along the rivers from the Lower Congo to Stanley Falls.

For his bravery, his discoveries, and his opening of central Africa to European trade and exploration, Stanley was knighted by King Edward VII. Although he had become a U.S. citizen in 1862, he decided to be a British subject again in 1895.

ALSO READ: AFRICA; EXPLORATION; LIVINGSTONE, DAVID.

STANTON, ELIZABETH (1815–1902)

Today we take it for granted that women can vote in elections, just as men do. But this was not always so. The fact that women have won the democratic rights they have, and continue to demand fair treatment and equality with men, is due to the pioneering struggles of women like Elizabeth Stanton.

Elizabeth Cady (Stanton was her married name) was born in Johnstown, New York, in 1815. Her father, Daniel Cady, was a Congressman and later became a New York Supreme Court judge. Elizabeth studied law in his office, and in 1840

▲ *Henry Morton Stanley on his march across Africa, accompanied by African porters and servants.*

▲ *Elizabeth Stanton, U.S. educator and feminist.*

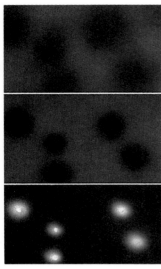

▲ *Stars begin their lives as thin clouds of hydrogen gas (top). As each cloud shrinks, its center heats up as its atoms are squeezed tighter (center). Eventually, this heat makes them begin to shine as stars.*

Because light takes so long to reach us from stars, some of the stars we see actually no longer exist!

▼ *The Crab Nebula is the wreckage of a star that exploded as a supernova. Very hot and brilliant stars die in this spectacular way.*

she married a lawyer named Henry Stanton. Her knowledge of law taught her how women were discriminated against, particularly in reference to owning property. She campaigned for changes in the state property laws. In 1848, she helped lead the first women's rights convention in the United States, which demanded woman *suffrage* (the right to vote).

Elizabeth Stanton worked closely with another leading women's rights pioneer, Susan B. Anthony. She wrote articles for the newspaper they ran together, the *Revolution*. With Matilda Joslyn Gage, she wrote three volumes of a six-volume *History of Woman Suffrage*.

ALSO READ: WOMEN'S RIGHTS.

STAR In the clearest night sky, you might see a few thousand stars with your unaided eye. These are only a handful of the hundred billion or more stars in our galaxy, the Milky Way. And the Milky Way is only one of even more billions of galaxies in the universe.

Most of these stars are so far away that the light they give off takes many years to reach the Earth. Their distances are measured in *light-years*— the distance that light, moving at 186,000 miles (300,000 km) a second, travels in a year. One light-year is about six trillion miles (9.7 trillion km). The farthest stars may be billions of light-years away. The nearest star is our sun, eight *light-minutes*

away (the distance light can travel in eight minutes). The next nearest star is slightly over four light-years away.

The sun is a fairly ordinary star. It is about 865,000 miles (1.4 million km) across and has 333,000 times as much mass (matter) as the Earth. Some stars are 50 times as wide, 500,000 times as bright, and have 100 times as much mass as the sun. Other stars have one-hundredth the width and one-tenth the mass and are only one-millionth as bright.

Make-up of Stars Most stars are about nine-tenths hydrogen gas. The remaining tenth is usually helium. They also contain small amounts of other elements.

Although stars are made up of gases, their centers are often extremely dense. The atoms of gas are pressed very tightly together. When atoms of gas are pressed tightly together, the gas usually changes to a liquid, and with even more pressure, it changes to a solid. Only under extremely high temperature will the gas remain a gas. Even a fairly cold star has a surface temperature of around 5,000° F (2,760° C). The temperature at the center of a star may be much higher, as high as several million degrees. At these temperatures, a gas can be very dense and still remain a gas. Some stars are so dense that a cubic inch from the center of the star, if weighed on Earth, would weigh 5,000 pounds (2,270 kg).

The tremendous heat and density of a star causes hydrogen to change to helium in a *thermonuclear reaction*. These reactions give off enormous amounts of energy in the form of heat and light. This is why stars shine.

Starlight *Magnitude* is the brightness of a star as seen from Earth. A star may appear to be bright either because it *is* bright or because it happens to be close to the Earth. The brightest stars are of zero or of nega-

▲ *Why do stars twinkle? Because their light travels through the Earth's atmosphere, which distorts, or bends, the light making the light appear to flicker.*

tive magnitude. Stars that are just visible to the naked eye are of sixth magnitude. The faintest stars that can be seen by using powerful telescopes are of twenty-second or higher magnitude.

Luminosity is a measure of the total energy given off by a star. This includes light, heat, radio waves, and other forms of energy. Almost all of this energy comes from the thermonuclear reactions in the center of the star. The luminosity of a star usually depends on its mass.

Astronomers—scientists who study bodies in space—not only measure the amount of light, but they also break down the light and other energy given off by stars. This breakdown can tell them what the star is made of, how hot it is, how fast it is moving, and where it is going. For instance, stars give off light of different colors, and these colors indicate the temperature of a star. Astronomers now know that the hottest stars are blue, and the coolest give off a red color.

The Life of a Star A star may last for a few million to ten billion years. A star is probably formed from a whirling mass of gas and dust. The mass contracts (shrinks), and as it contracts, it gets warmer and begins to glow. Eventually the temperature and pressure at the center of the star become high enough for thermonuclear reactions to take place. Over the next few million or billion years, the hydrogen in the star burns up, changing to helium. The star remains at about the same size and temperature.

When most of the hydrogen in the center of the star has been changed to helium, the star contracts again and becomes even hotter. This causes the thermonuclear reactions to spread to the outer layers of hydrogen. The outer layers swell up, and the star becomes a *giant*. The temperature in the center becomes still hotter, hot enough for the helium to take part in further thermonuclear reactions. Eventually all of the gases are used up, and the star shrinks up into a small, dense, dying star called a *white dwarf*.

The history of a star with a slightly larger mass is even more spectacular. The center may become so hot that an explosion takes place, spraying burning gases in all directions with tremendous energy and brightness. A star that undergoes an outburst like this is called a *supernova*, and it may be millions of times brighter than the sun. Only four supernovas have been seen in the Milky Way in the last thousand years. One of these is in the Crab Nebula, at whose center is a very small, dense, rapidly rotating body called a *pulsar*. A supernova was observed in the large Magellanic Cloud, the nearest galaxy to our own, in 1987.

ALSO READ: ASTRONOMY, CONSTELLATION, GAS, HYDROGEN, MILKY WAY, NUCLEAR ENERGY, OBSERVATORY, RADIO ASTRONOMY, SOLAR SYSTEM, SPACE, SPACE RESEARCH, UNIVERSE.

▲ *The great star cluster in the constellation Hercules may contain half a million stars.*

The brightest stars shine a million times more brightly than our sun. But these heavenly lighthouses are very rare; there are only about half a dozen in the whole Milky Way galaxy. Faint stars are by far the most common. The nearest star to our sun, Proxima Centauri, is just a small faint star, ten thousand times dimmer than the sun. We would never have seen it at all had it not been so close.

The brightest star in the sky is Sirius, the Dog Star. It is called this because it is the head of the constellation Canis Major, the Great Dog. You can find Sirius by following a line downward through Orion's Belt. Sirius gives out about 30 times as much light as the sun, but it is, of course, much farther away. It is so far away that light from the star takes more than eight years to reach us.

▲ *This monument to Francis Scott Key, composer of the words to "The Star-Spangled Banner," was erected in 1911 in Baltimore, Maryland.*

▼ *The legislative seat of each state government in the United States is located in the state capitol building. The Massachusetts State House in Boston, built in 1798, is one of the oldest and most impressive in the nation.*

STARCH see CARBOHYDRATE.

STARFISH see ECHINODERM.

STAR-SPANGLED BANNER

"The Star-Spangled Banner" is the national anthem of the United States. The words were written as a poem in 1814 by a young Baltimore lawyer, Francis Scott Key. The poem was made into a song using the music of "To Anacreon in Heaven," a popular English ballad of that time. In 1931, President Herbert Hoover declared "The Star-Spangled Banner" our national anthem.

"The Star-Spangled Banner" was written during the War of 1812. William Beanes, a well-known physician and a friend of Francis Scott Key, had been captured by the British. On September 13, 1814, Key went out to the British fleet anchored off the coast near Baltimore to persuade the admiral to release his friend. Although Key traveled under a flag of truce, the British held him on board ship for the night. They did not want him to report back on the position and strength of the fleet. That night, the British attacked Fort McHenry at Baltimore harbor. Key spent the night watching the attack from the deck of a British battleship. When dawn came, he was able to see the outline of Fort McHenry. The stars and stripes of the American flag were still flying over it. This deeply thrilling sight inspired Key to write "The Star-Spangled Banner." He wrote the first few lines on the back of an envelope. In the boat going back to Baltimore, he added more verses.

Within a week, many newspapers had printed the poem. The words were put to music and sung all over the United States. The original poem is now part of the Maryland Historical Society's collection.

ALSO READ: MARYLAND, NATIONAL ANTHEM, WAR OF 1812.

STATE GOVERNMENT

State government in the United States is the system of rule as established by the constitution of each of the 50 states. The government is made up of the governor and other officials, a system of law, and state government agencies. The voters of each state elect their governor and lawmakers.

State constitutions differ, but in one way all are alike. Each one provides the state with a government much like that of the Federal Government of the United States. Part of the state constitution is a bill (declaration) of rights. It lists certain important rights of the people. The state, county, and city governments must not interfere with these rights.

The state government has three separate branches. The executive branch, headed by the governor, enforces state laws. The legislative branch makes the laws. State lawmakers (senators and representatives) form a body called the legislature. In all the states except Nebraska, the legislature is *bicameral*, having two parts (houses) as Congress does. Nebraska's legislature consists of a single house and is called *unicameral*.

ORDER OF ADMISSION TO STATEHOOD

1.	Delaware	Dec. 7, 1787	26.	Michigan	Jan. 26, 1837
2.	Pennsylvania	Dec. 12, 1787	27.	Florida	Mar. 3, 1845
3.	New Jersey	Dec. 18, 1787	28.	Texas	Dec. 29, 1845
4.	Georgia	Jan. 2, 1788	29.	Iowa	Dec. 28, 1846
5.	Connecticut	Jan. 9, 1788	30.	Wisconsin	May 29, 1848
6.	Massachusetts	Feb. 6, 1788	31.	California	Sept. 9, 1850
7.	Maryland	Apr. 28, 1788	32.	Minnesota	May 11, 1858
8.	South Carolina	May 23, 1788	33.	Oregon	Feb. 14, 1859
9.	New Hampshire	June 21, 1788	34.	Kansas	Jan. 29, 1861
10.	Virginia	June 25, 1788	35.	West Virginia	June 20, 1863
11.	New York	July 26, 1788	36.	Nevada	Oct. 31, 1864
12.	North Carolina	Nov. 21, 1789	37.	Nebraska	Mar. 1, 1867
13.	Rhode Island	May 29, 1790	38.	Colorado	Aug. 1, 1876
14.	Vermont	Mar. 4, 1791	39.	North Dakota	Nov. 2, 1889
15.	Kentucky	June 1, 1792	40.	South Dakota	Nov. 2, 1889
16.	Tennessee	June 1, 1796	41.	Montana	Nov. 8, 1889
17.	Ohio	Mar. 1, 1803	42.	Washington	Nov. 11, 1889
18.	Louisiana	Apr. 30, 1812	43.	Idaho	July 3, 1890
19.	Indiana	Dec. 11, 1816	44.	Wyoming	July 10, 1890
20.	Mississippi	Dec. 10, 1817	45.	Utah	Jan. 4, 1896
21.	Illinois	Dec. 3, 1818	46.	Oklahoma	Nov. 16, 1907
22.	Alabama	Dec. 14, 1819	47.	New Mexico	Jan. 6, 1912
23.	Maine	Mar. 15, 1820	48.	Arizona	Feb. 14, 1912
24.	Missouri	Aug. 10, 1821	49.	Alaska	Jan. 3, 1959
25.	Arkansas	June 15, 1836	50.	Hawaii	Aug. 21, 1959

The judiciary, the third branch, consists of the state courts. When a person is accused of breaking a state law, one of these courts decides whether or not he or she is guilty.

The state constitution may be amended (changed) or may even be completely rewritten. But no changes in the constitution may be made without the consent of the people of the state.

ALSO READ: LOCAL GOVERNMENT, STATEHOOD, STATES' RIGHTS.

STATEHOOD When a land or territory becomes a state, it has reached statehood. It then has a government of its own. The United States is made up of 50 areas called states. Each state has its own government, partly independent and partly under the control of the government of the United States.

The United States of America was formed by the 13 original colonies that became states from 1787 to 1790. These states were Delaware, New Jersey, Georgia, Connecticut, Pennsylvania, Massachusetts, Maryland, South Carolina, New Hampshire, Virginia, New York, North Carolina, and Rhode Island. All the other states joined the Union formed by these original 13 states. They gained statehood when they were admitted to the Union.

After the Union was formed, parts of some states broke away to become independent states. Parts of Vermont had been claimed by New York and New Hampshire. In 1791, Congress voted to bring Vermont into the Union. Kentucky, which had been part of Virginia, was admitted as a state in 1792. Tennessee, once part of North Carolina, became a state in 1796. Maine separated from Massachusetts in 1820 and became a state. During the Civil War, West Virginia broke off from Virginia, which had seceded to join the Confederacy. West Virginia became a state of the Union in 1863. Texas and California once belonged to Mexico. Texas was admitted to statehood in 1845 and California in 1850.

Except for these states, and for the original 13 states, the remaining states

The actual flag that Francis Scott Key saw during the bombardment of Fort McHenry is preserved in the Smithsonian Institution, Washington, D.C. It is 30 by 42 feet (9 by 13 m) and has 15 alternate red and white stripes and 15 stars.

▲ *President Dwight D. Eisenhower congratulates Governor Michael A. Stepovich of Alaska in 1958 after the U.S. Senate decided to admit Alaska to the Union as the 49th state. Secretary of the Interior Fred E. Seaton holds a copy of an Alaskan newspaper headlined, "We're in."*

In the 1948 Presidential election, Strom Thurmond entered the contest as a States' Rights candidate, the only time the party has been represented.

were once territories. Congress divided large areas of land into territories. The early territories included parts of several states. When a territory had a sizable population, Congress voted to let it prepare for statehood. Delegates to a territorial convention drew up a constitution for the new state. The people of the territory then voted on the constitution. If approved by the voters, the constitution was sent to the U.S. Congress.

If Congress approved of the constitution, a bill to admit the territory as a state was passed. Congress might, however, have asked for changes in the constitution before granting statehood. The President then signed a bill granting statehood to the territory. This bill became a law that, unlike other laws, could not be repealed. Every territory that wanted statehood was granted it eventually.

ALSO READ: STATE GOVERNMENT, STATES' RIGHTS.

STATES' RIGHTS In the United States, the highest law is the U.S. Constitution. It lists the powers of the Federal Government.

The Federal Government has *only* the powers given it in the Constitution. The states and their people have all other powers of government (ex-

cept for powers that the Constitution forbids them to use).

States' rights are the powers that the Federal Government does not have. The matter sounds simple enough. But all through U.S. history there has been a tug of war—states' rights *versus* federal power.

Americans do not always agree on what the Constitution says about the division of power—state and federal. The argument of states' rights goes back as far as the Constitutional Convention, when the Federal Government was formed. The Federalist Party, led by Alexander Hamilton, believed in a strong Federal Government. Anti-Federalists, with Thomas Jefferson as their spokesman, wanted the states to keep many rights. The Northern states that depended on commerce feared that Congress would gain too much power over trade and navigation. The Southern states did not want their farm exports taxed. Some states would not ratify the Constitution until a Bill of Rights to protect individual citizens was promised.

In the early history of the country, the idea existed that a state could *nullify* a national law (declare the law not binding within the state). In 1798, Kentucky and Virginia protested against the Alien and Sedition Acts, which were laws passed to restrict the rights of immigrants. The New England states opposed the War of 1812 and threatened to secede.

In 1832, South Carolina wanted to nullify a tariff law passed by the Federal Government. President Andrew Jackson was ready to use troops against South Carolina to enforce the law. But Congress was able to smooth over the argument with a compromise bill.

Trouble came again in 1860. South Carolina feared that the Federal Government would act to end slavery. Its leaders decided that South Carolina must leave the Union to protect its rights. Most other slave states decided to do so, too. The Civil War followed. Since the end of that war, no state has seriously tried to leave the Union or to nullify federal law.

However, because of the growing power of the Federal Government, the argument about states' rights continues. What can people do when they feel that the Federal Government is interfering with the rights of their state? They may ask Congress to repeal a law that they consider unfair. Or they may bring a test case to the United States Supreme Court to see if a law will be declared unconstitutional. Often, neither course of action gives them what they want. The old question of states' rights is still very much alive.

ALSO READ: STATE GOVERNMENT, STATEHOOD, SUPREME COURT.

STATISTICS Statistics are organized collections of numbers. The won-lost record of a football team is a statistic. The number of people in the United States is a statistic. The amount of rain that fell last week in your city is another statistic.

An *average* is a common statistic. An average is one number that represents a group of numbers. If you wanted to find out the average age of a group of people, you do it in three different ways and obtain three different kinds of averages, called the *mean*, the *median*, and the *mode*.

The mean is obtained by adding several quantities together and dividing by the number of quantities. Suppose a group contains six people aged 7, 8, 10, 11, 12, and 12. To obtain the mean age, you add together all of the ages and divide by the number of people. In this case, the total of their ages would be 60 years. Dividing 60 years by 6 people, you get the mean age—10 years.

But now suppose someone 80 years old joins the group. The group now has 7 members and a total age of 140 years. The mean goes up to 20 years. But no one in the group is 20 years old, or anywhere near it. In this case, you might want to use the median—the number that lies in the middle of the group. Since there are seven members of this group, the median will be the age of the member that is older than three of the members, and younger than the other three. In a group of 7, 8, 10, 11, 12, 12, and 80, the median would be 11.

The mode is the number that occurs most frequently in a group. In this group the mode would be 12. Every other number occurs only once whereas 12 occurs twice.

Statistics are often used for comparisons and predictions. It would be hard to compare football teams with only a list of the games they played and the scores. You would have to read the results of each game and guess which team was best. It is much easier and fairer to add up the number of wins and losses for each team, calculate the fraction or percentage of games each team has won, and rank them according to this percentage. The same sort of statistical ranking is

◄ *A microcomputer is a useful aid, at home, school, or the office, for recording and evaluating statistics.*

When you throw a pair of dice they can come to rest in any one of 36 possible combinations. But your chances of getting some totals are greater than others. For example, your chances of getting a total of 7 are much greater than your chances of getting a total of 2. This is because there is only one way you can throw a total of 2 (1 + 1). But there are six ways you can throw a total of 7. Can you list those six ways?

used to compare students, nations, automobiles, and many other things.

Statisticians (people who study statistics) cannot always get all the information they need, so they make use of *samples*—small groups that are typical of larger groups. For instance, if you wanted to learn the average height of men in the United States, it would not be practical to measure all of them. But by measuring a sample of a few hundred typical men, you could get an average that would be very close to the national average. An opinion poll is based on a statistical sample. Statisticians have special ways of making sure that their sample is typical, and of predicting how much error there might be in their statistics.

■ LEARN BY DOING

You can experiment with statistics in various ways. Try counting the traffic that passes your home. How many cars and trucks pass by? What kinds of cars? How many people walk by? When is there a lot of traffic and when is there a little? Is there more traffic in one direction than another? ■

ALSO READ: OPINION POLL

STATUE   see SCULPTURE.

STATUE OF LIBERTY   The Statue of Liberty stands on Liberty Island (earlier called Bedloe's Island) in New York Harbor. It is one of the United States's most popular national monuments. It stands as a symbol of welcome to all who reach the United States by way of New York Harbor— either newcomers or those returning.

The Statue of Liberty was a gift to the American people from the people of France. It was proposed by the French historian, Édouard de Laboulaye, in 1865 to honor the alliance between the Americans and the French during the American Revolution. Money to construct the statue

was contributed by the French people. The statue was designed and made by the French sculptor, Frédéric Auguste Bartholdi. It was made out of copper sheets, hammered together by hand. The sheets were supported by a steel framework designed by Gustave Eiffel, who also designed the Eiffel Tower in Paris, France.

The copper statue was taken apart for shipment from France in 1885 and rebuilt in the United States. It was unveiled and dedicated by President Grover Cleveland on October 28, 1886.

The Statue of Liberty, formerly known as "Liberty Enlightening the World," represents a woman holding a torch in her uplifted right hand and a tablet, or law book, in her left hand. Inscribed on the tablet is "July 4, 1776," the date of the Declaration of Independence.

The statue is 151 feet (46 m) high and weighs 225 tons (204 metric tons). It stands on a pedestal or base 154 feet (47 m) high. An elevator inside the pedestal carries visitors to the foot of the statue, where they then walk up 168 steps inside the statue to the head. An observation platform is in the statue's crown. The American Museum of Immigration, opened in 1972, is located in the pedestal. In 1986, the statue was refurbished in honor of its 100th birthday.

On a plaque at the entrance to the statue are verses by the poet, Emma Lazarus. They read in part,

Give me your tired, your poor,
Your huddled masses yearning to breathe free,
The wretched refuse of your teeming shore.
Send these, the homeless tempest-tossed to me,
I lift my lamp beside the golden door!

For a long time, the statue's illuminated torch was a navigational aid for many ships. The Statue of Liberty was thus administered by the Lighthouse Board. In 1901, the U.S. War

▲ *The Statue of Liberty, looking out over the entrance to New York Harbor, stands as a monument to America's commitment to freedom and justice. The statue's 100th birthday was celebrated over the July 4th weekend in 1986. Over six million people came to this gala celebration, which included a parade of Tall Ships, a huge fireworks display, and more.*

Department took control of the statue, which was part of Fort Wood, a U.S. Army post. In 1924, the Statue of Liberty became a national monument. Nearby Ellis Island, the former immigration station for millions of Americans, was made part of this national monument in 1965.

ALSO READ: NEW YORK CITY, SCULPTURE.

STEAM ENGINE see ENGINE.

STEEL see IRON AND STEEL.

STEPHEN (about 1097–1154)
Stephen was king of England from 1135 to 1154. For much of his reign, England was torn by civil war.

Stephen was a grandson of King William I of England, known as "the Conqueror." Stephen was brought up in the court of the English king, Henry I. Before Henry died, he named his daughter, Matilda, to be his successor. But Matilda was not popular. She was married to a French nobleman and spent little time in England. After Henry died in 1135, the powerful English nobles chose Stephen to be king. Stephen was a weak ruler, and the nobles forced him to give them many privileges. Matilda invaded England in 1139. She was backed by her half brother Robert, Earl of Gloucester. Stephen was defeated and captured in 1141. But many of the nobles still refused to support Matilda.

Stephen was never strong enough to bring peace to the country. Matilda's son, Henry Plantagenet (the future King Henry II of England), invaded England several times. Stephen was finally forced to name Henry as his successor.

ALSO READ: ENGLISH HISTORY; HENRY, KINGS OF ENGLAND.

STEPHENSON, GEORGE (1781–1848) George Stephenson was an English engineer and inventor. He built some of the earliest steam locomotives to be used in Great Britain.

Stephenson was born in the mining village of Wylam near Newcastle. His father worked as a fireman on the steam-driven engine that hauled coal in the local mine. George's family was too poor to send him to school. At the age of 14, he went to work with his father and learned how to repair steam engines. In the evenings, he learned to read and write. In 1814, Stephenson built a steam-driven locomotive for hauling coal from a mine to the nearby port. He also invented one of the first safety lamps for miners.

Stephenson worked as an engineer on the first railroads using steam power. He encouraged the use of the new steam locomotives, instead of using horses to pull rail wagons. Stephenson's *Locomotion* was one of the first steam locomotives to run on the new railroads. In 1829, the Liverpool to Manchester Railway held a competition to find a locomotive that could safely haul a passenger train. Stephenson's *Rocket* won the competition. It was stronger and faster than any other locomotive of its time. Ste-

▲ *King Stephen of England. He was the only English king to bear that name.*

▲ *George Stephenson, pioneer of steam locomotion.*

▼ *Stephenson's* Rocket *locomotive won trials against rivals in 1829 because of its multi-tube boiler, a feature adopted by later locomotives.* Rocket *reached the then unheard-of speed of 36 miles (58 km) an hour.*

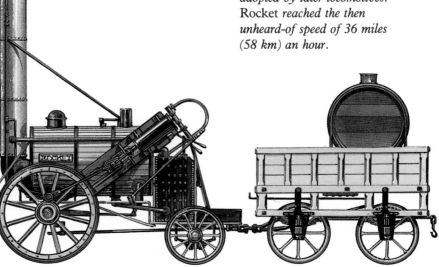

▲ *Robert Louis Stevenson, Scottish writer.*

▲ *The St. Lawrence Seaway as it passes through the city of Quebec, in Canada.*

phenson's son, Robert Stephenson, was also a well-known engineer. He built several great railway bridges in Europe and Canada.

ALSO READ: ENGINE, RAILROAD.

STEREO   see RECORDING.

STEVENSON, ROBERT LOUIS (1850–1894) Robert Louis Stevenson was a Scottish writer of books, poetry, and essays. He wrote the exciting tale of *Treasure Island* about the adventures of a young boy, Jim Hawkins, and pirate, Long John Silver, and their search for treasure.

Stevenson was born in Edinburgh, Scotland. He studied first to be an engineer, then a lawyer. Instead of entering either profession, he decided to take up writing. He soon became one of the most popular authors of his day.

Stevenson suffered from tuberculosis, but his illness did not stop him from leading an adventurous life. He journeyed through Europe and across the United States and lived in California for a year. In 1888, he sailed to the South Pacific, where he built a house on the island of Samoa. He spent the last four years of his life here at his estate, Vailima. When he died, he was buried on top of a mountain near his island home.

Stevenson's exciting tales include *Kidnapped* and *The Master of Ballantrae.* He wrote many travel books and the imaginative short stories, *New Arabian Nights.* Young people everywhere enjoy his collection of poems, *A Child's Garden of Verses.* They are about his own enjoyment of childhood and make-believe. Stevenson's tale *The Strange Case of Dr. Jekyll and Mr. Hyde* is one of the most famous horror stories ever written. *Across the Plains* tells of his trip across the United States.

ALSO READ: CHILDREN'S LITERATURE.

ST. LAWRENCE SEAWAY The St. Lawrence Seaway is an inland waterway that allows oceangoing ships to sail from the Atlantic Ocean almost halfway across North America through the Great Lakes. Ships can go all the way to the Lake Superior port of Duluth, Minnesota.

The seaway makes use of manmade canals and locks to connect natural bodies of water, such as the St. Lawrence River and the Great Lakes—Ontario, Erie, Huron, Michigan, and Superior. A vessel can sail more than 2,300 miles (3,700 km) from the mouth of the St. Lawrence to the western end of Lake Superior. In that distance, the ship is raised a total of 600 feet (183 m) from sea level to the higher level of Lake Superior. A ship enters a *lock* to be raised. Water pours into the lock to raise the water level. Then the ship sails out.

The seaway was jointly built and is jointly operated by the United States and Canada. It was opened to shipping in 1959. The costs of construction are being paid back by tolls from ships that use the waterway. Waterpower plants were also built along the seaway at the time it was constructed. The plants provide electricity to Ontario in Canada and to New York State.

Lake boats as big as oceangoing freighters carry wheat, barley, corn, oil, and coal eastward through the seaway. Iron ore mined in Labrador moves westward to steel mills in the midwestern United States. Tourists visit the seaway to watch the big ships go through the locks. Pleasure boats also use the seaway.

ALSO READ: CANAL, GREAT LAKES, SHIPS AND SHIPPING.

STOCKS AND BONDS The Muffin toy company is selling all the toys it can make. It could sell even more toys if it could expand, but in order to expand, it needs money. The Muffin family decide to sell stock in the company. The people who buy the shares of stock become part owners in the company. The company is no longer the Muffins' private company. It is now Muffin, Incorporated, and the stockholders vote on how to run it. Each share of stock carries one vote. Muffin, Inc. uses the money from the sale of stock to build a larger factory.

Muffin, Inc. is very successful. The value of the stock goes up. If stockholders decide to sell their shares, they can get more than they paid for them. Muffin could sell even more toys if it could get enough money to build another factory. The company decides to borrow the money by selling bonds. The people who buy the bonds do not own part of the company. They are just loaning the company money for a certain number of years. In return for their loan, they receive *interest*—a certain amount of money every year. After a number of years, the bonds become due, and the company repays the bondholders.

What happens if Muffin, Inc. cannot sell all of the new toys it is making? If the company loses too much money, it may go out of business. It sells its *assets*—the factory and anything else it owns—and pays the bondholders the value of their bonds, plus any interest that is owed on the bonds. If there is any money left over, the stockholders receive it.

Some companies issue both *common stock* and *preferred stock*. The preferred stockholders don't usually have a vote in company management, but if the company goes out of business, they get their money before the common stockholders do—but after the bondholders.

The stocks and bonds of many larger companies are traded—bought and sold—on stock exchanges. Much of this trading takes place in New York City in the financial district. The center of this district is Wall Street, and people often refer to the whole district by the name of that street. If you look in the financial section of the newspaper, you will see a long list of companies whose stock is traded on the New York Stock Exchange, the American Stock Exchange, and other exchanges. The paper will tell you how much a bond or share of stock has been selling for and how many shares were traded the day before. It will also tell you how high and how low the price has been that year. On the exchanges, stocks are usually traded in *blocks* of 100 shares. Any amount less than 100 shares is called an *odd lot*. On a busy day on the New York Stock Exchange, over 200 million shares may be traded.

ALSO READ: BANKS AND BANKING, CORPORATION.

STONE AGE The Stone Age is a period in early human cultural development when human beings first began to make tools and weapons. They made these tools and weapons out of stone. Long before the Stone Age, human ancestors are thought to have lived in trees. They were like apes and used their hands for swinging from branches. When they came down from the trees to look for food, they began to walk on two feet and use their hands in many new ways. They learned to use stones as weapons to help them get food. Their large brains made them intelligent. They worked out how to make better tools and weapons. Gradually these apelike creatures developed into human beings. Their use of stone tools was the beginning of civilization.

Scientists divide the Stone Age into three periods. The first of these is called the *Paleolithic* (old stone) period. The Paleolithic period began about one million years ago and ended about 15,000 B.C. During this period human beings developed the

▲ *Dealers on the Bourse, the Paris stock market. This elegant building seems an unlikely setting for the hustle, bustle, and computerized communications required for the modern international stock market.*

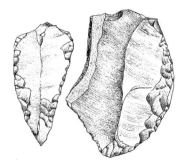

▲ *Two examples of Stone Age tools: a point (left), probably used as a spearhead; and a scraper, used to clean animal hides.*

▲ *This thumb-sized carving of a woman's head was made from mammoth tusk ivory, more than 20,000 years ago.*

▼ *Stonehenge is an impressive sight. Its massive stone blocks had to be hauled into place by muscle-power alone.*

hand ax, a crude weapon made of a piece of stone sharpened on one side by another stone. As the period progressed, they learned to refine this tool into knives and scrapers. They also learned to carve needles out of bone, and with them sewed clothes out of animal skins. They decorated their bodies with paints and shell ornaments. Fire was discovered during this period.

The second period, called the *Mesolithic* (middle stone) period, lasted from about 15,000 B.C. to 10,000 B.C. During this time, human beings began to build houses. They learned to make and use stone saws, spears, and bows and arrows.

The last period, the *Neolithic* (new stone) period, began in about 10,000 B.C. and lasted until about 3500 B.C. A great variety of stone tools was developed then. The plow and the wheel were invented, and agriculture was started. Animals were tamed. People began to live in more permanent communities. Finally, people discovered how to make the first alloy (bronze) from copper and tin. This was the beginning of a new, more complicated period of civilization called the Bronze Age. But even today, people in isolated parts of New Guinea live as men and women did in the Stone Age.

ALSO READ: ANTHROPOLOGY, HUMAN BEING, ICE AGE.

STONEHENGE Stonehenge is a mysterious, prehistoric monument. It stands on Salisbury Plain in Wiltshire in southwestern England. The main part of the monument is a group of giant stones. The people who built Stonehenge left no written records, so no one knows for certain how or why it was built.

Stonehenge was built about 4,000 years ago. Around the outside is a circular ditch with a bank inside it. Just inside the bank is a circle of 56 pits called Aubrey holes, which probably once held wooden posts. These holes were discovered by John Aubrey in 1666. At the center of Stonehenge is a circle of enormous stones about 13 feet (4 m) high. Flat blocks of stone lie across the tops of the high stones. Inside this circle are five pairs of even larger stones arranged in the shape of a horseshoe. Within these stones is another horseshoe of smaller stones, called bluestones.

Scholars have discovered that the bluestones come from mountains about 140 miles (225 km) away. No one knows exactly how the builders of Stonehenge carried these heavy stones over such a long distance. At the center of the bluestones is a great block of stone called the "Altar." If you stand at the Altar stone on the first day of summer (about June 21), you will see the sun rise over a stone called the "Heelstone."

For many years, people have believed that Stonehenge was some type of temple. An American astronomer, Gerald Hawkins, claimed that Stonehenge was actually a type of giant calendar. He showed that the stones and Aubrey holes mark the different positions of the sun and the moon during the year. He believed that people using Stonehenge were able to mark the beginnings of the seasons and forecast eclipses of the sun.

ALSO READ: CALENDAR, ECLIPSE.

STONE MOUNTAIN Near Atlanta, Georgia, a whole mountain of gray granite rises about 700 feet (213 m) into the air. This mountain, called Stone Mountain, is rounded, or shaped like a dome. On its north side, sculptors and their helpers have carved the world's biggest sculpture in *high relief* (sculpture that stands far out from its background). This large sculpture, 190 feet (58 m) high by 305 feet (93 m) wide, is a memorial to the Civil War leaders of the South. The sculpture shows Robert E. Lee, Jefferson Davis, and Thomas "Stonewall" Jackson riding their horses. Lee's horse, Traveller, is about 147 feet (45 m) long. Jackson's nose is four and a half feet (1.4 m) long.

The Stone Mountain Memorial was commissioned by the Daughters of the Confederacy in 1916. Several sculptors worked on the memorial over a period of about 50 years. Gutzon Borglum, who later carved Mount Rushmore National Memorial, was the first sculptor. Borglum began carving the relief in 1923. The U.S. Congress authorized the coining of a special half-dollar commemorating Stone Mountain to help support the project. But in 1924, Borglum left because of a disagreement. Augustus Lukeman was the next sculptor. He blasted away Borglum's work and started again. When money ran out in 1928, all carving had to stop. In 1963, the state of Georgia bought Stone Mountain and established a state park with recreational facilities there. The sculptor, Walter Hancock, was hired to complete the memorial. Working with Hancock was Roy Faulkner, who was on the mountainside for many years, using a thermo-jet torch for carving. Many others helped finish the memorial, which was dedicated in May 1970. It attracts thousands of visitors each year.

ALSO READ: GEORGIA; RUSHMORE, MOUNT; SCULPTURE.

STORES AND SHOPS Stores and shops are places where merchandise is set out, or displayed, and sold for money. A store usually sells several different types of merchandise. Most shops sell goods of only one type.

At the time of the Greek and Roman Empires there were many marketplaces where people bought food and other necessities. The early settlers in North America made their own clothes, furniture, and other things they needed. A farmer who wanted a new pair of shoes could go to a shoemaker and arrange a trade. The farmer might give the shoemaker a barrel of potatoes in exchange for the pair of shoes. This kind of trading is called *barter*.

As villages grew into towns, shops were opened, and people began to buy goods with money. Peddlers with horse-drawn wagons drove through the countryside and sold cloth, kitchen utensils, soap, and other goods for money.

People in small towns had to buy merchandise from a few small shops. Each shop usually sold only one product, such as food, clothing, pots and pans, or leather goods. As railroads were built across the nation, the towns grew larger and more people needed to buy goods of all kinds. To supply this demand, merchants built

▲ *This carving of Stonewall Jackson, Robert E. Lee, and Jefferson Davis is on Stone Mountain in Georgia. It is regarded as the world's largest sculpture. The figures are 90 feet (27 m) high.*

▼ *From cuddly toys to cream cheeses, you can buy almost anything in such supermarkets as this.*

▲ *More and more shops and stores in the United States and Canada are found inside vast galleries, or malls, like this impressive one in Toronto. Shoppers do not have to worry about the weather when walking from store to store.*

what were called *general stores*, which sold a variety of goods, usually in one room. The old general stores were similar to our *drugstores*, which sell goods such as candy, clothing, food, and school supplies, as well as medicines and toilet articles. The general store led to our modern *department stores*, which have several rooms, or departments, each one containing a different type of merchandise.

Some shops today still sell only certain kinds of merchandise. These are often called *specialty shops*. Other shops sell a variety of the same type of merchandise. Some bookstores, for example, sell not only books, but also greeting cards, stationery, and office supplies. Modern *supermarkets* sell many different kinds of food, cleaning supplies, and a variety of other items.

Many of the stores in our cities and towns are *chain stores*. A chain store is one of a number of stores owned by one company and selling similar merchandise. Many department stores, supermarkets, and drugstores are chain stores. Most dime stores or variety stores, which sell all kinds of inexpensive merchandise, are also of this type.

A different kind of store sells goods of all kinds by mail. These *mail-order* companies publish *catalogs* that describe their goods and also show pictures of many of them. Customers select what they want from the catalogs and send an order to the company. The goods are then sent to the customers by parcel post or by freight. Some of the mail-order companies also operate their own department stores, where goods are sold over the counters, as in any department store.

Some stores sell services, such as shoe repairing and dry cleaning. Stores called "service stations" sell parts as well as automobile services. They sell gasoline, oil, tires, and batteries. They also perform repair jobs on cars and trucks. When a person

drives into a service station to buy gasoline, he or she can ask the attendant to perform service checks on the car to be sure it's in good order.

A shop can be set up wherever anyone has anything to sell. On a hot summer day, youngsters may set up an old table on the street and sell lemonade. This is their shop. Many farms have fruit and vegetable stands by the roadside.

Years ago, people who bought something in a shop or store were expected to pay for it with cash. Many still do, but millions of customers today have *charge accounts*. Persons who have charge accounts can buy what they want without having to pay for it immediately. The store will send them a bill for their purchase later. If the bill is not paid within a reasonable time, an extra charge may be added to it. Most stores also allow people to use *credit cards*. These cards

▼ *Supermarket shopping is a similar experience to shoppers in countries all around the world.*

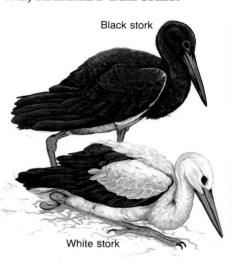
Black stork

White stork

▲ *The white stork is a common bird in parts of Europe during the summer. The black stork is found both in Europe and Africa.*

are given out by special companies or banks, which pay for the customers' purchases and then send them the bill themselves. Many stores will deliver purchases to the customers' homes. If the customers do not have charge accounts, they will usually be asked to pay "cash on delivery," or "C.O.D."

Stores sometimes advertise *bargain sales*. At these events, certain goods are sold at prices lower than "regular" prices. Most sales are *seasonal*. For example, clothing stores may lower prices of winter clothing at the end of winter, so that they will have more room to display new merchandise for spring and summer.

Many stores, especially department stores, lose some profits because goods are stolen, or *shoplifted*. In an effort to stop thefts, many stores now have closed-circuit television cameras, so that security people can watch suspicious customers from a central point in the store. Other stores have store detectives who pose as customers and walk around watching for shoplifters.

Many stores, especially department stores, employ men and women as *buyers*. Their job is to decide what kinds of clothing and other goods they should buy from manufacturers to be put on sale in the stores.

ALSO READ: ADVERTISING, SELLING.

STORK The stork is a large bird with long legs and a long neck. It has strong wings and is a good flier. Most storks live in marshes and near rivers. They usually eat frogs, fish, insects, birds, and small mammals. Because storks do not have a fully developed syrinx (a bird's vocal organ), they are almost voiceless. Some storks, however, make a clacking noise with their bills. Most storks travel in flocks except during the breeding season, when they pair off.

The most common stork is the white stork, which lives in Europe in the summer, but flies to India, Arabia, or Africa in the winter. It is about 3½ feet (1.1 m) tall and has a white body with black-tipped wings. Its bill and legs are red. The white stork builds its nest in the tops of trees or in roofs and chimneys that are not being used. A pair of white storks will return to their nest year after year.

One kind of stork, the wood stork, often called the wood ibis, lives in the southern United States. It is white with black wings and is about the same size as the white stork. The wood stork has a bill that curves downward. It nests in colonies in the trees.

Many people believe that the stork brings good luck. The Germans and the Dutch have laws protecting the storks that live and nest in their countries. The old belief that the stork brings the new baby into the home is thought to have originated because storks take very good care of their young.

ALSO READ: BIRD.

STORM see HURRICANE, TORNADO, WEATHER.

STOWE, HARRIET BEECHER (1811–1896) Harriet Beecher Stowe was a U.S. writer. She became known throughout the world for her book against slavery, *Uncle Tom's Cabin*. Harriet was born in Litchfield, Connecticut. Her father, Lyman Beecher, and her brother, Henry Ward Beecher, were both well-known preachers.

In 1836, Harriet married the Reverend Calvin Ellis Stowe, a professor in the Lane Theological Seminary in Cincinnati, Ohio. Mrs. Stowe and her husband were deeply concerned about the plight of runaway slaves.

Uncle Tom's Cabin was first published in an abolitionist (antislavery) newspaper, the *National Era*. When it was published in book form, it sold

▲ *Harriet Beecher Stowe, U.S. writer.*

▲ *Johann Strauss, Austrian composer.*

▲ *Igor Stravinsky, Russian-born composer, conducting an orchestral performance.*

over 500,000 copies in five years. *Uncle Tom's Cabin* is the story of Uncle Tom, a devoted black slave owned by a family named Shelby. Money troubles force the Shelbys to sell Tom. Uncle Tom saves the life of Little Eva, daughter of a well-to-do white man, who buys him. But Eva and her father die. Tom is sold again, this time to a cruel owner named Simon Legree, who whips Tom to death.

The book aroused Northern feelings against slavery. Some historians say the book helped bring on the Civil War. According to one report, Abraham Lincoln met Mrs. Stowe and said, "So this is the little lady who made this big war."

ALSO READ: SLAVERY.

STRAUSS, JOHANN (1825–1899)

The Austrian composer, Johann Strauss, was the most talented member of a family of musicians. Strauss was known as the "Waltz King." The waltz is a graceful dance that was popular in the 1800's. Strauss composed many tuneful and lilting waltzes, including the well-known "Blue Danube." Strauss and his father, Johann the Elder, were musical rivals for a time.

The young Johann was born in Vienna, Austria. His father conducted his own orchestra in Vienna. Johann the Elder also composed popular marches and waltzes. He did not wish his sons to have musical careers. But the young Johann began to write waltzes when he was a child. Johann and his brothers, Josef and Eduard, all became musicians.

In 1844, the younger Johann formed an orchestra of his own. It was successful right away and competed with his father's orchestra. After his father's death, Strauss joined the two together.

Strauss composed more than 400 waltzes. His "Emperor Waltz," "Tales from the Vienna Woods," and "Wine, Women, and Song" are still great favorites today. Strauss also composed several operettas.

ALSO READ: DANCING, COMPOSER, OPERA.

STRAVINSKY, IGOR (1882–1971)

Igor Stravinsky was a Russian-born composer. He was born near St. Petersburg (now Leningrad). As a young man, he studied musical composition under the Russian composer, Nicolai Rimsky-Korsakov. Stravinsky composed one of his first pieces of music for the wedding of Rimsky-Korsakov's daughter.

Stravinsky's first important musical works were written especially for Sergei Diaghilev, director of the Russian ballet in Paris, France. Stravinsky's first two ballets, *The Firebird* and *Petrouchka*, contained new rhythms and unusual harmonies and sounds. They were much admired. But the first performance of his ballet, *The Rite of Spring*, caused a riot among the audience. This was completely new music, full of savage, wild rhythms and strange *dissonance*—tones and chords that clash.

In the middle of his life, Stravinsky returned to more traditional forms of music, as in his choral (sung) work *Oedipus Rex*. His last works were based on a tone row, a random series of tones. Stravinsky became a U.S. citizen in 1945 and spent the last part of his life in the United States.

ALSO READ: COMPOSER; RIMSKY-KORSAKOV, NICOLAI.

STREETS AND ROADS

Roads are routes on which people and vehicles travel. Roads are usually established and maintained (kept up) by federal and state governments. Major roads are called *highways*. Roads within cities and towns are usually called streets.

Kinds of Streets and Roads Streets allow people to travel from place to place within a city or from the city to suburbs or rural areas. A street can have many different names, and the name often designates the type of street it is and the kind of traffic it is intended for. *Avenues* and *boulevards* are usually wide, important streets that receive a great deal of traffic. Most towns have a main street that goes through the most important business and shopping districts. *Expressways* are for fast-moving traffic that wants to cross all, or most, of a city. Consequently, expressways have few entrances and exits.

Highways, unlike streets, are usually built to avoid cities, or at least the most heavily traveled parts of them. When highways cannot be built around cities, they are often built over them. Elevated highways, often called *freeways*, have few entrances and exits to the cities beneath them, so traffic is disturbed very little. Large metropolitan areas often have several layers of elevated roads above their streets. You can drive along a street in a large city and see four separate highways above you! Vehicles enter and leave these roads (as they do most highways) by means of graded (sloped) "feeder" roads called *ramps*. Highways with entrance and exit ramps are called *limited-access*

roads. *Interstate* highways are wide limited-access roads that go through several states. State highways, built and maintained solely by state governments, connect at a state's borders with other highways. Toll roads, or turnpikes, are highways on which vehicles are stopped at certain points and charged a small fee (called a toll) for using the road.

Early Streets and Roads When an area is settled, people usually settle first along waterways so they will have a ready-made "highway." But their first real roads are the trails they use to go from one place to another. As communication and trade grow, more and better roads become necessary.

Ancient civilizations in Asia Minor and Egypt had fairly elaborate systems of good roads. (Egyptians built some of their roads for transporting materials to build the pyramids.) Most of the ancient roads surviving today are Roman roads. The Romans built four feet (1.2 m) thick roads of several layers of stone in all the provinces they conquered, including England. The word "highway" was first used in England to refer to these raised Roman roads.

Few good roads were built during the Middle Ages. But during the 1500's, as wheeled vehicles became more and more popular, new and better roads became necessary. (Carriages could not travel over very rough, muddy surfaces.) England began a system of toll roads in the

▲ *A highway winds across the rugged country of the Rocky Mountains. The United States has one of the most extensive national highway systems in the world.*

▼ *Road engineers have to be ingenious when designing a busy intersection. Traffic on several intersecting routes must move freely and safely, and the intersection structure must comply with strict building regulations. This series of junctions and overpasses is near Seattle, Washington.*

▼ *A street busy with buses, taxis, and cars in a U.S. city. Pedestrians crowd the sidewalks.*

1600's. In the late 1700's, John Loudon McAdam developed an improved system of road-building. McAdam placed layers of stone on well-drained earth covered with finer stones and sand and bound with gravel. This system, called *macadamization*, was widely used until the heavy trucks of the 1900's proved that macadamized roads could not bear the extremely heavy loads of the automobile age.

In the 1700's and 1800's, settlers in America gradually built roads as they explored and settled more of the new continent. The first roads in America were probably Indian trails. When settlers came, they used Indian trails (when they were known) for traveling until the trails became worn down to recognizable roads. As settlers moved west, they made "roads" by breaking trails through the rough countryside. Since the going was so rough, they usually chose the easiest routes rather than the most direct. The great western trails, such as the Santa Fe, were roads made in this way. (With the planning and improved methods of road construction developed recently, the roughness of the terrain does not matter so much, and more direct routes can be taken.) During the lat-

ter part of the 1800's, when railroads came into wide use, road construction was almost ignored. However, during the early 1900's, as the newly invented automobiles became popular, better roads became essential.

As soon as cities and towns began to grow, people needed streets. Ancient Greek and Roman cities had streets, some of which were paved (covered with hard, smooth stones). In western Europe, towns began paving some of their streets with stones in the 1200's. Towns developed main streets when the routes to most of the businesses and stores became worn by use. Side streets and residential streets came into being as the populations of towns grew and people needed routes to their homes. Since horse-drawn vehicles raised quite a bit of dust as they clattered along unpaved and litter-strewn streets, paved surfaces were soon necessary.

Round stones, called *cobblestones*, and bricks were widely used as paving materials until this century. Smoother surfaces are now used on streets so that motor vehicles can be driven safely and comfortably.

Construction of Streets and Roads Highway and street construction today is a complex industry. Civil engineers plan the route each road will take, whether it is an interstate highway or a city street. Roads are made as straight as possible. Curves and uphill and downhill grades are carefully engineered to be as gentle as possible.

The ground must be cleared and the soil drained before road construction can begin. Often more earth must be added to build up the road-

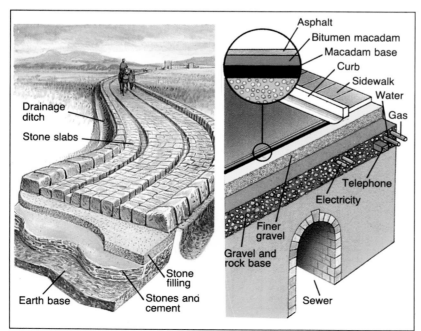

Drainage ditch
Stone slabs
Earth base
Stone filling
Stones and cement
Asphalt
Bitumen macadam
Macadam base
Curb
Sidewalk
Water
Gas
Telephone
Electricity
Finer gravel
Gravel and rock base
Sewer

◀ *Roman roads (far left) were among the first paved roads in the world. They were built by army engineers and had drainage. Modern roads (left) use drainage too, but also have a layer of concrete or macadam covered with tar, called bitumen or asphalt.*

bed. Foundations and concrete bases are then put down, the kind and amount depending on the type of road and the soil beneath it. The top layer—the road surface—usually consists of tar, asphalt, or concrete. Median strips (islands between traffic going in opposite directions) are constructed on wide highways.

ALSO READ: AUTOMOBILE, BUS, CARRIAGE, DRIVING, TRAFFIC PLANNING, TRUCKS AND TRUCKING.

STRESS
To scientists, stress means a force acting on an object. For example, if a metal wire is stretched, it gets longer and longer but finally snaps. Engineers designing bridges and airplanes test the materials used in construction to make sure they are strong enough to stand up to the stresses of everyday use.

Scientists have worked out that stress is the force acting on an object divided by the area of the solid on which it is acting. *Strain* is the change in size produced when an object is squeezed or stretched, divided by its original size. A law of physics states that for any material the stress divided by the strain is constant. This constant is called the *modulus of elasticity*, and it allows scientists to work out how stretchable a material is.

ALSO READ: ELASTICITY, FORCE.

STRINGED INSTRUMENTS
Any musical instrument that produces tone by means of vibrating strings is called a stringed instrument. As strings vibrate back and forth, they push the surrounding air outward in the form of sound waves that you can hear. Stringed instruments are divided into groups according to how the strings are made to vibrate.

Bowed Instruments Bowed instruments produce sound when a bow (long stick with horsehair stretched from end to end) is drawn across the strings. The horsehair is rubbed with a substance called *rosin*. The rosin roughens and sticks to the hair shafts so that the hairs will "grip" the strings slightly and cause them to vibrate.

The *violin*, *viola*, *cello* (or *violoncello*), and *bass viol* are the bowed instruments usually played today. All four are played in approximately the

▶ *This engraving of 1730 shows a maker of stringed instruments. He is carrying examples of his craft, among them a lute (rounded body), a violin, and (in his right hand) a cello. On his head is a case for a lute.*

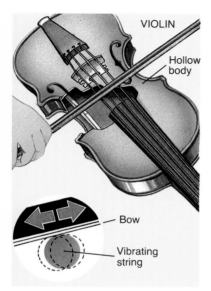

VIOLIN

Hollow body

Bow

Vibrating string

▲ *Stringed instruments have tight strings that vibrate to make a sound. The violin string vibrates when the hairs of the bow are drawn across it. The harder the bow is pressed down, the louder the sound. The vibration of the strings sets the hollow body of the violin vibrating too, making the sound louder.*

▼ *An acoustic guitar has a hollow body made of wood. When the strings are plucked, the vibrations are carried throughout the body and make it sound also. This sound comes from the sound hole beneath the strings.*

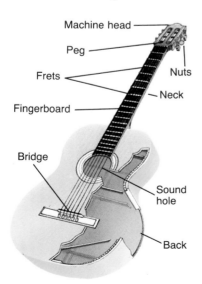

Machine head

Peg

Frets

Nuts

Fingerboard

Neck

Bridge

Sound hole

Back

same way. Each has a set of four strings made of sheep gut or nylon wrapped with wire. The highest string on a violin is just a single, thin wire of silver alloy. The strings are fastened to a *tailpiece* at the bottom of the instrument. From there they are stretched over a thin piece of wood, called the *bridge*, and up along the *fingerboard* to a *pegbox*, where each of the strings is wound around a peg. By turning a peg, a string can be tuned higher or lower.

As the player draws the bow across a string with the right hand, he or she uses the fingers of the left hand to press the string against the fingerboard at various places. This makes changes in pitch. The vibration of the strings causes similar vibrations to occur inside the hollow body (sound box) of the instrument.

The violin is the highest pitched of the four bowed instruments. It is held under the chin when played. The viola has the same shape as a violin and is played the same way, but it is one-seventeenth larger and the strings are tuned five tones lower. The cello is twice as big as a violin and is tuned eight tones lower than the viola. A cello can only be played from a seated position. The instrument is balanced between the player's knees and is supported by a metal rod at the bottom that rests against the floor. The bass viol (also called *double bass*) is twice as big as a cello and has a slightly different shape. The bass viol is the lowest pitched of all the stringed instruments. The instrument can be played standing or sitting.

All four of these bowed instruments are played in symphony orchestras. Composers have written much solo music for the violin and cello, so these two instruments are often played alone in recitals. The bass viol is important in jazz.

The greatest violin makers were various members of the Amati, Guarneri, and Stradivari families who all lived in the city of Cremona in northern Italy. From about 1550 to 1725, these craftworkers produced instruments of unparalleled construction and tone quality.

Plucked Instruments The *guitar*, *banjo*, *ukelele*, and *harp* are instruments whose tone is produced by plucking strings with the fingers. Plucked instruments are used in the performance of both classical and popular music—the guitar being especially popular. Guitars usually have six strings that are stretched from a bridge up the fingerboard to metal pegs that are used for tuning the instrument. Crossing the fingerboard at regular intervals are little ridges called *frets*, used to change the pitch.

There are three basic types of guitar, each used for performing different types of music. The *acoustic* or *classical guitar* is made of wood and has a circular sound hole located beneath the strings. Acoustic guitars are used in playing classical music and as accompaniment for folk songs. The *flamenco guitar* is like the classical except it has a thin plastic plate covering part of the front of the instrument. This protects the delicate wood from being scratched by the player's fingernails. Flamenco music is full of complicated chords and rhythms that take great skill and precision. The *plectrum* guitar is used for rock, jazz, and other popular music. It is larger and flatter than the classical guitar and is usually now made of a plastic material. The heavy steel strings are plucked with a plectrum, or pick. Plectrum guitars are often connected to electronic amplifiers to increase the volume and create special tonal effects for rhythm and lead guitar players.

Modern plucked instruments have developed from older instruments, such as the ancient Greek *kithara*, the *lyre*, the *psaltry*, the *lute*, and the *mandolin*. Other plucked instruments are the East Indian *sitar*, the Russian *balalaika*, the *dulcimer*, the Japanese *koto*, and the *zither*.

Hammered and Blown Strings

The *piano* is the best-known example of a stringed instrument whose tone is made by pressing a key which is connected to a hammer which hits the string.

The only stringed instrument whose tone is produced by a stream of air is the *Aeolian harp*. It consists of a number of gut strings of different thicknesses attached to a sound box. All strings are tuned to the same tone. A stream of air or a blowing wind makes the strings vibrate and produces harmonics (tones related to the pitch at which the strings are tuned).

ALSO READ: MUSICAL INSTRUMENTS, ORCHESTRAS AND BANDS, PIANO.

STUART, HOUSE OF see ENGLISH HISTORY.

STUYVESANT, PETER (about 1610–1672) Peter Stuyvesant was the last governor of the Dutch colony of New Netherland. This colony included parts of the present-day states of New York, Connecticut, New Jersey, and Delaware.

Stuyvesant was born in West Friesland in the Netherlands. He went to work for the Dutch West India Company and was made governor of the Dutch island of Curacao in the Caribbean Sea. In 1644, he lost a leg in a battle with Portuguese settlers.

Stuyvesant was appointed governor of New Netherland in 1646. The following year, he arrived in New Amsterdam (now New York City), the capital of the colony. He soon became a familiar figure, with his wooden leg trimmed with silver bands. Stuyvesant built New Amsterdam into a wealthy commercial center. But he angered the colonists by refusing to let them share in the government of the colony. He taxed the people heavily and dealt harshly with Protestant groups.

In 1664, the English laid claim to the New Netherland colony and sent a war fleet to New Amsterdam. The Dutch colonists refused to support Stuyvesant, and he was forced to surrender. The English renamed the colony "New York." Stuyvesant spent his last years in New York City on his farm, or *bouwerij*. A street named the Bowery was later built over the site.

ALSO READ: NEW YORK, NEW YORK CITY.

SUBMARINE The submarine is a ship designed for underwater use. The modern submarine is a watertight vessel with a welded, cigar-shaped *hull* (body). The body is called a *pressure hull* because it must withstand the enormous pressures of seawater at great depths.

Above the hull is a raised area that is the main deck of the ship when the vessel is riding on the water's surface. Above this deck is a tower that houses the submarine's control room. The control room is equipped with *periscopes*. A periscope is similar to a telescope, except that a periscope is bent and has mirrors inside. When the submarine is submerged, crew members can see things by raising the top of the periscope above the water's surface.

To submerge a submarine, water is sucked into large tanks, called *ballast tanks*, in the hull. The greater the amount of water in the tanks, the deeper the submarine will go. A submarine is brought to the surface by using compressed air to force the water out of the tanks. At the bow and stern of the ship are horizontal rudders, called *hydroplanes*, which keep the submarine steady when it is moving upward or downward.

The modern nuclear-powered submarine is armed with long-range *ballistic missiles*. These missiles carry atomic warheads and can be fired from underwater at targets thousands

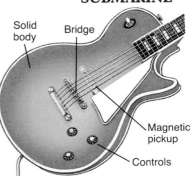

▲ *An electric, or plectrum, guitar has strings like an ordinary guitar. But its body is solid. When a string is plucked, a pickup under the strings give an electric signal. This signal is amplified through a loudspeaker to make the sound we hear.*

▲ *Peter Stuyvesant, last Dutch governor of New Netherland.*

▲ *David Bushnell's* Turtle *was the first submarine to go to war. It was used, unsuccessfully, during the American Revolution in an attempt to sink a British warship.*

of miles away. Most submarines carry *torpedoes*, large, bullet-shaped, self-propelled, underwater bombs. Torpedoes are used against enemy submarines and other ships.

The first submarine designed for war was a one-person, wooden, egg-shaped craft named the *Turtle*. It was invented in the 1770's by an American engineer, David Bushnell. The vessel was submerged by letting water into a ballast tank. It rose when the tank was emptied by a hand pump. In 1800, the U.S. inventor, Robert Fulton, built a 21-foot (6.4-m) submarine named the *Nautilus*. When submerged, the *Nautilus* was powered by a hand-cranked, four-blade propeller in the stern.

Submarine development was hindered by hostility from naval chiefs and by the lack of a suitable power plant. The first useful submarine with a good source of power was developed by the U.S. inventor, John Philip Holland, in 1898. His submarine was equipped with a gasoline engine for surface travel and an electric motor for underwater power. In 1906, the Germans began using diesel engines in submarines. With the development of the periscope and the selfpropelled

torpedo, the submarine became important in war. During World War I, the Germans made much use of submarines.

In the 1930's, underwater sound equipment was developed for communication and for detecting enemy ships. Rescue devices became part of the regular equipment of submarine crews. During World War II, the German navy developed a mechanism called the *snorkel*. Snorkels permit a submarine to recharge its batteries while cruising at periscope depth (shallow enough for a periscope to extend above the water's surface).

The most revolutionary development in underwater navigation is the use of nuclear energy to power submarines. Nuclear power provides almost unlimited energy and enables a submarine to keep going and to stay underwater for extremely long periods of time. The first nuclear-powered submarine was the U.S.S. *Nautilus*, in service from 1954 to 1980. In 1958 the *Nautilus* traveled from the Pacific Ocean to the Atlantic Ocean underneath the North Pole. Two years later, another American nuclear submarine, the *Triton*, circled the globe without coming to the sur-

▼ *A U.S. Navy submarine, which carries ballistic missiles that can be fired from underwater. The submarine's streamlined shape reduces water resistance. The diagram (bottom) shows in four stages how a submarine dives and rises. By blowing air out of buoyancy tanks, the vessel sinks. By blowing water out of ballast tanks, the vessel gains buoyancy and rises. The speed and angle of the dive or ascent are controlled by the finlike diving planes, and by varying the rate at which tanks fill and empty.*

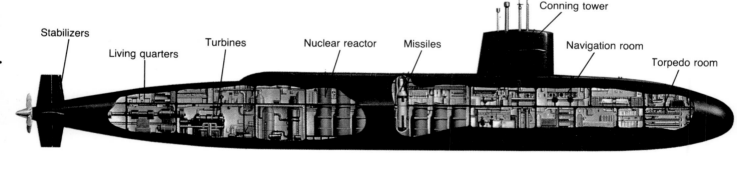

Stabilizers — Living quarters — Turbines — Nuclear reactor — Missiles — Conning tower — Navigation room — Torpedo room

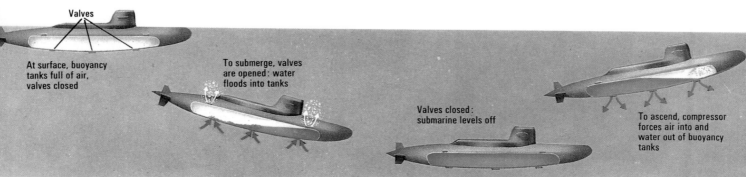

Valves

At surface, buoyancy tanks full of air, valves closed

To submerge, valves are opened: water floods into tanks

Valves closed: submarine levels off

To ascend, compressor forces air into and water out of buoyancy tanks

face. Today, the Navy has both nuclear-powered and diesel-powered submarines. Some submarines carry ballistic missiles. Another major development in underwater transport is the deep sea *submersible* used for exploration and research. It can also house diving crews for long periods working on projects like seabed oil pipelines.

ALSO READ: FULTON, ROBERT; NAVY; NUCLEAR ENERGY; OCEAN.

SUBTRACTION   see ARITHMETIC.

SUBURB
The suburbs are communities located on the outskirts of large cities. They are considered to be part of a city's metropolitan area because many of its residents travel into the city to work. Suburbs are of two types—*residential* and *industrial*. Residential suburbs are made up almost entirely of houses built on lots (small plots of land). Industrial suburbs are areas in which large business and industrial firms have set up factories and office buildings outside the city.

Since about 1900, people with enough money to buy land and houses have moved to suburban areas. The greatest movement to the suburbs occurred just after World War II. Many people moved to escape crowded city conditions.

As cities have grown, city governments have often *annexed* nearby suburbs (made them part of the city). This was necessary in order to settle problems of authority and jurisdiction. Nearby suburbs often use the city's water and electrical supply. Suburban *commuters* (people who travel into the city to work) use the city's roads and public services while at work. And many suburbs make use of city police and fire departments. But some suburbanites do not contribute anything to the city in return. They pay no city taxes to help support the needs of the city. By annexing a

suburb, the city government can levy taxes on the suburbanites.

For years, upper-income families have preferred the suburbs, leaving most of the poor in the cities. Poor people, although they may pay taxes, cannot contribute as much money to the city as wealthier people can. Some cities today grow poorer because the suburbanites with more money contribute little or nothing to them, even though they take advantage of the city's entertainment, transportation, jobs, stores, and other facilities. Some agreements, however, have been made whereby suburbanites who work in the city pay a "commuter's tax."

ALSO READ: CITY, COMMUNITY, LOCAL GOVERNMENT.

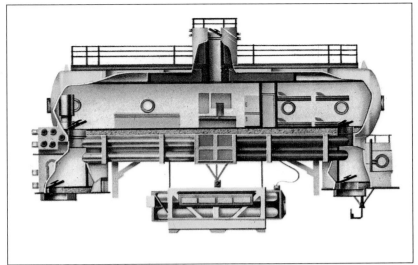

▲ *The US Navy Sealab III has quarters for a crew working long periods on the seabed. This submersible is a type of submarine.*

▼ *A typical suburban home in a U.S. city. The suburb offers its residents a comfortable environment and pleasant, open surroundings away from the noise and overcrowded streets of the city center, but near enough to commute to work.*

▲ *The world's first subway was opened in London, England, in 1863. Guests at the ceremony enjoyed riding in open wagons.*

SUBWAY The word "subway" is a U.S. term for an underground electric-powered railway system that provides rapid passenger service in densely populated city areas. In Britain the subway is called the "underground," or "tube." In other countries, subways are called "metros."

Subway trains are usually made up of several passenger cars, which are similar to railroad cars. A subway car may hold 100 to 200 passengers. Each car has its own electric motor and draws power from a "third rail" in the center or at one side of the tracks. A person, the *operator*, in a small cab at one end of the subway train controls the car motors, starting and stopping the train at various stations along the route.

Many subway systems are equipped with four pair of tracks. One pair is used for *local* trains going in one direction that stop at every station along the route. One pair is used for local trains going in the other direction. The other pairs of tracks are for *express* trains going in either direction that stop only at certain important stations.

When a train stops at a station, the doors are opened by the operator or they open automatically. Passengers get on and off before the doors close again. A train is allotted only a certain amount of stopping time at each station. As soon as that time is up, the doors close and the train pulls out, leaving the station clear for the next incoming train. During rush-hour periods, when thousands of people are going to and from work, trains may run as often as two minutes apart.

The movement of subway trains is coordinated at a central office by a *dispatcher*. The dispatcher watches a control board showing a map of the subway routes. Flashing lights on the control board tell the dispatcher where every train is at any time. The dispatcher makes sure that trains are moving at the proper speeds and time intervals. He or she also watches for distress signals from trains that have broken down.

Switchmen may send out signals to the operators along the line. They give instructions to slow down or speed up if it looks as if a group of trains is beginning to jam up. Sometimes they instruct an operator to skip one or two stations in order to keep the flow of trains moving. Operators can also signal to the central office if something happens to the train, the tracks, or the passengers.

Crews of track and tunnel inspectors make regular rounds to check the subway system. Their job is to locate any problems (tunnel leaks, rail damage, burned-out signal lights, etc.) and get them repaired.

In many cities, subway tracks come up above ground level when they leave the more heavily populated downtown areas. Overground tracks are usually raised above street level on steel girders. For this reason, they are called *elevated trains*, or *els*, for short. The downtown area of Chicago, known as The Loop, is so called because a circle of elevated tracks goes around the area.

The world's first subway line was opened in London, England, in 1863. This was before the time of electric railways, so the cars were pulled by horses. Later, steam locomotives were used until electrification was introduced in 1890. Boston was the first U.S. city to have a subway, opening

▼ *Modern subway systems provide fast public transportation in a number of the world's largest cities. This photograph shows a train on one of London's subway lines.*

its line in 1897. The New York City subway, which opened in 1904, has grown into the world's busiest. It is also the world's most complex subway network, with almost 230 miles (370 km) of track. The New York City subway carries more than one billion passengers each year. One of the most modern subways is San Francisco's BART (Bay Area Rapid Transit), which began operating in 1972. Many experts have acclaimed the Moscow subway as the best planned and operated system in the world. The Moscow trains were the first to use strong rubber tires on the wheels to cut down the noise. Metal wheels on metal tracks make much more noise.

Constructing a subway system is a time-consuming and often dangerous job. There are two basic ways of digging a subway. One is the *open-cut*, or *cut-and-cover*, method. The street pavement is removed and the tunnel area dug out. This cuts off the flow of traffic on the street until the open area can be braced with steel girders and covered with heavy timbers for the traffic to drive over. The *tube*, or *tunneling*, method of construction is used when a subway tunnel must be cut beneath bodies of water or beneath a city's maze of underground sewer and electrical systems. The workmen use a *tunneling shield* that is pushed along the planned route. The shield cuts up the earth and rock ahead of it, and the broken earth is

sent to the surface by conveyors. As the shield moves forward, the newly formed tunnel is supported with steel girders and tunnel liners that form the walls. This tunneling method does not disrupt the flow of traffic and can be used at much greater depths than can the open-cut method.

ALSO READ: CITY, RAILROAD, TRAFFIC PLANNING, TRANSPORTATION, TUNNEL.

SUDAN The Democratic Republic of Sudan is the largest country in Africa. It is more than one-fourth the size of the United States. The word Sudan can be translated as the "land of the blacks." Eight African countries border Sudan. Egypt is to the north. Ethiopia and the Red Sea form the eastern border, and Kenya, Uganda, and Zaire form the southern border. Libya, Chad, and the Central African Republic are on the west. (See the map with the article on AFRICA.)

The huge Sahara Desert lies in the northern sector, and the mountainous Nubian Desert reaches to the Red Sea in the east. The historic Nile River, longest in the world, divides the country and is the north-south means of communication and travel between the Mediterranean and African interior. At the capital city of Khartoum, the Blue Nile joines the White Nile to form the Nile.

▲ Top: *The control room of a subway system. The network is shown on an illuminated diagram, showing where each train is at any time. All signals and switches are controlled automatically. On some systems the trains are driverless, relying on automatic controls.*
Bottom: *A station on the Moscow subway, or Metro. The ornate stations were designed by leading Soviet architects and artists.*

SUDAN

Capital City: Khartoum (476,000 people).
Area: 967,570 square miles (2,505,813 sq. km).
Population: 25,000,000.
Government: Republic.
Natural Resources: Oil, gold, manganese, copper, asbestos, vermiculite.
Export Products: Cotton, peanuts, sesame, gum arabic.
Unit of Money: Sudanese pound.
Official Language: Arabic.

▲ *This man is a citizen of the Sudan, a hot, mostly arid land in Africa.*

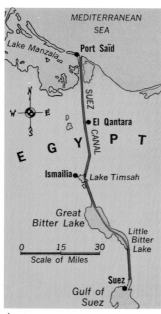

▲ *A map of the Suez Canal, showing the route from Port Said to Suez. The canal has no locks.*

Two groups of people live in Sudan. Arabic-speaking Muslims live in the central and northern parts. They make up about two-thirds of the population. Black tribes, speaking African languages, live in the south.

Sudan is the world's most important source of gum arabic, which is taken from the acacia tree to use in glue and candy. The country is known also for its fine cotton.

Sudan's ancient history revolves around the pharaohs of Egypt and the Nubian people of the south. Huge stones from the northern Nile region were used to build the beautiful temples and burial grounds of the ancient Egyptians. By the late 1500's B.C., Sudan was an Egyptian province and stayed under Egypt's rule for hundreds of years. At the time of Christ, Sudan was split into small, independent states. Some people were converted to Christianity. At the end of the 1200's, most people adopted the Muslim faith.

The history of northern Sudan is different from that of the south. In the south, primitive tribes lived in relative isolation until the 1900's, but the north spent centuries under foreign rule. Egypt, Rome, Byzantium, the Arabs, and the Turks all had loose controls over the area. From early in the 1800's until 1885, Turko-Egyptian rule prevailed. Then followed 13 years of rule by a religious leader known as the Mahdi. Anglo-Egyptian forces fought the revolutionary leader and his followers. British General Charles ("Chinese") Gordon, who had earlier put down the slave trade in Sudan, was sent to Egypt to lead the troops. He was beseiged and killed at Khartoum in 1885. In 1889, Sudan was put under joint Anglo-Egyptian administration. The area was then referred to as Anglo-Egyptian Sudan.

After World War II, Britain and Egypt gave up control of Sudan. The government of the new state was launched as a parliamentary democracy in 1956. Several military coups

▲ *These mud-brick houses are typical of village houses in Sudan.*

have wracked the parliamentary system. Major General Jaafar al-Numeiry took control of the government in 1969 and was elected Sudan's first president in 1971. He declared the country a socialist state and remained in power until he was overthrown in 1985. Civil war between the Muslim north and the mainly Christian south disrupted Sudan in the 1970's and 1980's.

ALSO READ: AFRICA, EGYPT, ETHIOPIA.

SUEZ CANAL The Suez Canal is an artificial (man-made) waterway that links the Mediterranean Sea with the Gulf of Suez, an arm of the Red Sea. It is considered the dividing point between Asia and Africa. The canal runs across the Isthmus of Suez, a desert area that connects northeast Africa with southwest Asia. This waterway lies in the northeastern part of Egypt. East of the canal is the Sinai Peninsula and Gaza Strip. Before the canal was built, ships from Europe and America had to travel around Africa to reach Australia, India, and the Far East.

The Suez Canal runs 109 miles (175 km) between Port Said on the Mediterranean and the port of Suez on the Gulf of Suez. The canal runs through flat desert land at sea level so that no locks are needed to raise and lower ships. Parts of the canal are only 194 feet (59 m) wide. Ships must wait to pass one another in a special bypass or in one of the lakes through which the canal flows.

The Suez Canal was constructed between 1859 and 1869. The project was directed by a French diplomat and engineer, Ferdinand de Lesseps. An international agreement stated that the canal would be open in peacetime and wartime.

After the war of 1948–1949 between Egypt and Israel, the Egyptians stopped Israeli ships from using the canal. In 1956, Egyptian president Gamal Abdel Nasser seized the canal. The Israelis then invaded the Egyptian Gaza Strip and the Sinai Peninsula. Egypt was also attacked by the British and the French, who feared that the canal would be closed to their shipping. The Egyptians immediately sank several ships in the canal to block it. The war was brought to an end by the United Nations. By 1957, the invading forces had been withdrawn and the canal was reopened. During the Six-Day, or Arab-Israeli, War of 1967, the Suez Canal was again blocked by sunken ships. With help from other countries, the Egyptians cleared the canal of debris and reopened it to shipping in 1975.

ALSO READ: CANAL, EGYPT, ISRAEL.

▼ *Ships passing through the Suez Canal. The canal has had to be widened and deepened for modern shipping.*

SUGAR Sugar is a sweet carbohydrate that is an important energy food for plants and animals. The white crystals we call sugar are actually *sucrose*. This natural sweetener is found in many plants, including sugarcane and sugar beets, which provide most of our sugar.

Other plants and fruits make different kinds of sugar. Corn and other cereal plants make *glucose*, or *dextrose*. Honey contains sugar and is made by bees from the *nectar* (sweet juice) of flowers. Maple sugar comes from the sugar maple tree. Green plants make sugar from sunlight, air, and water in a process called *photosynthesis*.

The human body needs sugar for quick energy. Chemicals in the small intestine break down the sugar and starches we eat into glucose, the only kind of sugar that can be used by body cells. Sugar does not contain minerals or vitamins.

Sugar (sucrose) is used to sweeten and preserve fruit in jellies and jams and is used in making other foods. The juice from sugarcane has been used as a sweetener for hundreds of years, but refined (processed) sugar was rare and costly for a long time.

Sugarcane is a grass plant that is often 20 feet (6 m) tall and looks like corn. It is grown in warm, tropical areas. The stalks are cut once a year. They are crushed to remove the liquid inside them. The sweet juice is boiled until crystals form, and then whirled in drums to separate crystals and liquid. As the sugar is refined, it changes from a dark brown, moist product (known in cooking as brown sugar) to a dry, white, fine-grained sugar. The thick syrup left after refining is called *molasses*.

Sugar beet is grown in some western states, in Canada, and in Europe. Liquid sugar is extracted from the sugar beet root and then crystallized.

ALSO READ: COOKING, PHOTOSYNTHESIS, PLANT PRODUCTS.

▲ *Ferdinand de Lesseps, a French engineer, directed the building of the Suez Canal. He also played a part in the building of the Panama Canal.*

▼ *Sugar is made either from cane or beet. This diagram shows how the beet and cane are processed, by extracting the juice and then filtering and heating it to make crystals of sugar.*

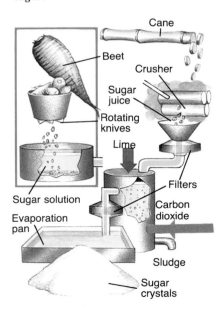

▲ *Cuneiform writing was invented in Sumer around 3000 B.C. The name means "wedge-shaped." The letters were made by pressing a pointed stick, or stylus, into soft clay.*

▲ *A sunny seaside beach attracts many people who are eager to soak up the summer sun's rays. However, too much exposure to sunlight can be harmful, especially to fair-skinned people.*

SULLIVAN, ARTHUR see GILBERT AND SULLIVAN.

SUMATRA see INDONESIA.

SUMER The Sumerians were an ancient people of the Middle East. They built up one of the earliest civilizations in the world. Their land, called Sumer, was in southern Mesopotamia (now part of Iraq). The first Sumerians settled in this area about 4000 B.C. They probably came from the southwestern hills of Persia (present-day Iran).

The Sumerian people were expert farmers. They built cities with magnificent temples and palaces. Sumerian artists carved impressive statues and made beautiful metalwork and textiles. The Sumerians invented one of the oldest forms of writing, called *cuneiform*. The Sumerians wrote myths, religious songs, business and legal records, and even essays. Cuneiform writing was used all over the Middle East for thousands of years. Most of the history of Sumer has been learned from writings on clay tablets in recent times.

Sumer was divided into many small city-states. The greatest of these was Ur. Abraham, the Biblical patriarch (founder) of the Hebrew and Arab peoples, was born in Ur about 2350 B.C. Sometimes, the king of a city-state would become powerful enough to rule over the whole of Sumer. But much of the time, the city-states fought one another, and so weakened the country. In the 2300's B.C., a powerful foreign king named Sargon conquered Sumer. Sargon was the ruler of Akkad, a kingdom in Mesopotamia. The empire of Sumer and Akkad was destroyed in 2230 B.C. by an invasion of people from Persia.

ALSO READ: ANCIENT CIVILIZATIONS, MESOPOTAMIA, PICTURE WRITING.

SUMMER

June brings tulips, lilies, roses,
Fills the children's hands with posies.
Hot July brings cooling showers,
Apricots and gillyflowers.
August brings the sheaves of corn,
Then the harvest home is borne.

These lines from a Mother Goose rhyme tell some of the good things about the lovely season called summer. In the northern half of the world, the Northern Hemisphere, summer begins about June 21 and ends about September 23. It is the hottest season of the year. In the southern half of the world, the Southern Hemisphere, summer lasts from about December 22 to March 21, while it is wintertime in the northern half.

In summer, the crops planted in spring grow to their fullest. The leaves on the trees turn a darker shade of green, and fruit ripens. By September, many crops and fruits are ready to be harvested. June is the month when most flowers first begin to bloom. Roses burst into fragrance, and the sun-warmed scent of purple clover fills the air. Bees dart from flower to flower gathering nectar and filling their combs with honey. Most wild animals and birds are busy raising their young and finding them food.

The hottest days of the summer, between early July and mid-August, are sometimes called the "dog days." This is the time when the Dog Star, Sirius, rises and sets at the same time as the sun. People in northern countries celebrate June 24 as "Midsummer Day." The evening of June 23, or "Midsummer Eve," is traditionally a time for lighting bonfires. People used to believe that the fires would frighten away the witches and evil spirits that were supposed to gather on this night. The play *A Midsummer Night's Dream*, by the English playwright, William Shakespeare, tells about the adventures of a group of people on this magical evening.

July and August are the most popular months for summer vacations. Many people from the hot cities travel to the beach or the mountains, where the air is cooler. Independence Day, with its parades, speeches, and fireworks, falls on July 4. The Canadians celebrate their national holiday, Dominion Day, on July 1. Labor Day, on the first Monday in September, is the last official holiday of summer in the United States.

ALSO READ: AUGUST, JULY, JUNE, SEASON, SEPTEMBER.

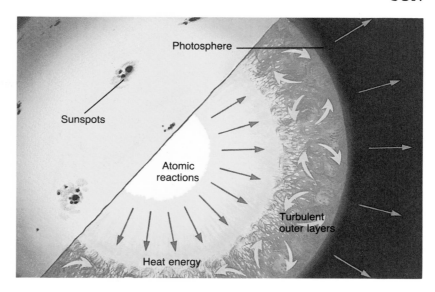

SUN The sun is a star—a ball of hot gas. The sun is about 865,000 miles (1,392,000 km) across with a mass (amount of matter) about 300,000 times that of the Earth. The sun is one of a family of some 100,000 million stars in our galaxy. It is not a very large or bright star, but it is special to us because it gives us life.

The sun is the source of almost all of the heat and light on Earth. Plants would never have grown, fuels such as coal, petroleum, and natural gas would never have formed, and human beings would never have lived if the sun had never shone on the Earth. The sun also keeps the Earth and the other planets in orbit. Without the gravitational pull of the sun's mass, all the planets would fly out into space.

The sun is about 93 million miles (150 million km) from the Earth. Its light, traveling at about 186,000 miles (300,000 km) a second, takes approximately eight and one half minutes to reach the Earth. The temperature over most of the surface of the sun is about 11,000 degrees Fahrenheit (6,000°C). In dark areas called sunspots, the temperature is about 3,600° F (2,000°C) cooler. It is not certain what causes sunspots, but they often occur in connection with strong mag-

netic fields. Sunspots are most common every 11 years or so, and this period is called the sunspot cycle.

The temperature in the center of the sun is much higher, about 25,000,000° F (14,000,000°C). The center is also much denser than the surface. The surface of the sun is less dense than the air we breathe. But a cubic foot of matter from the center of the sun is so dense it would weigh about 6,000 pounds (2,700 kg) on Earth. This tremendous heat and density at the center of the sun results in thermonuclear reactions. Atoms collide with each other and their nuclei fuse (join together); energy is given off. In the sun, atoms of hydrogen are constantly being changed to atoms of helium by thermonuclear reactions. When all the hydrogen has changed to helium, the sun will begin to burn the helium and make heavier atoms. It is estimated that the sun has been burning for about five to eight billion years and has about another 30 billion years to go. Scientists have also estimated that in every second, the sun sends out as much energy as three billion power stations could produce in a year. Solar power as a major energy source has yet to be fully harnessed.

ALSO READ: ASTRONOMY, LIGHT, NUCLEAR ENERGY, SOLAR POWER, SOLAR SYSTEM, STAR, UNIVERSE.

▲ *The sun is a yellowish star—one of medium temperature. Very cool stars are reddish, and very hot ones are bluish white. The sun's outer layers are turbulent. Sunspots indicate regions of intense magnetic activity below the surface, known as the photosphere. The photosphere is heated by atomic reactions deep inside the sun.*

Because there is so much matter in the sun, its strength of gravitation is enormous. An object on the sun's surface would weigh 28 times as much as it would on Earth. An average man would weigh over two tons on the sun.

▲ *Sun Yat-sen, founder of the Republic of China.*

Any Friday the 13th is supposed to be a very unlucky day. There is at least one Friday the 13th in any year, and there can be a maximum of three. The next year with three of these unlucky days will be 1998.

SUN YAT-SEN (1866–1925) Sun Yat-sen was a Chinese Nationalist revolutionary leader and founder of the Chinese republic. He is considered the "Father of His Country" by the People's Republic of China and the Nationalist Chinese of Taiwan.

He was born in a small farming village in Chungshan district in Kwangtung province. In 1879, Sun went to Hawaii, where he attended an English missionary school. Later, he studied medicine in Canton and Hong Kong, but he became interested in working for the independence of China. China was ruled by the Manchu dynasty (ruling family) at that time.

After participating in a revolutionary plot, Sun had to leave China for his own safety. He lived in exile from 1895 to 1911 in various places—Hawaii, the United States mainland, Japan, and England. He spread propaganda among Chinese people living overseas.

Sun expressed his ideas in his *Three Principles of the People.* These principles were "nationalism, democracy, and people's livelihood." People's livelihood meant a socialism that would provide food, shelter, and clothing for everyone.

In 1911, while still living abroad, he founded the Kuomintang ("Nationalist People's Party"). The establishment of this party helped to form a republic to follow the Manchu dynasty when it was overthrown that year. Sun returned to China and became temporary president of the republic, but resigned in favor of Yuan Shih-k'ai (the Manchu emperor's former minister) to secure stability for the new republic. When he thought Shih-k'ai was assuming too much power, Sun led the Kuomintang in creating the Republic of South China with its capital in Canton.

His political activities and thinking between 1911 and his death in 1925 involved him in the leadership of the Kuomintang. He tried to cement an alliance with the Chinese Communists and, with Soviet aid, to build a united China.

ALSO READ: CHIANG KAI-SHEK, CHINA, MAO TSE-TUNG.

SUPERSONIC FLIGHT see AIR FORCE, AIRPLANE.

SUPERSTITION Do you ever knock on wood or cross your fingers to try to make sure something good will happen? These actions are superstitions. A superstition is a belief that a certain object, sign, or act has a meaning, even though it is not reasonable or logical to think so.

Most superstitions began as beliefs connected with primitive religion or magic. Long ago, people believed that the gods sent omens, or signs, to tell what was going to happen or to warn of coming danger. An eclipse or a strange heavenly body, such as a comet, was often believed to be an omen. People also thought that evil spirits could be kept away by magical *charms.* A charm might be an object, a magical diagram, or even a verse or saying.

In some parts of the world, people still believe in the *evil eye*—a belief that certain persons can harm others just by looking at them. In America and Europe, a rabbit's foot is a favorite good-luck charm. Finding a horseshoe or a four-leaf clover is considered good luck. An old rhyme goes, "See a penny, pick it up, and all the day you'll have good luck." But having a black cat cross your path is thought to be unlucky. So is the number 13. Some hotels and other buildings do not number a thirteenth floor. When the thirteenth of the month falls on a Friday, superstitious people consider it an especially unlucky day. Fewer people nowadays take superstition seriously. Superstitions are harmless as long as they are not taken too seriously.

Here is a superstition from a Mother Goose rhyme:

If you sneeze on Monday, you sneeze for danger;

Sneeze on a Tuesday, kiss a stranger;

Sneeze on a Wednesday, sneeze for a letter;

Sneeze on a Thursday, something better.

Sneeze on a Friday, sneeze for sorrow;

Sneeze on a Saturday, joy tomorrow.

ALSO READ: ASTROLOGY, FOLKLORE, FORTUNE-TELLING, GHOST, MAGIC, RELIGION, WITCHCRAFT.

SUPPLY AND DEMAND

The term supply refers to the quantity of goods that can be sold at certain prices. The term demand refers to a consumer's ability and desire to buy. Both supply and demand are usually *elastic*. This means that both factors can change according to prices and to the amount of money that people have to spend for goods.

For some goods, the supply or the demand is *inelastic*. An inelastic supply cannot increase regardless of how great the demand is and how much the price increases. An inelastic demand will not change regardless of how the supply changes. The supply of great paintings and the demand for penicillin are both relatively inelastic.

Stores raise and lower their prices according to the supply and demand of goods. If many people wanted to buy a certain toy for five dollars, the stores might raise the price of the toy to six dollars because the demand was so great.

When workers earn high wages, they are likely to buy such things as television sets, tape recorders, new refrigerators, or new automobiles.

These goods are in demand, and stores keep stocking them to provide the supply. But if workers lose their jobs or are given cuts in their pay, they are more likely to use their money for necessities, such as food, rent, and clothing. Then the stores have a supply of television sets, cassette players, and other goods that they cannot sell because there is no longer a demand for luxuries.

ALSO READ: ECONOMICS, STORES AND SHOPS, TRADE.

SUPREME COURT

The Supreme Court is the highest court in the United States. Its establishment was authorized by the Constitution with the statement, "The judicial power of the United States shall be vested in one Supreme Court, and in such inferior [lower] courts as the Congress may from time to time ordain and establish." The Supreme Court heads the judicial branch of the Federal Government.

The Supreme Court consists of eight associate justices and one chief justice. They are appointed by the President with the approval of the U.S. Senate. Justices are appointed for life, and their salaries cannot be lowered while they serve. These rules were established so that Supreme Court justices would be free from political pressures that might influence their decisions. Until they resign, justices can be removed from the court only by impeachment and conviction, but this has never been done.

▲ *When a ship's passenger crosses the equator for the first time, he or she may be asked to "pay homage to Neptune, King of the sea." This amusing ceremony, known as "crossing the line" was practiced by sailors, who have always been particularly superstitious.*

THE SUPREME COURT 1989

Name	Born	State
William J. Brennan, Jr.	1906	New Jersey
Byron R. White	1917	Colorado
Thurgood Marshall	1908	New York
Harry A. Blackmun	1908	Minnesota
William H. Rehnquist	1924	Arizona
John Paul Stevens	1920	Illinois
Sandra Day O'Connor	1930	Arizona
Antonin Scalia	1936	Virginia
Anthony M. Kennedy	1936	California

Joseph Story of Massachusetts was the youngest justice ever named to the U.S. Supreme Court. He was appointed in 1811 at age 32 and served for 34 years until his death in 1845.

Sandra Day O'Connor, former Arizona appeals judge, became the first woman justice on the Supreme Court when she was sworn in on September 25, 1981.

▼ *The pond skater can walk on the surface of a pond. Its body is supported by surface tension, and its weight just dents the surface of the water.*

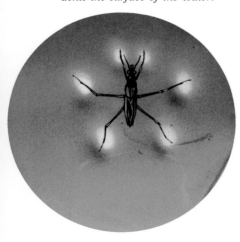

The Supreme Court has two kinds of *jurisdiction* (authority). In cases affecting ambassadors and other public ministers and cases in which a state is one of the parties, the Supreme Court has *original* jurisdiction. That is, the Supreme Court is the first and only court to hear these cases. The court also has the power—called *appellate* jurisdiction—to hear appeals in other cases that are affected by federal law, "with such exceptions and under such regulations as the Congress shall make." (An *appeal* is a request to a higher court to try a case again.) Appellate jurisdiction accounts for most of the cases that come before the court. The Supreme Court has appellate jurisdiction over both state courts and lower federal courts.

When five or more justices agree on a decision, a ruling is made. One of the justices writes the *majority opinion*—a statement of the court's decision and its reasons. A justice who agrees with the decision but for different reasons may write his or her own opinion, called a *concurring opinion*. A justice who disagrees with the majority opinion may write a *dissenting opinion*.

The Supreme Court has the power to declare a law unconstitutional through its ruling on a specific case. This power, called *judicial review*, is not directly authorized by the Constitution. But it has been considered an "implied power" since Chief Justice John Marshall, in *Marbury* v. *Madison* in 1803, ruled that the Court has this power. Judicial review is the source of much of the Supreme Court's power. Judicial review enables the Supreme Court to overrule some of the decisions of the other two branches—executive and legislative—of the Federal Government, as well as some state laws.

ALSO READ: CONSTITUTION, UNITED STATES; COURT SYSTEM; IMPEACHMENT; MARSHALL, JOHN; O'CONNOR, SANDRA DAY.

SURFACE TENSION Everything is made of tiny molecules, and molecules that are close together attract each other. Most molecules in a liquid are surrounded by other molecules, so they are pulled in all directions. But the molecules on the surface of the liquid have more neighbors below than above and tend to be pulled downward. This makes the surface of the liquid like a skin, and this skin is called surface tension. Surface tension can support light metal objects such as needles.

■ LEARN BY DOING

You can easily demonstrate surface tension. Fill a drinking glass nearly full of water. Wash a fork and a sewing needle with soap and water. Rinse and dry them thoroughly. Place the needle on the fork and gently lower the fork into the water. The needle will float. The needle is made of steel, and since steel is heavier than water, you would expect the needle to sink. Instead, it floats because the surface tension of the water holds it up.

You can make the floating needle sink by lessening the surface tension. Dry the needle and float it again. Now, drop three or four grains of soap powder or detergent into the water. The needle sinks, because the soap or detergent lowers the surface tension so much that it can no longer hold up the needle. ■

The rising of liquid in a narrow tube or between narrow flat surfaces is called *capillarity*. Capillarity is caused by attraction between molecules and the effect of surface tension. To show capillarity, put a drinking straw into a glass of water. The water in the straw will rise above the water level in the glass.

When the straw is first placed in the water, the molecules of water are attracted by those molecules of the straw just above the level of the water.

The attraction between the water molecules and those of the straw is greater than the attraction between the water molecules themselves. Therefore, the water molecules are pulled upward. The water molecules cling together due to attraction. The rising water molecules pull other water molecules up with them. The water continues to rise in the straw until the weight of the water equals the upward pull of the surface tension.

ALSO READ: ATOM, PHYSICS, PLANT, SOAPS AND DETERGENTS.

SURFING Surfing is the sport of riding a long, flat board on the crest of an ocean wave. It is an exciting activity that demands skill, a good sense of balance, and quick reflexes.

Surfing began in Hawaii. When the explorer, Captain James Cook, first visited that island in 1778, he found that surfing was a popular sport among the natives. They held surfing contests and awarded prizes to the winners. Hawaii is still one of the best places for surfing because of the giant waves that break there.

The only equipment needed for surfing is a surfboard, which is shaped something like an ironing board. The best surfboards are made of plastic foam covered with a coating of fiberglass and resin. Most boards are about ten feet (3 m) long and two feet (60 cm) wide. They weigh from 20 to 25 pounds (9 to 11 kg). A small tail fin attached to the bottom of a surfboard helps make it easier to control.

A surfer starts out by lying on his or her stomach on the board and using hands and arms to paddle out to the point where the waves begin to break. Then, each surfer looks out to sea and waits for the approach of a big wave. When the wave begins to come in, the surfer gets into a kneeling position on the board and begins to paddle the water with both hands. As

the board begins to slide down the front of the wave, the surfer stands up, putting one foot in front and one behind. The surfer can steer by shifting the weight on the rear foot from left to right. He or she tries to stay close to, but ahead of, the white surf at the top of the wave.

People should not try surfing until they are good swimmers and have had expert instruction. Many people train for surfboard riding by first doing some body surfing. A body surfer swims to the top of a wave and then lets the wave push him or her to shore. This helps a beginner develop a sense of balance.

ALSO READ: SPORTS.

SURGERY Surgery is the branch of medicine that treats injuries or diseases through manipulation and operation. An operation usually requires cutting into the body, while manipulation, such as the setting of simple bone fractures, does not require cutting. Surgery can be described as minor or major. Minor surgery includes procedures that can usually be performed in a doctor's office, such as closing small wounds and setting simple fractures. Major surgery includes operations to correct conditions that may endanger the patient's life. Major operations, such as removing an appendix, correcting heart conditions, and brain surgery, are performed in a hospital.

Surgical instruments are highly specialized. Hundreds of instruments may be used in a single operation. Sharp *scalpels* (knives) and scissors are used for cutting, *forceps* (pincers) for grasping and pulling, *clamps* and *hemostats* for closing off blood vessels, *retractors* for holding back folds of skin, and *probes* for exploring. Special instruments may be designed for a particular operation or for use by a particular surgeon.

Major surgery is performed in spe-

▲ *Ideal surfing water is found along the west coast of the United States, Hawaii, and around Australia. The Pacific sends in large rollers, providing good sport for surfers.*

▲ *The British surgeon Joseph Lister used carbolic acid to prevent infection in surgical wounds. He found that dressings soaked in acid killed the germs that caused infection. Lister also tried a carbolic spray (illustrated) to create an antiseptic mist around the operating table.*

Circus acts often entertained American audiences with a "grand exhibition of laughing gas," in the days before anesthetics became a common aid in operations. The gas was guaranteed to make those who inhaled it "laugh, sing, dance, speak, or fight."

cial operating rooms in a hospital. Hundreds of surgical instruments are kept ready for use in operating rooms. The patient lies on an operating table that can be turned and tilted so that a surgeon can work more easily. Special lights keep the operating table brightly lit. If there is time, the patient will be thoroughly prepared for the operation. He or she will be given various tests and may be put on a special diet. The skin area where the *incision* (cut) is to be made will be shaved and cleaned. If the operation is an emergency, the patient will receive the quickest care possible to prepare him or her for surgery. Before the operation, the anesthetist will give the patient an *anesthetic*—a drug that causes unconsciousness or deadens the nerves in the area to be operated on.

The nurses hand the instruments to the surgeons. One surgeon is usually in charge, but assistants may take over at different times during the operation. When the operation is completed, the incision is *sutured* (sewn up) and the patient is sent to the recovery room. After a few hours in the recovery room under constant observation, the patient is sent to his or her own hospital bed.

History of Surgery Surgery began about 10,000 years ago. Skulls of prehistoric people have been found with surgically cut holes in them. The great Greek physician, Hippocrates,

taught surgeons to control infection by washing surgical wounds with boiled water or wine. Ancient surgeons also knew how to use sutures. The art of surgery was almost lost during the Middle Ages. It was more than a thousand years before surgery returned to the level to which Greek and Roman surgeons had brought it.

Modern surgery began in the mid-1800's, when the British surgeon, Joseph Lister, developed sterilization to kill the germs on surgical instruments. This greatly decreased deaths from infections. Modern surgeons use electronic instruments, such as *cryogenic probes*, that can freeze and destroy damaged tissues. Beams of light from devices called lasers are used to weld torn eye retinas in place and for delicate brain surgery. Organs, including kidneys and hearts, have been transplanted from living or dead donors to living recipients with varying amounts of success. Complete artificial hearts have been used as temporary surgical aids. In the future, more artificial organs and parts of organs may be inserted by surgery.

Surgery today is divided into several specialized fields. Neurosurgeons specialize in brain surgery, and cardiological surgeons in heart surgery. Orthopedic surgeons repair broken and deformed bones. Plastic surgeons improve the appearance and the functioning of the exposed parts of the body.

ALSO READ: ANATOMY; ANESTHETICS; LISTER, JOSEPH; LASERS AND MASERS; MEDICINE; X RAY.

▼ *A patient undergoing surgery. The surgeon and the surgical team assisting in the operation wear gloves and masks to protect the patient from infection. They use sterilized instruments and dressings.*

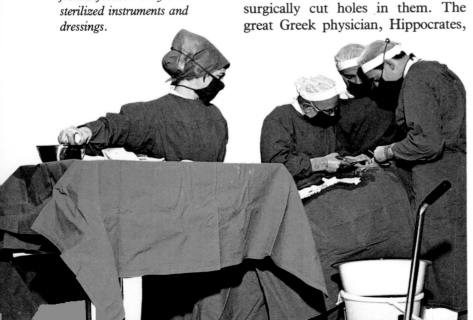

SURINAME People of many races live together in Suriname (spelled also Surinam), a small country on the north central coast of South America. (See the map with the article on SOUTH AMERICA.) Each group of people follows its own customs and religion. The largest group of people are the Creoles, who are mainly of Euro-

SURINAME

Capital City: Paramaribo (180,000 people).
Area: 63,042 square miles (163,265 sq. km).
Population: 400,000.
Government: Military Council.
Natural Resources: Bauxite, forests.
Export Products: Bauxite, alumina, rice, citrus fruit.
Unit of Money: Guilder.
Official Language: Dutch.

pean and black ancestry. The second largest group are the Hindustanis (East Indians), and the third are the Javanese (Indonesian). There are also Bush Negroes (descendents of former slaves who fled to the interior), Amerindians (American Indians), and Chinese.

Suriname, formerly called Dutch Guiana, is about the size of Wisconsin. The land is divided into three main parts—the coastal lowland, the savanna plains, and the rain forest in the interior highlands. The savanna is a narrow band of sandy soil covered mostly by low shrubs. The interior is a big, sparsely inhabited area of densely forested hills.

The climate of Suriname is tropical. It is warm and damp the year around, but trade winds often blow in from the northeast. The capital and largest city, Paramaribo, looks much like a Dutch city. Other cities are Nieuw Nickerie, Totness, and Moengo.

Most of the farmland is located along the Atlantic coast. Crops of rice, bananas, cacao, coffee, coconuts, fruits, and sugarcane are grown here. Cattle and sheep are raised. The bauxite (ore for aluminum) deposits found here are some of the richest in the world.

In the early 1500's, Spanish explorers sailed along the coast, but the first colony in Suriname was established by an English explorer. Occupied alternately by the English and the Dutch, Suriname was given to the Dutch by the English in 1667. In exchange, the Dutch gave up any claim to New Amsterdam (New York City). Suriname was a Dutch colony until 1948, when it was granted partial self-government. It became an independent part of the Kingdom of the Netherlands in 1954. Suriname was granted complete independence in 1975. A group of military officers took control of the government in 1980 and abolished the legislature.

ALSO READ: SOUTH AMERICA.

SURREALISM Try an experiment. Take a pencil, think a minute, and then write down the first words that come into your mind exactly as you think of them. Pay no attention to the meaning of the words and do not change a word for a better one—for that would interfere with the pure act of creation. What kind of writing do you produce this way?

A group of French writers working in the 1920's under the leadership of poet André Breton called this method surrealism. Writing in this way, they felt, one could record as accurately as possible the thoughts of the *unconscious mind* (the part of one's thinking processes that one is unaware of). As a result, their writing sometimes made little sense to the ordinary reader. For example, Paul Eluard wrote this well-known surrealist saying: "Elephants are contagious." Such a phrase means little to a reader, unless he or she

▲ *A surrealist painting,* At Four O'Clock in Spring, the Hope, *by Yves Tanguy.*

realizes that surrealists are more interested in free expression than in making sense in the usual way.

Surrealistic painting became more widely known than surrealistic writing in the 1920's and 1930's. The psychologist, Sigmund Freud, had presented some exciting discoveries about dreams—how they reveal a person's innermost thoughts and how they relate to the unconscious mind. The surrealist painters, among them Salvador Dali, used many dream symbols from Freudian psychology. Like the surrealist writers, the painters felt that art could come out of the unconscious mind—untouched by a person's educated values. For this reason, they painted pictures of dreams. Have you ever tried to draw a picture of a dream you have had? You may find all kinds of actions, objects, and people that would ordinarily never be together.

The dreamlike picture shown on page 2359 is by the French artist, Yves Tanguy. It is entitled *At Four O'Clock in Spring, the Hope*. The title is surrealistic, because you know that "four o'clock in spring" makes no sense if you think of it in a matter-of-fact way. The yellow bird rising over the bank symbolizes spring, and its bright yellow color symbolizes hope. The patch of white cloud and the green, misty look give a dreamy feeling to the picture.

Some filmmakers have used surrealism in movies. The surrealistic dreams of a character in a film can be very effective art. The Swedish director Ingmar Bergman used this technique in *Wild Strawberries*. In the movie, a character dreams that he is in his coffin, and scenes from his life pass by. A clock with no hands adds another surrealistic touch.

It is not always possible to turn a dream directly into a painting or a film or to write a poem without thinking beforehand. Nonetheless, surrealists achieve some surprising and unusual effects in their work.

ALSO READ: MODERN ART, SYMBOLISM.

SURVEYING Surveying is the science of measuring the exact distances and directions between points on the Earth's surface. The drawing of maps and boundaries and the construction of roads and buildings depend on surveying.

Various instruments are used in surveying. Small areas may be surveyed using a compass to determine direction and a measuring tape to measure distance. For larger areas, a *level*, a *transit*, or a *plane table* may be used.

A level is a telescope mounted on a tripod (a three-legged stand). The level is so named because it has a device that the surveyor can use to make the telescope exactly level. Then the surveyor can determine how much higher or lower other points are.

A transit is similar to a level. The telescope in a transit can be rotated horizontally and vertically. So a transit can be used to measure both the horizontal and vertical directions of an object.

A plane table is a drawing board mounted on a tripod. An *alidade*, a telescope mounted on a ruler, is set on a piece of paper attached to the table. When the surveyor sights a point

▼ *This surveyor is checking that the multi-story steel structure he is helping to build is plumb (straight and true).*

through the alidade, he or she draws a line on the paper to show the direction to the point.

The surveyor does not sight a point simply by looking through the telescope but works with a helper called a rodman. The rodman holds a long measured rod at the exact point the surveyor wishes to sight. The surveyor can determine the distance of the point by measuring the length of the rod as it appears through the telescope.

Surveying is a very old science. It probably began in ancient Egypt. But modern surveying, like most modern sciences, has many specialized methods and branches. *Plane* surveying is used for areas so small that they are not much affected by the curve of the Earth's surface. *Geodetic* surveying is used for areas large enough that this curvature makes a difference. *Topographic* surveys show positions and elevations (heights above sea level) of points on the Earth's surface. *Hydrographic* surveys show coastlines and other features that are important for water navigation. *Aerial* surveying is done from an airplane. Photographs taken from the plane are placed together to give a picture of a large part of the Earth.

Today, much of the Earth's surface has been surveyed. All over the United States you will find *benchmarks*, brass markers placed by the United States Geological Survey to show the elevation of particular points. These markers are useful in building roads and houses.

ALSO READ: BANNEKER, BENJAMIN; GEOGRAPHY; GEOMETRY; MAP; MASON-DIXON LINE.

SWAMPS AND MARSHES

Low-lying swamps and marshes are areas of very wet land. In some cases, shallow water may stand above the spongy ground. Swamps and marshes are generally considered to be the

▲ *Nauset Marsh on Cape Cod in Massachusetts is an area of low-lying land close to the Atlantic Ocean. Swamps and marshes are rich in plant and animal life. Because many swamps have been drained, conservationists are seeking to protect some swamps as wildlife reserves.*

same thing, but the difference lies in the kinds of plants that grow in these wet areas. Swamps are covered with trees and shrubs, as well as smaller plants. Marshes are usually treeless and have grasses and other small plants.

Coastal swamps are formed when high tides wash over land that does not drain well. Swamps also form near rivers in areas that are lower than the riverbed. When rivers overflow their banks in these areas, the floodwater cannot run back into the river, and a swamp is formed. As lakes grow larger, swampy areas form near their shores.

A *bog* is a section of wet, spongelike land that has no drainage. The ground becomes waterlogged and grasses or other plants decay. Layer upon layer of this decomposed vegetable matter gradually compresses into a mass we call *peat*. Peat bogs are extensive in Ireland and other northern countries.

Swamps and marshes are found in virtually every country in the world. Large swamps are found at the deltas, or mouths, of the Mekong River in Vietnam, the Amazon River in Brazil, and the Congo River in Zaire. Well-known marshes are at or near the deltas of the Rhône River in France, the Guadalquivir River in Spain, and the Danube River in Romania.

In the United States, the Everglades, a vast watery region (actually a

The Okefenokee Swamp in southern Georgia and northeastern Florida is a refuge for more than 200 types of birds and about 50 kinds of fish. Animals include bears, deer, wildcats, raccoons, opossums, otters, and alligators.

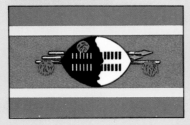

Freshwater creeks meandering through a salt marsh wash mud down to the coast. The mud accumulates around the roots of salt-tolerant plants. In time, these plants will create low-lying islands, making new land.

river) in Florida, is a combination of swamp and marsh. The Okefenokee Swamp covers a large area in southeastern Georgia. The Dismal Swamp covers about 500 square miles (1,300 sq. km) of northeastern North Carolina and southern Virginia. The southern states bordering the Gulf of Mexico have swamps filled with mangrove and cypress trees and other tropical vegetation. Many birds, fish, and small animals, such as otters and beavers, live and breed in the swamps and marshes of the United States.

ALSO READ: ANIMAL DISTRIBUTION, ECOLOGY, EVERGLADES, LAKE, RIVER, SEACOAST.

SWAN see DUCKS AND GEESE.

SWAZILAND The Kingdom of Swaziland in southeast Africa is almost completely surrounded by the Republic of South Africa. Mozambique borders it on the east. (See the map with the article on AFRICA.)

Swaziland is a country of high plateaus, with forested mountains in the western portion. The landscape looks something like the Appalachian Mountain regions of the United States. In the west, the climate is temperate, with chilly nights during the winter months. The central and eastern areas are subtropical.

Swaziland has many important minerals, including iron ore, asbestos, and coal. Agriculture is important to the economy, and many crops are grown for export. The forests yield large quantities of wood pulp.

Some Swazis work in neighboring South Africa. Others are employed in industries in Swaziland, but most of them work on small farms. The official language is English. Most Africans speak Siswati (a Bantu dialect), while English and Afrikaans (one of the languages of South Africa) are spoken by the whites who live in the country.

The Swazis are a people of Bantu origin who broke off from other Bantu-speaking groups about 1750. They are related to the Zulu and Xhosa people. Their highly developed warrior system was much feared by white settlers and pioneers.

Swaziland is a former British protectorate that became independent in 1968. King Sobhuza II, a member of one of Africa's last ruling dynasties, became head of state. The king, known as the Ingwenyama (Lion), shared ruling power with his mother, the Inlovukali (Lady Elephant). In 1973, the king abolished the country's constitution and took full control of the government. A new constitution was proclaimed in 1978, and a new parliament with limited powers was opened in 1979. King Sobhuza died in 1982, and in 1986 a new king, the youthful Mswati III, succeeded to the throne.

ALSO READ: AFRICA, SOUTH AFRICA.

SWAZILAND

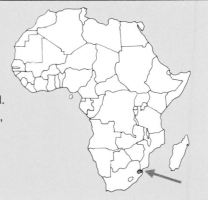

Capital City: Mbabane (52,000 people).
Area: 6,704 square miles (17,363 sq. km).
Population: 760,000.
Government: Constitutional monarchy.
Natural Resources: Iron ore, asbestos, coal.
Export Products: Sugar, cotton, wood pulp, iron ore, asbestos, citrus fruits, meat.
Unit of Money: Lilangeni.
Official Language: English.